HEROES
OF THE RESTORATION

HEROES
OF THE RESTORATION

BOOKCRAFT
Salt Lake City, Utah

Library of Congress Catalog Card Number: 96-78897
ISBN 1-57008-291-X

First Printing, 1997

Printed in the United States of America

Contents

1   President Gordon B. Hinckley   *1*
Joseph, the Seer

2   Elder Robert D. Hales   8
Oliver Cowdery

3   Elder Marlin K. Jensen   *24*
Martin Harris
A Life Worth Remembering

4   Elder Russell M. Nelson   *35*
Orson Hyde

5   Elder Jeffrey R. Holland   *58*
Heber C. Kimball
Common Man, Uncommon Servant

6   President James E. Faust   *71*
Edward Partridge
A Man like unto Nathaniel of Old

7   Elder Cecil O. Samuelson   *81*
David W. Patten

8   Elder Carlos E. Asay   89
     Orson Pratt

9   Elder John H. Groberg   99
     Parley P. Pratt
     Apostle of the Lord

10   Elder Merrill J. Bateman   118
     Willard Richards
     Integrity to the Trust

11   Elder John K. Carmack   135
     George A. Smith
     Chronicler of Church History

12   Elder M. Russell Ballard   148
     Hyrum Smith

13   Elder Joe J. Christensen   161
     Samuel Harrison Smith
     He Was There

14   Elder Spencer J. Condie   172
     Lorenzo Snow

15   Elder L. Tom Perry   183
     John Taylor
     A Man of Eloquence

16   Elder Joseph B. Wirthlin   194
     Newel K. Whitney
     Faithful Steward, Steadfast Saint

17   President Thomas S. Monson   211
     Wilford Woodruff

18   Elder Neal A. Maxwell   219
     Brigham Young

     Index   231

1

President Gordon B. Hinckley

Joseph, the Seer

The time was the night of September 21–22, 1823. The place was an upper bedroom of the simple log cabin of Joseph Smith Sr. Joseph Jr., before retiring for the night, reflected on what had occurred in his life during the three years that had passed since he had experienced a remarkable and transcendent vision. He called upon the Lord in prayer. He discovered a light appearing in his room, which continued to increase until the room was lighter than at noonday. A personage appeared at his bedside, standing in the air, his feet not touching the floor.

When Joseph looked upon the personage he was afraid, but the fear soon left him.

The personage called him by name, saying that he was a messenger sent from the presence of God, that his name was Moroni; that God had a work for Joseph to do, and that his "name should be had for good and evil among all nations, kindreds, and tongues, or that it should be both good and evil spoken of among all people" (see Joseph Smith—History 1:29–33).

Here was a boy, a youth seventeen years of age. The circumstances in which he lived were those of the rural poor. He had not traveled widely. He had no friends among the affluent and influential of the world. His name was Joseph, a common name, and Smith the most common of surnames. And yet he was told that this "name should be had for good and evil among all nations, kindreds, and tongues."

The wonder of the story of Joseph Smith is that it has all come to pass. His life's odyssey began with his birth on December 23, 1805, in a little-known Vermont village. It ended 38½ years later, on June 27, 1844, with gunshots in Carthage, Illinois. Between those polar dates runs the story of one who "has done more, save Jesus only, for the salvation of men in this world, than any other man that ever lived in it" (D&C 135:3). Such was the appraisal of a companion who knew him well and who was with him at the time of his death.

Can anyone who is acquainted with his life and who has drawn inspiration from his writings doubt that the hand of the Almighty was manifest in his tutoring and in his ministry? His life was filled with events which molded a man into a prophet.

Perhaps it all began with the typhus fever he suffered as a little boy, followed by the terrible infection that settled in his leg and began to destroy the bone. This was while his family resided in Lebanon, New Hampshire. The medical decision was to amputate the infected limb. It now seems more than coincidence that perhaps the only surgeon then in the United States who had developed a procedure that could save the leg was Dr. Nathan Smith, who taught medicine at the academy in Hanover, only a few miles away.

But the saving of the leg was not to be accomplished without intense suffering. All who have read his mother's account are familiar with what happened. It is difficult to imagine how the little boy stood the pain, as his father held him in his arms and his mother walked and prayed among the trees of the farm to escape his screams, while without anesthesia or antiseptics the surgeon opened the flesh of the leg and broke off the infected portions of bone.

Joseph came to know at the tender age of seven the meaning of physical suffering. He was to know it again at Kirtland when he was tarred and feathered by an angry mob; at Liberty, Missouri, in the cold winter of 1838–39, while he languished in a dungeon cell; and again in Carthage when the shots of the mob rang out that sultry June afternoon.

Through the poverty endured by his family, he developed a sensitivity to the needs of others. The New England years, particularly in New Hampshire and Vermont, exposed him to the problems of the poor. The soil his father farmed yielded frugally. The hills among which they lived were of granite, with relatively thin topsoil, and frost frequently came late in the spring and early in the fall. In fact, it was the July frost of 1816, which killed their crops, that compelled their decision to move to western New York.

Then, in the education of a boy for the great work of the Almighty, there came the religious revivals with their high-pitched oratory and their confusing claims. Out of anxious concern over wanting to be right, on a spring morning the boy went into the woods to pray, to ask the Source of all wisdom and knowledge the way to truth. He had read in the family Bible the words of James: "If any of you lack wisdom, let him ask of God, that giveth to all men liberally, and upbraideth not; and it shall be given him" (James 1:5). That was a day of transcendent education with an introduction by the Eternal Father and instruction from the resurrected Lord. Surely no other experience of mortal man had been so great or so enlightening as that given this boy of fourteen years. Then followed the tutoring by Moroni, with both warning and instruction given on many occasions, including delivery of the ancient record.

The work of translation was an education in itself as the history of once-great nations, and of their prophets and leaders, was spelled out word by word. There was also a bestowal of divine authority, first under the hands of John the Baptist and subsequently under the hands of Peter, James, and John. There were revelations in which the voice of God was heard again and the channel of communication between God and man was reopened. All of these most remarkable experiences were preliminary to that 1830 April sixth when the Church of Jesus Christ was organized anew in these the latter days.

With the naming of various offices, with the formation of quorums, and with the designation of responsibilities, the young prophet laid the doctrinal and organizational foundation of the Church as it has functioned ever since. Coupled with this development was the unrelenting work of preaching the word and the establishment of governing branches wherever there were converts. And there was always the moving—first from western New York to Kirtland, where the land rises gently from Lake Erie. This gathering to the Ohio community—the first move of the Saints—is seldom noted, as if it were a small undertaking. Actually it was one of the most difficult. At that early date there was little of discipline in the membership, and the administrative organization was not perfected. But at the suggestion of Joseph, new converts left their farms and homes, their comforts and security, without ever seeing the place to which they were going. They knew only that it was to be a gathering place and that their prophet had counseled them to go. No matter the risks, the hazards, the lack of housing, the uncertainty of provisions, they went. How can one with objectivity note such loyalties and not recognize Joseph Smith, even in those days of his very young manhood, as a leader of remarkable qualities?

In Kirtland they built their first temple, the forerunner of all that have been built since. They had not the means to construct so substantial a building, but they did it out of a spirit of love for and devotion to God, whose house it was designated, and at the instance of their leader. Simultaneous with the establishment of Kirtland, they were building another center in Missouri to the west. This was to be their Zion, the place of gathering. The plans of their prophet were unique and remarkable. Here he spoke of building a city of twenty thousand—small enough to avoid the congestion and miseries of the great unfriendly metropolises of the East and Europe but large enough to provide the social opportunities that give graciousness to living, with farmland surrounding, thus combining the advantages of both urban and rural living. And when this was built, there would be another, and on and on to fill the earth.

While all of this planning and building was going forward, he was engaged in a revision of the King James Bible, in the development of doctrine, in sending missionaries as far afield as the British Isles, and in other bold undertakings. One is led to marvel at the energies of the man. The breadth of his vision, the intensity of his activity, are explained only by his great sense of mission and the inspiration of heaven that quickened his understanding. He was a man possessed by a sense of destiny, and that destiny was nothing less than the building of the kingdom of God on the earth.

But the hope of Kirtland was shattered with tar and feathers, with insults and threats of worse to come. And the dream of Zion was blasted with rifle fire, the burning of homes, the wolf-cries of night-riding mobs, death at Haun's Mill and Crooked River, the evil expulsion order of Governor Boggs, the painful march to the bottomlands of the Mississippi, then the crossing of the river to a temporary asylum at Quincy.

Their prophet did not make that journey with the fleeing exiles. He was in a cold and miserable basement cell in the jail at Liberty, Missouri. One can only imagine the misery of that winter in those circumstances. The ceiling of that cell was six feet one-half inch from the floor, too low for a tall man to stand straight. There was no door, only a hole in the ceiling through which the slop pail was raised and the distasteful food lowered. Slit, barred windows at the level of the ceiling let in a little sunlight and also the bitter cold. Here Joseph and his associates spent four months of that winter. Here it was that he cried out on one occasion, "O God, where art thou?" In the revealed response to that prayer was this remarkable prophecy resonant of the earlier words spoken by Moroni: "The ends of the earth shall inquire after thy name, and fools shall have thee in derision, and hell shall rage against thee; while the pure in heart, and the wise, and the noble, and the virtuous, shall seek counsel, and authority, and blessings constantly from under thy hand. And thy people shall never be turned against thee by the testimony of traitors." (D&C 122:1–3.)

There followed Nauvoo, the City of Joseph, the miracle city of Illinois. He planned it. The swamps were drained, streets platted; a beautiful community rose from the river up to the hill where the temple was built. Homes were constructed of brick and mortar, sturdy and well-planned, as if these people were to live here for generations. Sounds of industry filled the air—of hammer on anvil, of the cutting of stone, of saw and lathe and plane. Beauty and stability rose from that swampland. This was the zenith of the Prophet's mortal career.

But there also arose a miasma of jealousy and hate and disloyalty. There were traitors among the ranks, and over in Missouri Governor Boggs grew angry in his frustration over attempts to get at Joseph. A brew of dark evil smoldered. Joseph knew a storm was coming. With the vision of a prophet, he spoke one day in Montrose, on the west side of the river, telling those about him that there would be more affliction and that the Saints would be driven to the Rocky Mountains, where they would become a mighty people.

He never saw that day. June 27, 1844, was the hour of his tragedy. A mob, their faces blackened to hide their identity, took his life and that of his brother Hyrum that hot afternoon. That night was the darkest of all nights through which the Saints had lived in Nauvoo. The Prophet, not yet thirty-nine years of age, was dead.

He and Hyrum were buried in the soil of Nauvoo. Today their grave sites are visited by thousands who come from over the earth. He has been gone these many years. But his spirit is immortal. "Mingling with Gods, he can plan for his brethren" (William W. Phelps, "Praise

to the Man," *Hymns,* no. 27). He is the great prophet of this dispensation. His praises are sung in the congregations of the Saints across the
world. As was promised in the dungeon cell at Liberty, "the pure in
heart, and the wise, and the noble, and the virtuous . . . seek counsel,
and authority, and blessings constantly from under [his] hand" (D&C
122:2).

More than a century and a half have passed since he spoke to his
beloved people in Nauvoo. Standing on the summit of this reach of
time, we are inclined to exclaim: "What God hath wrought through
the instrumentality of his servant Joseph!"

The Church of Jesus Christ of Latter-day Saints, established in
this the dispensation of the fulness of times, flourishes in a world of
secularism. It is a refuge of spirituality. It has been buffeted and
ridiculed. It has been persecuted and driven. It has been belittled and
wounded. It has reeled from the blows of adversity hurled against it.
But never has it taken a step backward. The little handful who gathered under Joseph's direction in the Whitmer home in 1830 have become a mighty congregation of millions. The provincialism of that beginning in the towns and villages of western New York has blossomed
into a great cosmopolitan society of many languages and many cul-
tures, but one faith.

The burden of its work is the gospel of salvation. Its cause is the
cause of peace. Its challenge lies in teaching eternal truth. Its victory
lies in accomplishing the work of God.

Its story is unique. It is heroic. It is tremendous. Joseph's was the
vision, divinely given. For it he lived, and for it he gave his life, sealing his testimony with a martyr's blood.

Congregations throughout the world sing in their native tongues,
"We thank thee, O God, for a prophet." They are singing of him who
stands at the head of the work of the Almighty in this the final dispensation of God's work on the earth.

Said one who loved him: "When a man gives his life for the cause
he has advocated, he meets the highest test of his honesty and sincerity
that his own or any future generation can in fairness ask. When he dies
for the testimony he has borne, all malicious tongues should ever after
be silent and all voices hushed in reverence before a sacrifice so complete." (Ezra Dalby, Ms, December 12, 1926.)

> Great is his glory and endless his priesthood.
> Ever and ever the keys he will hold.
> Faithful and true, he will enter his kingdom,
> Crowned in the midst of the prophets of old.
> (*Hymns*, no. 27.)

I stand humbly in his lengthened shadow, fifteenth in line to hold the keys first given him in these latter days. He stands as my leader, my model, my prophet, my seer and revelator. I am overwhelmed. I am humbled. I am profoundly and deeply grateful. God be thanked for His chosen servant, whom He nurtured and taught, to whom He appeared and spoke, who under divine direction was visited by those who anciently held precious keys and authority, and whose image stands before the world as an instrument in the hands of the Almighty bringing to pass the great work of immortality and eternal life for all of the sons and daughters of God.

2

Elder Robert D. Hales

Oliver Cowdery

Throughout the history of mankind there have been periods, called gospel dispensations, when the blessings of the priesthood have been given through prophets to the inhabitants of the earth. The Prophet Joseph Smith was commissioned by the Lord to preside over the restoration of His church in the era known as the last dispensation or the dispensation of the fulness of times. This dispensation restored all priesthood keys, blessings, ordinances, and doctrines necessary to prepare the faithful and obedient Saints of this and previous dispensations to return to the presence of God the Father and His Son Jesus Christ and to prepare the earth and its inhabitants for Christ's second coming. Oliver Cowdery's life story shows him as a witness of these historical events at the side of the Prophet Joseph Smith.

While the Savior was living on the earth He organized His Church. Following His crucifixion and His atoning sacrifice, with one exception His faithful Apostles suffered a martyr's death. Thus, the priesthood and the Lord's church were taken from the earth, and men's uninspired doctrines prevailed in what is known as the Great Apostasy. During the ensuing Dark Ages the light of the gospel was extinguished from the earth. The sixteenth century, however, brought the Reformation, a movement in Europe in which men such as Martin Luther, John Calvin, John Wycliffe, and John Knox, feeling that in some respects the church of the day was in a state of apostasy, took steps to reform it.

These men were, by their own admissions, merely reformers attempting to change incorrect practices—that is, none claimed direct revelation from God to bring back the ancient Christian church and its teachings. But they nonetheless served a useful purpose in preparing the world for the dawning of the Restoration.

DAWNING OF THE RESTORATION

In the first decade of the eighteen hundreds two baby boys, each destined to play pivotal parts in the restoration of the Church of Jesus Christ, were born in Vermont. Joseph Smith was born on December 23, 1805, in South Royalton, Windsor County. On October 3 of the following year Oliver Cowdery was born in Wells, Rutland County. Though they lived in adjacent counties and shared a common ancestor, their families were not acquainted.

Joseph's and Oliver's early lives, however, followed remarkably parallel courses. Vermont was home to both boys. No doubt these two young men shared similar interests—growing up at the same time in contiguous areas—as they played young boys' games and spent time roaming and exploring the mountain vales that surrounded their homes.

The environment where they lived was a remarkable refinement in their lives. There is a great similarity between the New England area and upstate New York. During the Ice Age, glaciers brought with them rocks that literally covered the eastern landscape. When the ice receded and in course of time the country was settled, the thin soil remaining had to be cleared of rocks, brush, and trees. Pure Yankee ingenuity turned rolling hills littered with piles of rocks into sturdy rock homes and thousands of miles of rock fences. This was a hard life that produced men with a strong inner strength who clearly understood the law of the harvest—that one does not get something for nothing.

The beautiful northeastern landscape also had a powerful influence on the lives of the early colonizers of this area. No artist's palette can replicate the breathtaking panorama of the colorful autumn season of this northeastern seaboard. The harshest of winters produces a Currier and Ives scene at every vista, and in the springtime the hundreds of variations of the color of green are almost overwhelming.

This combination of hard work and the beauty of nature created some of the greatest American statesmen, poets, and writers. The practicality of rigorous physical labor produced the humility necessary to an appreciation of the wonders of nature and the gifts of God, thus bringing these men to a heightened level of spirituality and creativity. It was in this environment that the United States Constitution and the Bill of Rights had been produced only a quarter of a century before Joseph Smith and Oliver Cowdery were born, creating the right setting for the freedoms that were a prerequisite to the Restoration.

The Smith family moved to Palmyra in western New York when Joseph was just a boy. His principal occupation through his adolescent years was helping on the family farm, working in various family businesses, and hiring out to work for others, mostly doing farm labor. While family circumstances precluded Joseph from spending large amounts of time acquiring a formal education, he did learn to read and write. Though principally absorbed in the day-to-day routine of farm chores, Joseph was preoccupied with questions about religion. The matter of his personal salvation particularly troubled and perplexed him. Much of his energy was focused on discovering answers to his questions about finding the true church of Jesus Christ.

Oliver, too, worked at odd jobs and was exposed to the rigors of farm life. However, he appears to have been predisposed to concern himself with matters of the mind; he devoted considerable energy to discovering and developing his literary skills, honing his powers of personal expression. His interest and preparation in this realm foreshadowed his role of giving indispensable service to the Restoration.

In 1825 Oliver moved to western New York to live with his brothers and work in surrounding communities. He experimented with several occupations, such as clerking, blacksmithing, and farming, none of which provided the satisfaction he seemed to be seeking. When a teaching post opened in Manchester in the winter of 1829, Oliver seized the opportunity.

CONVERSION

More than mere chance brought nineteen-year-old Oliver Cowdery to the western reaches of New York state. It was there that he heard rumors of Joseph's visits with angels and his work in translating the gold plates. Believing that "there must be some truth in the story of the plates, . . . he intended to investigate the matter."[1]

Oliver was willing and eager to pursue his new profession and was in serious need of a place to board. In time, the irresistible prospect of a warm bed, adequate meals, a friendly fireside, and lengthy discussion about the spiritual work of Joseph Smith Jr. drew him to the Smith household.

At this time Joseph was in Harmony, Pennsylvania, dealing with another matter that would soon bring these two men together in doing the Lord's work. Joseph had matured and married, and he was now ready to begin the translation of the gold plates. He had made attempts to do so with Martin Harris as his scribe, but a combination of circumstances had frustrated the work. Joseph's wife, Emma, and his brother Samuel had also tried to help by acting as scribe, but problems persisted. Joseph found himself in desperate circumstances. By this time he not only was left without a scribe but also lacked the financial means to provide for himself and his wife. In this condition, Joseph said, "I cried unto the Lord that he would provide for me to accomplish the work whereunto he had commanded me."[2]

Meanwhile, living in the Smith home in Manchester, New York, Oliver talked directly with the Smiths about Joseph's work and learned more about the marvelous spiritual manifestations Joseph had experienced, such as the First Vision and obtaining the golden plates. Lucy Mack Smith, the young prophet's mother, later recalled that Oliver became so preoccupied about the gold plates and all the other things that had happened to Joseph that he remarked, "The subject . . . seems working in my very bones, and I cannot, for a moment, get it out of my mind."[3]

One of the central themes of the Restoration is the sequence of fervent, sincere, prayerful petitions that were answered by revelations to guide the participants to do the Lord's bidding. Oliver received his desired witness "one night after he had retired to bed, [when] he called upon the Lord to know if these things were so."[4] "[The] Lord appeared unto . . . Oliver Cowdery and shewed unto him the plates in a vision and . . . what the Lord was about to do through [Joseph] . . . therefore he was desirous to come and write for [Joseph] and translate."[5]

It was at this perilous point that virtually simultaneous prayers seeking divine guidance from the Lord by both Joseph Smith, in search of a scribe, and Oliver Cowdery, in a petition for confirmation of the truth, were answered by God to provide the second witness that was needed for the required revelations that would advance the restoration of the Church of Jesus Christ in these latter days.

Assured of the divinity of the work and enthused with the prospect of his own participation, Oliver visited Joseph in Harmony, Pennsylvania.

TRANSLATION OF THE BOOK OF MORMON

Of their first meeting Oliver fondly recalled: "Near the time of the setting of the sun, Sabbath evening, April 5th, 1829, my natural eyes, for the first time beheld this brother [Joseph Smith]. He then resided in Harmony, Susquehanna County, Pennsylvania. On Monday the 6th, I assisted him in arranging some business of a temporal nature, and on Tuesday the 7th, commenced to write [being scribe as Joseph dictated the translation of] the Book of Mormon. These were days never to be forgotten—to sit under the sound of a voice dictated by the inspiration of heaven, awakened the utmost gratitude of this bosom!"[6]

Having inquired of the Lord concerning this man he had just met, the Prophet Joseph Smith received the revelation found in section 6 of the Doctrine and Covenants. Oh, how the Lord must have loved Oliver!

In this revelation the Lord gave Oliver beautiful and important counsel. He reminded Oliver of the night he had prayed for and received a witness of the divinity of the work Joseph was called to do.

> Verily, verily, I say unto you, if you desire a further witness, cast your mind upon the night that you cried unto me in your heart, that you might know concerning the truth of these things (D&C 6:22).

The Lord further counseled Oliver:

> Behold thou hast a gift, and blessed art thou because of thy gift. Remember it is sacred and cometh from above. . . . If thou wilt do good, yea, and hold out faithful to the end, thou shalt be saved in the kingdom of God . . . ; for there is no gift greater than the gift of salvation. . . . Thou hast inquired of me, and behold, as often as thou hast

inquired thou hast received instruction of my Spirit. If it had not been so, thou wouldst not have come to the place where thou art at this time. (D&C 6:10, 13–14.)

The fact that Oliver was in the presence of the Prophet Joseph Smith was not coincidence or happenstance. It was a result of two men being directed by the Spirit.

The revelation continues as a foreshadowing of Oliver's life and calling as the second witness to the Restoration: "I tell thee these things as a witness unto thee—that the words or the work which thou hast been writing are true. Therefore be diligent; stand by my servant Joseph, faithfully, in whatsoever difficult circumstances he may be for the word's sake. Admonish him in his faults, and also receive admonition of him. Be patient; be sober; be temperate; have patience, faith, hope and charity." (D&C 6:17–19.)

In preparation for the trials and tribulations that were to follow, Oliver could not have received greater inspired counsel: "Treasure up these words in thy heart. Be faithful and diligent in keeping the commandments of God, and I will encircle thee in the arms of my love. Behold, I am Jesus Christ, the Son of God. . . .What greater witness can you have than from God? . . . You have received a witness; for if I have told you things which no man knoweth have you not received a witness? . . . Therefore, fear not . . . let earth and hell combine against you, for if ye are built upon my rock, they cannot prevail." (D&C 6:20, 21, 23, 24, 34.)

SECOND WITNESS

Many marvelous events were now taking place as the Church of Jesus Christ was being restored in these latter days, and throughout this time Oliver was privileged to be at Joseph's side, both as a scribe and as a second witness.

Jesus taught that "in the mouth of two or three witnesses every word may be established" (Matthew 18:16). The law of witnesses and testimony has been evident in every dispensation. Oliver Cowdery was provided as a witness to Joseph Smith and the Restoration in the same manner as the Lord appointed Aaron to serve by the side of

Moses. Joseph prayed for assistance to complete the translation of the Book of Mormon, and in answer to his prayer Oliver Cowdery was given to him as both a scribe in that translation and a witness of the divinity of the events of the Restoration. Similarly, Moses cried to the Lord for assistance because he was slow of speech and tongue. Aaron was provided in answer to Moses' prayer, not only to be a spokesman, but also to bear witness with Moses that the Lord had spoken. Unfortunately, both Aaron and Oliver eventually forgot their roles as witnesses and aspired to equality with the prophets they were sent to sustain.

Oliver was given the unique blessing of being the second witness of the Restoration. He had seen visions, he had seen angels, he had seen the gold plates of the Book of Mormon, and he had seen the Lord. Joseph Smith, as Prophet, was sustained by Oliver Cowdery's witness to the translation and truthfulness of the Book of Mormon; the restoration of the Aaronic Priesthood and the Melchizedek Priesthood under the hands of John the Baptist and Peter, James, and John; and the restoration of the keys of the priesthood on April 3, 1836, in the Kirtland Temple with visitations of the Savior, Moses, Elias, and Elijah. The priesthood and the keys of this dispensation were bestowed on Joseph and Oliver so that we would have two testimonies as to the critical elements of the Restoration. All the above were among the most remarkable events witnessed in the history of the world.

God established the divine law of witnesses so that there would be witnesses to attest to the significant bestowals and proclamations that affected the people on earth. Ancient Apostles such as Peter, James, and John repeat in the New Testament writings their testimony about the Lord Jesus Christ so that we can have more than one witness of the life of our Savior. Both the Bible and the Book of Mormon are witnesses of Jesus Christ. Even God the Father bears witness of His Son Jesus Christ when he introduces Him: "This is my beloved Son. Hear him!" (See Matthew 3:17; Matthew 17:5; Mark 9:7; Luke 9:35; 2 Peter 1:17; D&C 93:15; Joseph Smith—History 1:17; JST, Matthew 3:46.)

To come to an acceptance of the validity of a witness, there must be some tests against which the testimony of the witness is measured. Was there a need for a witness? Was it happenstance, or was there prayerful desire on the part of the witness? Was the witness chosen by the Lord? What was the depth of the integrity of those claiming to be witnesses? Were they teachable? Were they trustworthy? Were they actual witnesses of the event? Did the witness stand the test of time? Did the consecrated testimony of the witness withstand tribulation—all manner of persecution, personal privation, and the cross-examination of historical scholars and nonbelievers? Oliver Cowdery meets each of these qualifications of a valid witness.

Once joined with Joseph in the work of the Restoration, Oliver's essential role in the marvelous work was to stand next to Joseph as a witness—a second witness—to the restoration of fundamental gospel truths and powers. His was the responsibility, along with Joseph, to experience firsthand the literal restoration and then testify boldly of it so that all mankind could be blessed and benefit thereby.

Oliver bore strong testimony of the Book of Mormon, for he had seen the gold plates, first in a vision and then when an angel of the Lord literally laid them before his eyes and those of Joseph Smith and David Whitmer. He bore powerful testimony of the truthfulness of the translation of the Book of Mormon because he was present when Joseph Smith dictated its translation and he heard the voice of the Lord declaring that the plates had been "translated by the gift and power of God" (The Book of Mormon: Another Testament of Jesus Christ, "The Testimony of Three Witnesses"). Through letters and other written documents Oliver bore testimony of visits from John the Baptist, Peter, James, and John, and even the Lord Jesus Christ in the events that restored to the earth the ordinance of baptism by immersion and the Aaronic Priesthood and the Melchizedek Priesthood, which hold the keys of binding on earth what is bound in heaven, the laying on of hands for the gift of the Holy Ghost, and the keys to preach the gospel to every nation, kindred, tongue, and people. He boldly and firmly testified of and defended Joseph Smith as a prophet of God.

Oliver's testimony of these things was powerful and eloquent, yet straightforward and simple. In describing the power of that testimony, Wilford Woodruff recalled, "I have seen Oliver Cowdery when it seemed as though the earth trembled under his feet. I never heard a man bear a stronger testimony than he did when under the influence of the Spirit."[7]

DISASSOCIATION

Despite all his loyalty, sacrifice, and experience in the early days of the Church, Oliver strayed for a time and eventually separated from the Church. Though their beginnings were similar and the Lord brought them together to accomplish His purposes, the lives of Joseph Smith and Oliver Cowdery, at least for a while, separated.

For ten lonely years Oliver was alienated and estranged from those with whom he had forged friendships in the fiery furnaces of affliction and persecution. For a decade Oliver was, at various times, the object of ridicule, scorn, pity, and sympathy.

What happened to Oliver Cowdery? How and why does one prepared by God from childhood to stand as a witness of holy and sacred events stray from the straight and narrow way, forsaking all that the testimony means but still holding fast to the witness? How could Oliver separate himself from his dedicated involvement as the second witness of the restored church?

Oliver became disaffected from the Church because of the frailties of the natural man. Many conditions could have contributed to his disassociation. Pride certainly could have been one element. In a revelation given through Joseph in April 1830 Oliver was cautioned to beware of pride: "Behold, I speak unto you, Oliver. . . . Behold, thou art blessed. . . . But beware of pride, lest thou shalt enter into temptation." (D&C 23:1.)

July 1830 brought another strong warning when the Lord cautioned: "In me he [Oliver] shall have glory, and not of himself, whether in weakness or in strength, whether in bonds or free" (D&C 24:11).

A few recorded incidents in Oliver's life allow us to understand the devastating effect pride can have in one's life. In the early interactions Oliver had with Joseph Smith, he was not always content to be *just* the scribe as Joseph translated the Book of Mormon. He wanted to do more than he was asked to do in his calling. It was as if he coveted Joseph's role and divine priesthood authority as the translator.

This dissatisfaction led Oliver to attempt to correct the Prophet in the specific wording of revelations. On one occasion, Oliver wrote to the Prophet about a phrase in Doctrine and Covenants 20:37, said the phrase was in error, and then added: "I command you in the name of God to erase those words." Joseph received Oliver's demand with

"sorrow and uneasiness" and responded to him, asking "by what authority he took upon him to command me to alter or erase, to add to or
diminish from, a revelation or commandment from Almighty God."[8]

While Joseph was translating the Book of Mormon, Oliver may
have felt he was better qualified to be the translator because he was
better educated than Joseph. However, when Oliver was given the opportunity to translate, he failed in his attempt to do so. In a subsequent
revelation he was admonished to be patient and was asked to be content to perform his duties as a scribe. "Behold, I say unto you, my son,
that because you did not translate according to that which you desired
of me, and did commence again to write for my servant, Joseph Smith,
Jun., even so I would that ye should continue until you have finished
this record, which I have entrusted unto him" (D&C 9:1).

Another example of pride in Oliver's life involves a stone owned
by Hiram Page, one of the Eight Witnesses to the Book of Mormon.
By the use of this stone Hiram Page obtained purported revelations for
the guidance of the Church. Oliver was one of those who believed
these so-called revelations, and perhaps this sparked within him a desire to act and be like the Prophet. At the very least, it was a serious
error of judgment. By a special revelation given through the Prophet
Joseph the Lord set Oliver straight on the matter of revelations for the
Church and assigned him to correct Hiram Page.

> Behold, I say unto thee, Oliver, that. . . . no one shall be ap-
> pointed to receive commandments and revelations in this church ex-
> cepting my servant Joseph Smith, Jun., for he receiveth them even as
> Moses.
>
> And thou shalt be obedient unto the things which I shall give
> unto him, even as Aaron, to declare faithfully the commandments
> and the revelations, with power and authority unto the church. . . .
>
> And thou shalt not command him who is at thy head, and at the
> head of the church.
>
> For I have given him the keys of the mysteries, and the revela-
> tions which are sealed, until I shall appoint unto them another in his
> stead. . . .
>
> And again, thou shalt take thy brother, Hiram Page, between
> him and thee alone, and tell him that those things which he hath
> written from that stone are not of me and that Satan deceiveth him.
> (D&C 28:1–3, 6–7, 11.)

Later the Lord would reiterate this principle (see D&C 43:1–7).

These incidents in Oliver's life are great teaching moments for every priesthood holder and every member of the Church. Apparently Oliver forgot his important supportive role to a prophet of God, taking upon himself more authority than he was granted through the callings he had been given. The result for Oliver was the loss of his priesthood authority, which led to a decade of disassociation from the Church.

Jealousy and backbiting may have developed within Oliver with the emergence of powerful and devoted priesthood leaders who stood by the Prophet's side. The human trait of finding fault with the emerging leaders of the Church and not being able to take direction or correction from those brethren who served with Joseph could have been another component in Oliver's disassociation. Another element could have been the fact that after the closeness experienced during the remarkable early events of the Restoration, Oliver was separated from the Prophet Joseph because different missionary assignments put many miles between them.

Whatever the reasons, we know that for a period of time he lost his precious gift of faith and was separated from the Church. Oliver had allowed some little differences to canker his soul, and thus he lost opportunities for great blessings.[9]

There is a phrase in the scriptures: "But whosoever continueth not to receive, from him shall be taken away even that he hath" (JST, Matthew 13:12). During the period of Oliver's absence from the Church, that which he had was taken away; and, sadly for him, upon his return the time and opportunity to regain what was once his had passed.

> And from this time forth I appoint unto him [Hyrum Smith] that he may be a prophet, and a seer, and a revelator unto my church, as well as my servant Joseph;
>
> That he may act in concert also with my servant Joseph; and that he shall receive counsel from my servant Joseph, who shall show unto him the keys whereby he may ask and receive, and be crowned with the same blessing, and glory, and honor, and priesthood, and gifts of the priesthood, that once were put upon him that was my servant Oliver Cowdery;

That my servant Hyrum may bear record of the things which I shall show unto him, that his name may be had in honorable remembrance from generation to generation, forever and ever (D&C 124: 94–96).

Thus the special calling that Oliver had once had was given to Hyrum Smith.

One can only imagine the aching sorrow that must have been in Oliver's heart that would have given him a melancholy countenance during the time he was disassociated from the Church. William Lang, a student who apprenticed in Oliver Cowdery's legal office, said of Oliver: "His manners were easy and gentlemanly. He was polite, dignified, yet courteous. . . . With all his kind and friendly disposition, there was a certain degree of sadness that seemed to pervade his whole being. . . . He was modest and reserved, never spoke ill of anyone, never complained."[10]

Phineas Young, brother-in-law to Oliver, was very close to him. Phineas labored with Oliver and wrote him letter after letter over a period of years. In response to a letter Oliver had penned in which he expressed some of his grievances and feelings that he had been personally injured by some of his friends, Phineas wrote back and said: "Never mind all that; suppose there was some grievance. You know the gospel is true; you know your testimony; you know where you belong."[11]

Oliver knew the importance of that of which he had been a part, and he knew that he should come back to the Church. Joseph had an intensely strong desire for Oliver to come back, and it was on his mind even until his death. There was no other man on earth who really knew just who Oliver was and what he could have become.

About a year before the Martyrdom the Prophet Joseph Smith asked that a letter be written to Oliver Cowdery asking him if he had not fed upon husks long enough, a clear reference to the parable of the prodigal son.[12]

The letter reads as follows:

City of Nauvoo April 19, 1843

An epistle of The Twelve, in Council assembled, to Oliver Cowdery, one of the witnesses to the Book of Mormon.

Dear Brother;–

We are assembled together for the purpose of taking steps, for the upbuilding of Zion. . . . Among other things that came before us, was that of the situation of Oliver Cowdery[.] We reflected upon the time when we had met together, when we were brethren, when we were one, & took sweet counsel together.

We thought perhaps our old, long esteemed friend might by this time have felt his lonely solitary situation; might feel that he was a stranger in a strange land, & had wandered long enough from his Fathers house, & that he might have a disposition to return. If this is the case, all that we have got to say, is, your <u>brethren</u> are ready to receive you, we are not your enemies, but your ~~friend~~ brethren. Your dwelling place you know ought to be in Zion—Your labor might be needed in Jerusalem, & you ought to be the servant of the living God.

In the bonds of the New & Everlasting Covenant we remain your <u>unchangeable</u> friends <u>in</u> the Gospel.[13]

The letter was signed by Brigham Young, Heber C. Kimball, Parley P. Pratt, William Smith, Orson Pratt, Willard Richards, Wilford Woodruff, John Taylor, and George A. Smith.

RETURN TO FULL FELLOWSHIP
WITH THE CHURCH

Four years after Joseph's martyrdom in 1844 Oliver Cowdery found his way back to Nauvoo and then continued his journey across the territory of Iowa to the camp of the Latter-day Saints at Kanesville, where he made his plea to reenter the Church, testifying that he was not asking to come back for any place or position, but merely to be a humble member of the Church. At that time he bore witness to the truthfulness of the Book of Mormon and the Restoration.

In all humility Oliver said: "I have sustained an honorable character before the world during my absence from you, . . . I am out of the church. I know the door into the church [baptism], and I wish to become a member thro the door. I wish to become a humble private member. I do not come here to seek honor."[14]

UNWAVERING TESTIMONY OF
THE RESTORATION

The foibles of the natural man caused Oliver to disassociate himself from the body of the Church from 1838 to 1848, but, to his credit, at no time in his life did he deny his testimony. Oliver Cowdery bore unwavering witness and testimony of the Book of Mormon and the restoration of the Aaronic and Melchizedek Priesthoods from 1829 till his death in 1850.

During the period of his disassociation from the Church, Oliver practiced law in the state of Michigan. While he was participating as prosecutor in a murder trial, the attorney for the defendant tried to shift the focus of the trial from his client to Oliver Cowdery, who was then the county attorney. With sneers and jests he challenged Oliver about his association with Joseph Smith, his visit with an angelic messenger, and his witness of the Book of Mormon.

Finally, when the defendant's attorney had completed his argument, Oliver Cowdery's turn came to reply, and everybody in the court room strained their necks to catch a glimpse of Mr. Cowdery. He arose as calm as a summer morning, and in a low but clear voice which gradually rose in pitch and volume as he proceeded, said:

"If your honor please, and gentlemen of the jury, the attorney on the opposite side has challenged me to state my connection with Joseph Smith and the Book of Mormon; and as I cannot now avoid the responsibility, I must admit to you that I am the very Oliver Cowdery whose name is attached to the testimony, with others, as to the appearance of the angel Moroni; and let me tell you that it is not because of my good deeds that I am here, away from the body of the Mormon church, but because I have broken the covenants I once made, and I was cut off from the church; but, gentlemen of the jury, I have never denied my testimony, which is attached to the front page of the *Book of Mormon,* and I declare to you here that these eyes saw the angel, and these ears of mine heard the voice of the angel, and he told us his name was Moroni; that the book was true, and contained the fulness of the gospel, and we were also told that if we ever denied what we had heard and seen that there would be no forgiveness for us, neither in this world nor in the world to come."[15]

In 1887 David Whitmer wrote a statement in which he reported Oliver Cowdery's deathbed testimony of the truthfulness of the Book of Mormon. "I will say once more to all mankind, that I [David Whitmer] have never at any time denied the testimony or any part thereof. I also testify to the world, that neither Oliver Cowdery or Martin Harris ever at any time denied their testimony." Oliver's last words to David were, " 'Brother David, be true to your testimony of the Book of Mormon.' "[16]

Oliver Cowdery always maintained his first testimony that God had sent an angel and revealed to him that the Book of Mormon was true. We can read from Brigham Young's April 1855 general conference address: "Oliver Cowdery . . . never denied the Book of Mormon, not even in the wickedest days he ever saw."[17]

Lucy P. Young, stepsister to Oliver, stated in a letter of 7 March 1887 to Brigham Young Jr.: "Just before [Oliver] breathed his last, he asked to be raised up in bed so he could talk to the family and friends and he told them to live according to the teachings of the Book of Mormon and they would meet him in heaven. Then he said lay me down and let me fall asleep in the arms of Jesus and he fell asleep without a struggle."[18]

Oliver Cowdery's history teaches a lesson for each member of the Church—to express gratitude each day for the blessings we have received from having the gospel in our lives. In our prayers we need to ask the Lord to strengthen us that we will not waver in our times of persecution or tribulation, that we can rise above the wrongs and differences and trials of mortality, and that we may hold true to our covenants so that we will be able to testify and to be witnesses of the Lord Jesus Christ and the restoration of The Church of Jesus Christ of Latter-day Saints in these latter days.

NOTES

1. "Mormonism," Kansas City Daily Journal, 5 June 1881.

2. In Dean C. Jessee, ed., The Personal Writings of Joseph Smith (Salt Lake City: Deseret Book, 1984), p. 8.

3. Lucy Mack Smith, History of Joseph Smith (Salt Lake City: Bookcraft, 1956), p. 139.

4. In Dean C. Jessee, ed., *The Papers of Joseph Smith*, 2 vols. (Salt Lake City: Deseret Book, 1989), 1:289.

5. *The Personal Writings of Joseph Smith*, p. 8.

6. Oliver Cowdery Letter to W. W. Phelps, 7 September 1834, in *Messenger and Advocate* 1 (October 1834): 14.

7. Wilford Woodruff, Address 3 March 1889, Provo, Utah, in Brian H. Stuy, ed., *Collected Discourses Delivered by President Wilford Woodruff, His Two Counselors, the Twelve Apostles, and Others*, vol. 1 (Burbank, California: B. H. S. Publishing, 1987), p. 220.

8. *History of the Church* 1:105.

9. See Dean C. Jessee, ed., *The Papers of Joseph Smith*, 2 vols. (Salt Lake City: Deseret Book, 1992), 2:227–31; Donald Q. Cannon and Lyndon W. Cook, *Far West Record: Minutes of The Church of Jesus Christ of Latter-day Saints, 1830–1844* (Deseret Book, 1983), pp. 162–71.

10. William Long, *History of Seneca County* (Springfield, Ohio, 1880), p. 365; quoted in Richard L. Anderson, "Oliver Cowdery's Non-Mormon Reputation," *Improvement Era*, August 1968, p. 22.

11. Quoted by Clifford E. Young, Conference Report, October 1954, p. 103.

12. See *History of the Church* 5:368.

13. Council of the Twelve, Letter Draft, 19 April 1843, Nauvoo, Illinois, to Oliver Cowdery; Luna Y. Thatcher Collection, Church Historical Department.

14. Pottawattamie High Council, Minutes, 5 November 1848, typescript, Church Historical Department.

15. B. H. Roberts, *Comprehensive History of The Church of Jesus Christ of Latter-day Saints*, 6 vols. (Salt Lake City: Deseret News, 1930), 1:142–43.

16. David Whitmer, *An Address to All Believers in Christ* (Richmond: Missouri: The Author, 1887), p. 8.

17. In *Journal of Discourses* 2:257.

18. Lucy P. Young, Letter, 7 March 1887, to Brigham Young Jr., Church Historical Department.

3

Elder Marlin K. Jensen

Martin Harris
A Life Worth Remembering

I am interested in the role that "remembering" plays in the way we live our lives. It seems to me that one purpose of the gospel ordinances and of the scriptures is to influence for good our current choices and behavior by reminding us of events of times past, especially the Savior's life and atonement. Nephi, for example, once read to his brethren from the brass plates that they "might know concerning the doings of the Lord in other lands, among people of old" and that he "might more fully persuade them to believe in the Lord their Redeemer" (1 Nephi 19:22–23). There is also much value in remembering circumstances from the history of the Church in this final dispensation that can positively affect the way we conduct our lives today. Perhaps that is why Alma begins the searching series of questions to Church members of his day by inquiring whether they have "sufficiently retained in remembrance" certain essentials of their dynamic history (Alma 5:6).

No period of Church history exceeds the early period of the Restoration for spirit, drama, pathos, and memorable men and women. Oliver Cowdery's well-known exclamation that "these were days never to be forgotten" was heartfelt and true. Among the "unforgettable" figures of that period is Martin Harris, best known as one of the Three Witnesses of the Book of Mormon. His life is worthy of being studied and remembered for its strengths as well as its weaknesses, and especially for the evidence it provides of God's personal involvement in the lives of His children as He brings to pass His eternal purposes. I personally find the following elements of Martin's life especially instructive and memorable.

MARTIN HARRIS AND THE PROPHET JOSEPH

Among the most interesting and satisfying aspects of a study of Church history are the human relationships that emerge. The relationship between Martin Harris and Joseph Smith first captured my attention when our family was called in 1993 to serve for two years in the New York Rochester Mission of the Church. Within less than twelve hours after arriving in Rochester we boarded the mission van and headed east on Route 31, which leads from Rochester to Palmyra. As Route 31 merged into Main Street in Palmyra and we saw for the first time the famed "four-corner" churches (houses of worship of four different denominations, constructed after the First Vision, located on the four corners of the same intersection), the "lo, here" and "lo, there" confusion and excitement described by the Prophet Joseph in his history took on new meaning (see Joseph Smith—History 1:5). We then drove a mile or so south on Stafford Road to the hundred-acre Smith farm, where missionary guides reverently ushered us through the family home. Later we walked unescorted across Crooked Creek along a tree-lined path to the Sacred Grove.

After a spiritually moving experience together as a family in a small clearing in the Grove, we traveled another mile south and east to the Hill Cumorah, speculating along the way about which route Joseph might have taken on that long-awaited night in September of 1827 when Moroni finally permitted him to receive the plates. After thoroughly inspecting "the Hill" (it did not take us long to pick up Palmyra-area jargon) we drove back to Palmyra, past the Grandin building where the Book of Mormon was first printed, and then north on Maple Road toward Wintergreen Hill and the Martin Harris farm. As we crossed over the Erie Canal and drove through the verdant countryside, I could easily imagine the Smith boys walking there in the early morning hours of a summer's day to keep their field-work engagements with local farmers.

Standing on the upper end of the Harris farm looking back toward the village of Palmyra, I began for the first time to appreciate the opportunity the mission would give our family to learn the geography of the Restoration. Until then I had not realized how much a personal acquaintance with the places, the distances, and the physical features of the land of the Restoration would help us to comprehend the human dimensions and the relationships that were part of the principal characters of that period in Church history. Over the next two years this became a great blessing in our acquiring greater perspective about essential facts concerning the Restoration, learning about things not just as they "really are" and "really will be" (Jacob 4:13) but also as they "really were."

For instance, the thought came to me some time later that Martin Harris could certainly be considered the "senior citizen" of the Restoration. He was thirty-six in 1820 when the fourteen-year-old Joseph Smith experienced the theophany that would radically change millions of lives, including Martin's. Martin learned about Joseph's experience from conversations with him and other Smith family members as they worked on Martin's farm. Because of intense persecution, the Smiths were very selective about sharing Joseph's story, so Martin must have enjoyed a closeness and confidence with them. Joseph, in turn, was undoubtedly grateful for Martin's willingness to accept the miraculous nature of his experiences and for his early and very critical financial support. In his own account, Joseph says with an obvious sense of relief that in the midst of his family's afflictions "we found a friend in a gentleman by the name of Martin Harris" and then adds, perhaps to further show his gratitude, that Martin was "a farmer of respectability" (Joseph Smith—History 1:61). These written lines are brief, but what one reads between them speaks volumes concerning the relationship Martin and Joseph enjoyed and what it must have meant to the sensitive young prophet to have an older man of Martin's stature believe in him. The faith of early converts must have been strengthened by the knowledge that a man twice Joseph's age, and who by 1828 had been married for twenty years, had five children, and had acquired a 320-acre farm and erected a substantial home, would commit himself so early and so completely to Joseph and the fledgling restoration movement.

MARTIN HARRIS AND LUCY HARRIS

The changes the gospel required did not come without some jolting domestic adjustments for Martin. Although his first wife, Lucy, initially appeared to be sincerely interested in the Restoration, she quickly became suspicious and hostile toward Joseph Smith and his family. It is difficult to determine just what the relationship between Martin and Lucy was before they became involved with the Prophet Joseph. However, Mother Smith offers the telling observations in her history that "[Lucy] considered herself altogether superior to her husband" and that Martin "always allowed her to keep a private purse in order to satisfy her singular disposition."[1]

Martin's response to Lucy's escalating opposition to his involvement with Joseph was admirable, and it can serve as a model for those who may find themselves spiritually unequally yoked in marriage. He was patient and understanding, kept her informed of his religious activities, and did all he could to involve and please her.

Even the well-known episode of the lost 116 pages of the Book of Mormon manuscript appears to have been motivated by Martin's desire to appease Lucy. Toward the end of his life, in speaking of this traumatic experience, Martin told William Pilkington, "Willie I loved my wife and wanted to please her. . . . I found out Willie that the Lord could get out of patience as well as a human."[2]

Shortly before Martin left Palmyra to join the Saints gathering in Ohio in May of 1831 he sold 151 acres of his farm to satisfy the $3000 debt he had incurred to help finance publication of the Book of Mormon. At that time Lucy and he separated, and she and the children went to live on a part of the farm deeded to her pursuant to an agreement of separation. The home in which they lived still stands, and even now when visiting the premises one feels a certain sadness and sense of "what might have been." Martin made at least one trip back to Palmyra in 1836, when undoubtedly he made a last attempt to reconcile with Lucy. This apparently failed, and Lucy died later that summer.

If Martin's marriage to Lucy represents one of his tutoring tests in life, it seems to me he did very well with it. A knowledge of their relationship provides an understanding of the Savior's declaration that when one takes up his cross, a "man's foes shall be they of his own household" (Matthew 10:36). On the other hand, one must also feel compassion for Lucy and the children. Their relatively prosperous and stable lifestyle was radically disturbed by Martin's "call" to the Lord's service and his faithful response to its demands. From her perspective, Lucy's unmet expectations in the marriage were just as great as Martin's. For both of them, dealing with the wrenching effects of the Restoration on their lives took exceptional courage and fortitude, regardless of the merits of their differing views of Joseph Smith and his mission.

MARTIN HARRIS AND HIS PALMYRA NEIGHBORS

President David O. McKay taught that the gospel of Jesus Christ is to "make bad men good and good men better." In terms of everyday living, Martin Harris was already at least a very good man by the time he accepted the claims of Joseph Smith. If his believability as a witness of the Book of Mormon depends upon his character, it is clear from contemporary accounts that his neighbors considered him an honest, industrious citizen and farmer. As part of a serial history of Palmyra published in the *Palmyra Courier* in 1872, James H. Reeves observed that until his connection with Mormonism Martin Harris "was an industrious, hard-working farmer, shrewd in his business calculations, frugal in his habits, and what was termed a prosperous man in the world."[3]

The one thing Martin's neighbors could never seem to reconcile was how he could sign his name to the statement of the Three Witnesses in view of the reputation for good character and honesty he had always enjoyed. What did not occur to many of them then (and to many who read the Book of Mormon today) is that the testimony of one so stable and competent in ordinary life ought to be given equal credibility in spiritual matters.

MARTIN HARRIS AND THE
REVELATIONS OF THE LORD

Because of the prominent role Martin Harris played in the coming forth of the Book of Mormon and the early organization of the Church, a number of revelations in the Doctrine and Covenants contain counsel and admonitions to him. The most poignant reference is a reprimand by the Lord in section 3, verses 12 and 13, relating to the loss of the 116 pages of the first Book of Mormon manuscript. Here the Lord refers to Martin as a "wicked man." My study of Martin's life leads me to believe that Martin was certainly not wicked at heart, but generally desired to do what was right. However, his belief in the mission of Joseph Smith was at the time not sufficiently strong for him to withstand alone the pressures of family and friends, and he wanted to convince them of the value of his labors in acting as Joseph's scribe by showing them the manuscript.

Martin's "wickedness," as does much of ours, consisted of insisting that his own will be done contrary to the will of the Lord. The assertion of "my will" in opposition to "thy will" is at the root of most transgression and contrasts sharply with the submissiveness Abinadi attributes to the Savior in describing "the will of the Son being swallowed up in the will of the Father" (Mosiah 15:7). Martin then compounded the error of his first transgression by breaking the promise he had made to show the manuscript only to a few specified individuals. This pattern of one sin being succeeded by another is also a common occurrence in our lives. Usually the initial transgression is followed by lies designed to cover up, minimize, or justify the wrong. We often seek first to hide our sin and then, when that fails, to blame others for causing it or to otherwise rationalize it away.

The consequences of Martin's "wickedness" were serious—he was relieved of his duties as scribe, and Joseph temporarily lost his gift to translate—but the encouraging fact to me is that Martin was able to humbly repent and again find favor with the Lord. He was later deemed worthy to act as one of the three special witnesses of the Book of Mormon, participate in the selection of the first Quorum of the Twelve in this dispensation, and serve on a committee to assemble the revelations and commandments of the Lord—all significant spiritual duties.

A common thread that runs through several of the other revelations directed to Martin concerned his obligation to provide financial support for the emerging Church. I am reminded of a one-liner employed years ago by my student-ward bishop as he made a plea to our poverty-stricken ranks to pay what was then called the ward budget assessment. "Remember," he said, "we have to make the coins roll, to help the stone roll!" Martin came to understand this principle well as the Lord commanded him not to covet and to give freely to the

printing of the Book of Mormon (see D&C 19:26), to lay his monies
before the bishop of the Church as one of the pioneers of the law of
consecration (see D&C 58:35), and to devote his monies for the proclaiming of the word (see D&C 104:26).

It did not take long for me years ago, as a young bishop, to become
impressed with the close correlation between a strong conviction of
the truth of the restored gospel and one's willingness to contribute
money, time, and other means to the building of the kingdom. Judged
by this standard, Martin stands very tall among those early stalwarts
God called to help restore His church. The 151 acres of choice farm
ground Martin sold in 1831 to raise the $3,000 needed to pay Book of
Mormon publication costs are worth at least $150,000 today, which
gives us some comparative idea of the substantial value of Martin's
assistance. Such considerations may also help us be a little more sym-
pathetic toward Lucy Harris's suspicions at the time, and toward Martin's desires to show the Book of Mormon manuscript to his family
and to obtain from professors Anthon and Mitchell independent veri-
fication of the accuracy of Joseph's translation. Martin was putting his
property and money where his heart was, and the fact that he consistently did so in those early years is a testimony to his generosity and to
his strong belief that the mission of the Prophet Joseph was authenti-
cally divine.

MARTIN HARRIS AS A
BOOK OF MORMON WITNESS

In 1829, shortly after Oliver Cowdery and David Whitmer had
done so, in a wooded area near the Whitmer farm in Fayette, New
York, Martin Harris was privileged to behold the plates from which the
Book of Mormon was translated and, in the presence of an angel, to
hear the voice of the Lord declaring that the translation had been done
by the Lord's power and that Martin was to bear record of what he saw
and heard. A few months later the Lord reaffirmed Martin's important
calling as a witness. In a powerful and poetic passage of scripture He
told Martin: "And thou shalt declare . . . it upon the mountains, and
upon every high place, and among every people that thou shalt be permitted to see" (D&C 19:29). Martin's life after receiving this divine di-

rective had as its one notable constant his unwavering testimony of the experience he had had in the Whitmer woods.

For the first eight or nine years thereafter, Martin was a loyal associate and follower of the Prophet Joseph Smith. He was present at the organization of the Church on April 6, 1830, and was baptized that day. He gathered with the Saints in Ohio in 1831, journeyed to Missouri in 1831 and again with Zion's Camp in 1834, and engaged in missionary work in various locations. Martin's enthusiasm for the restored Church started to wane by 1837 as the Church at Kirtland began suffering from internal dissension and apostasy became rife. In September of that year Martin Harris was dropped from the Kirtland high council. It appears that by December he had been excommunicated from the Church because of his affiliation with dissenters.

Thereafter Martin began uncharacteristically to vacillate in his religious feelings. Over the next several years he affiliated in succession with a group of apostates led by Warren Parrish; the Shaker organization of Ann Lee; James J. Strang's movement; the Church of Christ organized by William E. McLellin, formerly one of the Twelve Apostles; and lastly he joined with the Prophet Joseph's brother William in organizing a church. At every juncture along this rocky path Martin had every reason to deny his testimony of the Book of Mormon and thereby gain some advantage for himself, but he stood firm in his witness.

A statement he made in an interview in Kirtland with David B. Dille, a missionary journeying from Utah to England in 1853, is representative of his unwavering conviction during this period of apostasy: "Do I not know that the Book of Mormon is true? Did I not hear the voice of God out of Heaven declaring that it was truth and correctly translated? Yes I did and you know I did for I see that you have the spirit of it."[4] In 1869 when Martin bore a similar testimony to William H. Homer, another visitor from Utah, Martin was asked how he could bear such a wonderful testimony after having left the Church. Martin replied: "Young man, I never did leave the Church, the Church left me."[5]

Over the years Martin's feelings gradually softened and he was eventually invited and assisted to move west and rejoin the Saints. In 1870, at age eighty-seven, he traveled from Kirtland to Salt Lake City with Elder Edward Stevenson, a member of the First Council of the

Seventy, who was acting under President Brigham Young's direction. A wonderful reunion with family and friends ensued and Martin was rebaptized, spoke and bore testimony to the divine authenticity of the Book of Mormon in October general conference, and then went to live with a son, Martin Harris Jr., in Smithfield, Cache County, Utah.

Martin Harris died on July 9, 1875, in Clarkston, Utah. William H. Homer, a brother-in-law of Martin Harris Jr., was present in Martin's final hours and recorded his impressions as follows:

> I stood by the bedside holding the patient's right hand and my mother at the foot of the bed. Martin Harris had been unconscious for a number of days. When we first entered the room the old gentleman appeared to be sleeping. He soon woke up and asked for a drink of water. I put my arm under the old gentleman, raised him, and my mother held the glass to his lips. He drank freely, then he looked up at me and recognized me. He said, "I know you. You are my friend." He said, "Yes, I did see the plates on which the Book of Mormon was written; I did see the angel; I did hear the voice of God; and I do know that Joseph Smith is a Prophet of God, holding the keys of the Holy Priesthood." This was the end. Martin Harris, divinely chosen witness of the work of God, relaxed, gave up my hand. He lay back on his pillow and just as the sun went down behind the Clarkston mountains, the soul of Martin Harris passed on.[6]

Martin's dying declaration of his testimony of the Book of Mormon was consistent with the witness he had borne for nearly fifty years. In the beginning the calling of Martin and the other witnesses to the Book of Mormon may have been as much for Joseph Smith's benefit as for the benefit of the world. Lucy Smith, in her history, says that the Prophet came home weeping for joy after the witnesses had seen the plates under the direction of an angel of God because, he said, "I feel as if I was relieved of a burden which was almost too heavy for me to bear, and it rejoices my soul, that I am not any longer to be entirely alone in the world."[7] The calling of the witnesses also fulfilled the Lord's law of witnesses (see 2 Corinthians 13:1) and complied with His pattern of providing the testimony of witnesses whenever He has established a new dispensation of the gospel.

On a more personal level, I must honestly ask myself the question:

If Martin saw what he claimed he saw and knew what he claimed he knew, why did he become disaffected from the Prophet Joseph and the Church and spend over thirty years away from the main body of the Saints? My answer is a simple one: If I know what I know, why do I do as I do? To some greater or lesser degree, all of our lives deviate from strict adherence to gospel standards and requirements, and thus we are all "disaffected" or estranged from God to some extent. Despite all the ebbing and flowing of Martin's life, he was undeviating in his witness of the Prophet Joseph's mission and the truth of the Book of Mormon. This fact provides an important anchor to my faith in the Prophet Joseph and the restored gospel.

CONCLUSION

Martin Harris deserves to be remembered. Recalling his struggles and challenges helps me see more clearly the inconsistencies in my own life and makes me want to make ever more congruous the relationship between what I know and what I do. It also helps me realize that no life can be measured without viewing it as a composite of all one has done (and omitted to do) over an entire lifetime. Martin ended his life in full fellowship in the faith, loyal to the restored gospel and devoid of bitterness. Finally, remembering him makes me very grateful that for Martin Harris and for all of us "the keeper of the gate is the Holy One of Israel; and he employeth no servant there" (2 Nephi 9:41). Only our infinitely empathetic and merciful Savior will ultimately know Martin Harris and each of us well enough to make a fair judgment concerning his and our eternal destinies. And that is something really worth remembering!

NOTES

1. Lucy Mack Smith, *History of Joseph Smith* (Salt Lake City: Bookcraft, 1956), pp. 115–16.

2. William Pilkington Jr., *Autobiography*, 1938, p. 16, Church Historical Department.

3. *Palmyra Courier*, 24 May 1872, as quoted by Richard L. Anderson in "Martin Harris, the Honorable New York Farmer," *Improvement Era* 72 (February 1969), p. 18.

4. David B. Dille Reminiscence, 1886, typescript, p. 4, Church Historical Department.

5. William Harrison Homer, "The Passing of Martin Harris," *Improvement Era* 29 (March 1926), p. 470.

6. Ibid., p. 472.

7. Lucy Mack Smith, *op. cit.*, p. 152.

4

Elder Russell M. Nelson

Orson Hyde

Lessons that I have learned from studying the life of Orson Hyde have been both powerful and fundamental. Before getting into the fascinating detail of Elder Hyde's sojourn in mortality, we would do well to remember the dialogue between God and Abraham that reveals the purpose of our life upon the earth:

> Now the Lord had shown unto me, Abraham, the intelligences that were organized before the world was; and among all these there were many of the noble and great ones;
>
> And God saw these souls that they were good, and he stood in the midst of them, and he said: These I will make my rulers; for he stood among those that were spirits, and he saw that they were good; and he said unto me: Abraham, thou art one of them; thou wast chosen before thou wast born.
>
> And there stood one among them that was like unto God, and he said unto those who were with him: We will go down, for there is space there, and we will take of these materials, and we will make an earth whereon these may dwell;
>
> And we will prove them herewith, to see if they will do all things whatsoever the Lord their God shall command them. (Abraham 3:22–25.)

As you become better acquainted with Orson Hyde you will no doubt conclude, as have I, that he along with Abraham was fore-ordained for the ministry he was to perform. In addition, he was sub-jected to trials and testing to see if he would obey the commandments of the Lord. Those tests came in many ways. As you read on, you will find the thread of hardship woven through the fabric of his life's story. Now in retrospect, that thread looms prominently as a fiber of strength that helped Orson Hyde to accomplish all that the Lord re-quired at the very strenuous time in which Brother Hyde and his asso-ciates lived. I have concluded that this remarkable man did indeed fulfill the purpose for which he was sent to the earth, and that he did it with courage and faith.

Deprived of parents early in life, Orson Hyde pensively wrote of his gratitude to "a kind Providence who ever watches, with care, over the lonely orphan and hears the plaintive cry of the young sparrows, bereft of their parent mother."[1]

Born 8 January 1805 to Sally Thorpe and Nathan Hyde of Ox-ford, New Haven County, Connecticut, Orson was one of eleven chil-dren. He was seven years old when his mother died. His father was later drowned while attempting to swim a river in Derby, Connecti-cut. After the death of Orson's mother, young Orson was placed in the foster care of Nathan Wheeler. Six years later, in 1818, Mr. Wheeler moved to a farm he had purchased in Kirtland, Ohio, and sent for Orson and Mr. Wheeler's nephew, Nathan Wooster, the spring of the following year. Of that difficult move Orson wrote: "This was a hard trip for a youngster [fourteen years of age] to perform on foot, with knapsack upon the back, containing clothes, bread, cheese, and dried beef for the journey, and obliged to keep up with a strong man, travel-ling from 30 to 38 miles per day, until we had performed the entire distance of 600 miles."[2]

At the age of eighteen he separated himself from Mr. and Mrs. Wheeler. Orson described details of his "first debut into the world with the following outfit. One suit of home-made woollen clothes (butternut colored). Two red flannel shirts, also home-made. Two pairs of socks, one pair of coarse shoes on the feet, one old hat and six and a quarter cents in clean cash."[3]

Such was the start in life for this great Apostle whose name is everlastingly etched in the history of the Church, having been mentioned in six sections of the Doctrine and Covenants (see D&C 68:1–12; 75:13; 100:14; 102:3–4, 34; 103:40; 124:128–29).

At age eighteen he was literally on his own. He worked in a small iron foundry and then learned to card wool. He later went to Kirtland, Ohio, where he gained employment as a clerk in the store of Sidney Gilbert and Newel K. Whitney. Orson's religious bent took him first to the Methodist faith, then to the Campbellite group. There he was impressed with its chief advocate, Sidney Rigdon, and with the doctrine of baptism by immersion for the remission of sins. Rigdon also subsequently served as tutor for Orson's study of English grammar.

CONVERSION TO THE CHURCH

In the autumn of 1830 Orson Hyde was a pastor of the Campbellite churches in Elyria and Florence, Ohio, where he first encountered Samuel H. Smith, Ziba Peterson, Frederick G. Williams, and Peter Whitmer. They preached of a "golden bible" and "Mormonism." After an initial negative response to the men and their teachings, he conceded "that the 'Mormon' bible might be the truth of heaven."[4] In the summer of 1831 he returned to Kirtland to investigate more fully. Of that experience he wrote:

> After about three months of careful and prayerful investigation, reflection and meditation, I came to the conclusion that the "Mormons" had more light and a better spirit than their opponents. I concluded that I could not be the loser by joining the "Mormons," and as an honest man, conscientiously bound to walk in the best and clearest light I saw, I resolved to be baptized into the new religion. Hence, I attended the Saints' meeting in Kirtland, Sunday, October 30, 1831, and offered myself a candidate for baptism, which was administered to me by the hands of Elder Sidney Rigdon; was confirmed and ordained an elder in the Church on the same day under the hands of Joseph Smith, the Prophet, and Sidney Rigdon.[5]

Thus Orson Hyde was baptized, confirmed, ordained, and prepared for his lifelong saga as a leader in The Church of Jesus Christ of Latter-day Saints.

Exposure to the Destiny of the Church

From the writings of Wilford Woodruff we gain additional insight concerning the destiny of the Church as revealed by the Prophet Joseph Smith to a small group of leaders:

> [At Zion's Camp] the Prophet called upon the elders of Israel with him to bear testimony of this work. Those that I have named (Oliver Cowdery, Brigham Young, Heber C. Kimball, the two Pratts, Orson Hyde, and others) spoke, and a good many that I have not named bore their testimonies. When they got through the Prophet said:
>
> "Brethren, I have been very much edified and instructed in your testimonies here tonight, but I want to say to you before the Lord, that you know no more concerning the destinies of this church and kingdom than a babe upon its mother's lap. You don't comprehend it. . . .
>
> "It is only a handful of priesthood you see here tonight, but this church will fill North and South America—it will fill the world."[6]

Young Orson Hyde—and others assembled—gained a global perspective even though Orson's experience at that time had been limited to a small sector of one country.

Missionary Service Begins

Soon after his baptism Orson Hyde was ordained a high priest by Joseph Smith and appointed as a missionary to labor with Hyrum Smith, older brother of the Prophet. They labored among Orson's old Campbellite friends, baptized many, and established two or three branches of the Church. Later, Orson was sent on another mission, this time with a younger brother of the Prophet, Samuel H. Smith. In the spring of 1832 they journeyed by foot eastward, without purse or scrip, to New York, Massachusetts, Maine, and Rhode Island, returning home to Ohio in late December. Orson's personal description of that missionary experience bears citation here. It would make good reading for any present-day missionary who feels the difficulties of duty:

> This was one of the most arduous and toilsome missions ever performed in the Church. To travel two thousand miles on foot, teach-

ing from house to house, and from city to city, without purse or scrip, often sleeping in school houses after preaching—in barns, in sheds, by the way side, under trees, and etc., was something of a task. When one would be teaching in private families, the other would frequently be nodding in his chair, weary with toil, fatigue and want of sleep. We were often rejected in the afterpart of the day, compelling us to travel in the evening, and sometimes till people were gone to bed, leaving us to lodge where we could. We would sometimes travel until midnight or until nearly daylight before we could find a barn or shed in which we dare to lie down; must be away before discovered least suspicion rest upon us. Would often lie down under trees and sleep in day time to make up loss.[7]

In Kirtland, the School of the Prophets met in early 1833, most often in a room above Newel K. Whitney's store, where Brother Hyde had been employed. Orson Hyde was the instructor, and the Prophet Joseph Smith presided. Selected priesthood holders were invited to attend; probably no more than twenty-five men were enrolled at a time.[8]

Elder Hyde taught in a unique manner, as exemplified by his explanation of the nature of our premortal existence:

> We understood things better there than we do in this lower world. . . .
> . . . It is not impossible that we signed the articles thereof with our own hands,—which articles may be retained in the archives above, to be presented to us when we rise from the dead, and be judged out of our own mouths, according to that which is written in the books. . . .
> The vail is thick between us. . . . But our forgetfulness cannot alter the facts.[9]

The strength of Elder Hyde's theological wisdom has been a great resource to the Church, then and now. For example, when Elder Harold B. Lee became President of the Church, he quoted Elder Hyde:

> The day after this appointment, following the passing of our beloved President [Joseph Fielding] Smith, my attention was called to a paragraph from a sermon delivered in 1853 in a general conference by Elder Orson Hyde, then a member of the Twelve. This provoked some soul-searching in me also.

The subject of his address was "The Man to Lead God's People," and I quote briefly from it:

". . . It is invariably the case that when an individual is ordained and appointed to lead the people, he has passed through tribulations and trials, and has proven himself before God, and before His people, that he is worthy of the situation which he holds . . . that when a person has not been tried, that has not proved himself before God, and before His people, and before the councils of the Most High, to be worthy, he is not going to step in and lead the Church and people of God. It never has been so, but from the beginning some one that understands the Spirit and counsel of the Almighty, that knows the Church, and is known of her, is the character that will lead the Church."[10]

Missions in 1834 took Brother Hyde to Pennsylvania, New York, and later to Jackson County, Missouri. Because men of Zion's Camp had started traveling from Kirtland toward Missouri, Brother Hyde went by Florence to collect debts that were owed to him. He joined the camp near Dayton and reported, "[I] turned in myself and my money to strengthen the camp."[11]

Elder Hyde's desire to "strengthen the camp" was surely laudable. Meanwhile, the experiences of Zion's Camp strengthened its men. Elder Neal A. Maxwell so explained:

The roster of the participants included the names of such men as Jedediah M. Grant, Orson Hyde, David W. Patten, Heber C. Kimball, Orson Pratt, Parley P. Pratt, George A. Smith, Hyrum Smith, Joseph Smith, Nathan Tanner, Wilford Woodruff, and Brigham Young. The lessons learned and the yield for the future can scarcely be calculated by us, but out of this seeming "furnace of affliction" came the refined cadre who, because of their experience, could call the cadence for future treks and who could pass through even sterner tests.

"All these things" gave those men vital experiences that were for their good—and for the later good of those who would follow these tempered leaders.[12]

Orson married Marinda Nancy Johnson on 4 September 1834 in a ceremony performed by Sidney Rigdon. Marinda's two brothers, Luke and Lyman Johnson, were named in the Doctrine and Covenants, along with Orson Hyde, as missionaries and "faithful elders" (D&C 68:7).

CALL TO THE HOLY APOSTLESHIP

Elder Hyde, age thirty, was ordained an Apostle and set apart as a member of the original Quorum of the Twelve Apostles on 15 February 1835 under the hands of the Three Witnesses—Oliver Cowdery, David Whitmer, and Martin Harris.[13] His two aforementioned brothers-in-law were also called to the Quorum of the Twelve Apostles in February 1835.

THE RESTORED GOSPEL IS TAKEN TO CANADA

In 1832, when the Church was only about two years old, the restored gospel was taken to Canada by Joseph Young, Brigham Young, and others. The Prophet Joseph Smith, Sidney Rigdon, and others preached in Upper Canada in 1833. Parley P. Pratt opened the mission in Toronto in 1836. He carried with him a letter of introduction to John Taylor, then a minister in the Methodist Church. Elder Pratt taught the gospel to John Taylor and his associates. All but one was converted and baptized. Elder Pratt sent word for some Apostles to come and provide assistance. Orson Hyde went in answer to that request. In July 1836 Orson proselyted with Elder Pratt for several weeks. They organized several branches of the Church before they returned to Kirtland.

The literary skills of Orson Hyde were put to work when he prepared a doctrinal tract, *A Prophetic Warning to All the Churches, of Every Sect and Denomination* . . . , published in Canada in 1836. This was the first tract to be used for proselytizing purposes. The following winter Orson engaged in reading Hebrew.

MISSION TO ENGLAND

After missionary labors in New York and Canada, the important call came for Elder Hyde to begin the work in England in the spring of 1837 with Elders Heber C. Kimball, Willard Richards, John Goodson, Isaac Russell, John Snyder, and Joseph Fielding. The Church at this time was barely seven years old.

On 3 April 1836, only a year prior to this mission call, the sacred keys of the priesthood were bestowed under the direction of the Lord by heavenly messengers—Moses, Elias, and Elijah—upon the Prophet Joseph Smith and Oliver Cowdery in the Kirtland Temple (see D&C 110:11–16). Those keys included the authority to gather Israel from the four parts of the earth—meaning missionary activity—along with keys to perfect the Saints and to redeem the dead.

Orson's call to England meant he was to leave his wife and their two children. The youngest child, Laura Marinda, was an infant born in May 1837. While this chapter focuses on the great work of Elder Hyde, it is well to remember the natural feelings of husband, wife, and little children through their protracted periods of separation.

In England the elders concentrated their missionary efforts in the area of Preston and the nearby valley of the River Ribble, where in eight months they baptized about two thousand souls.[14] From 1839 to 1841, nine members of the Quorum of the Twelve Apostles labored in Britain and added another four thousand converts to the Church. In a relatively short time, the twelve Apostles established the foundation for the most successful missionary program of the Church in the nineteenth century, organized an extensive emigration program, and established a major publication program. Elder Hyde was placed in charge of the publication *The Latter-day Saints' Millennial Star*. Appropriately, the autobiography of Orson Hyde was published in that journal in 1864.[15]

Strength came to the Church from the vigor of its early converts. In 1850 more members of the Church resided in Britain than in all of North America. Moreover, the British Isles comprised the springboard for the Church to reach the continental countries of France, Scandinavia, Italy, Switzerland, and Germany. Elder Marion G. Romney spoke of his personal legacy from those early missionaries to Great Britain: "My grandfather, Miles Romney, heard the first missionaries, Heber C. Kimball, Orson Hyde, and Willard Richards, preach on the streets in Preston, England, in 1837. He heard them on Market Square; he followed them to the Cockpit where they did much of their preaching in those early days. He joined the Church early in 1838, emigrated to Nauvoo in 1842, and now has about 2,500 descendants in the Church."[16] President Romney's citation shows that a rich harvest continues to be reaped from the seeds planted by these missionaries more than 150 years ago.[17]

SENIORITY IN THE QUORUM OF THE TWELVE

Elder Hyde returned to Kirtland on 21 May 1838. When Brigham Young became President of the Church, Elder Orson Hyde was sustained as President of the Council of the Twelve. He was so sustained for many years. Later in 1838 an event occurred that would carry implications regarding Elder Hyde's seniority in the Quorum. This circumstance was described by Elder John A. Widtsoe:

Orson Hyde, then just recovering from a serious illness,[18] had yielded to the importunities of Thomas B. Marsh to sign a vicious paper against Joseph Smith. Brother Hyde was promptly cut off from the Church, and of course lost his apostleship. The charges against the Prophet were, however, shown to be unfounded. Brother Hyde repented and was restored to his position as an Apostle on June 27, 1839. This incident made Brother Hyde a junior rather than a senior member of the Council. In matters of seniority, in case of an excommunication, the length of service dates from the time of re-entry, should they occur, into the Quorum. When this matter was considered by the First Presidency and the Council of the Twelve, John Taylor assumed the presidency of the Council.[19]

The separating action cited above occurred on 4 May 1839, and the priesthood office was restored to Elder Hyde less than eight weeks later. President John Taylor expressed his own views of this incident:

Orson Hyde and Orson Pratt had both of them been disfellowshipped and dropped from their quorum, and when they returned, without any particular investigation or arrangement, they took the position in the quorum which they had formerly occupied, and as there was no objection raised, or investigation had on this subject, things continued in this position for a number of years. . . . I stated that, personally, I cared nothing about the matter, and, moreover, I entertained a very high esteem for both the parties named; while, at the same time, I could not help but see, with [Elder George A. Smith], that complications might hereafter arise, unless the matters were adjusted. Some time after, in Sanpete, in June, 1875, President Young brought up the subject of seniority, and stated that John Taylor was the man that stood next to him; and that where he was not, John Taylor presided.

He also made the statement that Brother Hyde and Brother Pratt were not in their right positions in the quorum. Upon this statement, I assumed the position indicated [as President of the Quorum].[20]

MISSION TO PALESTINE

Full confidence in Orson Hyde was evident in a letter from the Prophet Joseph Smith dated 14 May 1840, when Elder Hyde was called to undertake a great and historic mission to Palestine with Elder John E. Page, also one of the Twelve. The letter to them said in part: "Brethren, you are in the pathway to eternal fame, and immortal glory; and inasmuch as you feel interested for the covenant people of the Lord, the God of their fathers shall bless you. Do not be discouraged on account of the greatness of the work; only be humble and faithful. . . . He who scattered Israel has promised to gather them; therefore inasmuch as you are to be instrumental in this great work, He will endow you with power, wisdom, might and intelligence, and every qualification necessary."[21]

Elder John E. Page failed to fill the appointment; hence, Elder Hyde proceeded alone. Once again, this meant a long period of separation from his Marinda and their children, increased in number to three since an infant daughter, Emily Matilda, had been born in Nauvoo the preceding December.

Elder Hyde crossed the ocean to England and traveled to Germany, staying in Bavaria, where he learned the German language. There he wrote the first LDS German tract, *Ein Ruf aus der Wüste* (*A Cry out of the Wilderness*), published in Frankfurt, Germany, in 1842. This publication included sixteen essays on such topics as the Godhead, the use of scripture, faith, repentance, baptism, confirmation, the sacrament of bread and wine, confession of sins and Church discipline, children, revelations, lay priesthood, baptism for the dead, prayer, holidays, washing of the feet, and patriarchal blessings.[22]

From Germany, Elder Hyde went to Constantinople, to Cairo, to Alexandria, and, after encountering many hardships, finally reached the Holy City. On the morning of Sunday, 24 October 1841, he went up on the Mount of Olives and dedicated and consecrated the land for the gathering of Judah's scattered remnants. He also erected a pile of stones there as a witness and erected another such monument upon Mount Zion, according to a vision given to him prior to leaving Nauvoo and to the predictions of the Prophet Joseph Smith.

This dedicatory prayer was carefully crafted and has been a model for later Apostles when they have been authorized to dedicate countries for the sacred purposes of the Lord. But this dedication was unique—the land was dedicated for the gathering of the Jews and of Israel to their ancient inheritance. This prayer is without parallel in Church history. It is reproduced in its entirety in the appendix to this chapter because of its historical import and literary significance. The reader will be well rewarded for studying its entire text. As you read, notice not only the powerful prophecies contained therein but also the faith and plaintive longings for family and fellow Apostles that permeate this prophetic prayer.

Exactly 138 years after that prayer was given—24 October 1979—President Spencer W. Kimball dedicated the Orson Hyde Memorial Garden in Jerusalem. On more than one occasion President Kimball told me how deeply he felt about the significance of that moment. He admired Elder Hyde greatly. He was particularly thankful that the Orson Hyde Memorial Garden featured a plaque on which the words of Elder Hyde's dedicatory prayer were inscribed. They now inspire countless visitors who come there to learn about Elder Hyde's remarkable mission to the Holy Land and to perceive the prophetic vision and hope he held for the Jewish people.

Some authors have suggested that Elder Hyde was of Jewish lineage. This cannot be confirmed. One of his descendants, Myrtle Stevens Hyde, studied this question carefully and wrote, with reference to Elder Hyde's book *Ein Ruf aus der Wüste:* "In recent years, this book has been translated back into English. In it Orson wrote of himself (English typescript, page 81): 'I am not a Jew, neither am I a son of a Jew; but I am a friend of the Jews.'" Sister Hyde's extensive genealogical research on their common ancestry led to the conclusion that "Orson Hyde's alleged Jewish progenitors [would be] based on a statement so broad as to fit vast millions of earth's people." She succinctly phrased her response to the question, "Was Orson Hyde a Jew?" "We don't know."[23]

Elder Hyde had embarked on his mission to Israel after April conference in 1840; he returned home nearly three years later, in December

1842. Today, even the thought of one of the Twelve being absent that long from meetings of the Quorum, unless physically unable to attend, is inconceivable. Actually, if one of us is away even for two or three weeks, he feels as though he has missed important chapters in the history of the Church—and indeed he has in this rapidly expanding work.

President Ezra Taft Benson observed another dimension in Brother Hyde's dedication of Palestine. He wrote: "This concern for a homeless people and the sending of this apostle were done at a time when the Mormons themselves were virtually homeless, having been dispossessed of their lands and possessions in Missouri."[24]

KEYS CONFERRED UPON THE TWELVE

Orson Hyde participated in an event of great importance shortly before the martyrdom of the Prophet Joseph Smith. The Prophet, who held all the keys of the kingdom, bestowed upon the Twelve Apostles all the keys and all the ordinances of the priesthood. Elder Hyde wrote:

> Before I went east on the 4th of April [1844] last, we were in council with Brother Joseph almost every day for weeks; said Brother Joseph in one of those councils, "There is something going to happen; I don't know what it is, but the Lord bids me to hasten and give you your endowment before the Temple is finished." He conducted us through every ordinance of the holy priesthood, and when he had gone through with all the ordinance he rejoiced very much, and said, "Now if they kill me, you have got all the keys, and all the ordinances, and you can confer them upon others, and the hosts of Satan will not be able to tear down the kingdom as fast as you will be able to build it up"; and now, said he, "On your shoulders will the responsibility of leading this people rest."[25]

Elder Wilford Woodruff documented the same experience in his own words: "They [the Twelve] received their endowments, and actually received the keys of the kingdom of God, and oracles of God, keys of revelation, and the pattern of heavenly things; and thus addressing the Twelve [Joseph] exclaimed, 'Upon your shoulders the kingdom rests, and you must round up your shoulders and bear it, for I have had to do it until now.'"[26]

I reflect upon this event with considerable empathy, realizing the close relationship between Orson Hyde and Sidney Rigdon. Sidney had baptized Orson, tutored him in English grammar, and performed his marriage, yet Sidney's name was not mentioned among those who had received those priesthood keys. In connection with this event, Orson specifically mentioned that Brother Rigdon, who was not one of the Twelve Apostles, "did not attend our councils."[27]

ADDITIONAL ACTIONS AND PRONOUNCEMENTS

The martyrdom of Joseph and Hyrum Smith, 27 June 1844, placed upon the shoulders of the Apostles the very burdens of leadership foreseen by the Prophet. The actions and pronouncements of Orson Hyde contributed to the base on which the Church was to stand, not only then but now. Elder Ezra Taft Benson, for example, when speaking of temporal welfare, quoted a statement of Elder Hyde. Elder Benson wrote: " 'There is more salvation and security in wheat,' said Orson Hyde years ago, 'than in all the political schemes of the world' (in *Journal of Discourses* 2:207). The revelation to produce and store food may be as essential to our temporal welfare today as boarding the ark was to the people in the days of Noah."[28]

To Orson Hyde, President Joseph Fielding Smith attributed our understanding of Joseph Smith's prophecy regarding possible future risks to the Constitution of the United States of America. President Smith wrote:

> The statement has been made that the Prophet said the time would come when this Constitution would hang as by a thread, and this is true. There has been some confusion, however, as to just what he said following this. I think that Elder Orson Hyde has given us a correct interpretation wherein he says that the Prophet said the Constitution would be in danger.
>
> Said Orson Hyde: "I believe he said something like this—that the time would come when the Constitution and the country would be in danger of an overthrow; and said he: 'If the Constitution be saved at all, it will be by the elders of this Church.' I believe this is about the language, as nearly as I can recollect it."[29]

Orson Hyde was a man of great versatility. His missionary labors are well known. He also filled many assignments of a temporal nature. In 1849, for example, he was "duly appointed and authorized . . . to receive, solicit and gather tithing and donations in the United States."[30]

In September 1850 he was called to assist in the management of the Perpetual Emigrating Fund, having received this charge from the First Presidency:

> We wish all to understand, that this fund is PERPETUAL, and is never to be diverted from the object of gathering the poor to Zion while there are Saints to be gathered, unless He whose right it is to rule shall otherwise command. Therefore we call upon President Orson Hyde and all the Saints, and all benevolent souls everywhere, to unite their gold, their silver, and their cattle, with ours in this perpetual fund, and cooperate with Bishop Hunter in producing as many teams as possible, preparatory for next spring's emigration, and let the poor who are to be helped, go to work with their might, and prepare wagons of wood for their journey.[31]

SEPARATION OF POLITICS FROM RELIGION

As an Apostle bearing heavy temporal responsibilities, Orson Hyde received timeless counsel from President Brigham Young. It is as relevant for Church leaders today as it was when given to Elder Hyde in 1855: "Mingle as little as possible with the politics of the day, and above all *never* use the priesthood or the influence thereof to promote party questions or designs; it is condescending far too low to bring the authority of the high heaven's King to mingle in the party strifes which agitate the political world in this degenerate age."[32]

ADDITIONAL RESPONSIBILITIES

Elder Orson Hyde was true to that trust. When the majority of the Saints left Nauvoo for Iowa Territory early in 1846, he was asked to remain behind to supervise the completion and dedication of the Nauvoo Temple. Public dedicatory services were conducted under the leadership of Elder Orson Hyde and Elder Wilford Woodruff on 30

April and 1 May 1846. It should be noted that other parts of the temple had been dedicated as they were finished; the public dedication was for the entire structure.

From October 1846 to January 1847, Elder Hyde presided over the British mission. In September 1848 President Brigham Young and other Church leaders returned to the Salt Lake Valley, leaving Elder Hyde to oversee the camps of Saints in the Midwest. During this time Elder Hyde served as editor and publisher of the *Frontier Guardian* (1849–1852).

President Brigham Young had asked Elder Hyde to remain in Kanesville to supervise the movement of Latter-day Saints to the West. The town's location on the Missouri River was particularly advantageous for several thousand European converts who had postponed their migration to America until a new gathering place and headquarters in the West had been established. By sailing to New Orleans, steamboating to St. Louis, and then going upriver to Kanesville, these immigrants were spared the rigors of overland travel at least that far. (One of my great-grandparents, Neils Christian Anderson, who converted to the Church in Sweden in 1853, was among those who were gathered to Zion via this route.) Significant is the fact that Oliver Cowdery was rebaptized in Kanesville by Elder Orson Hyde in November 1848, thereby ending years of estrangement from the Church that Brother Cowdery had helped to organize in 1830.

The date of 6 April 1853 marked the occasion of the laying of the cornerstones for the Salt Lake Temple. Elder Orson Hyde delivered the prayer on the laying of the northeast cornerstone.[33]

In 1855 Brigham Young, then also serving as territorial governor of Utah, called Orson to head the Carson Valley Nevada Mission. At that time the area that now comprises the state of Nevada was included within the original boundaries of Utah Territory as established by Congress in 1850. Brother Hyde was asked to organize a county government there.

Later, President Young called Elder Hyde to supervise the settlement in the Sanpete-Sevier district of Utah, where, as one of the Twelve Apostles, he was also to serve as president of the Sanpete stake.[34] In that capacity he served as a member of the committee for the construction of the Manti Temple.[35]

Through all of these accomplishments, Elder Hyde stood tall as a family man. He and Marinda had ten children. The first two were born in the Kirtland area of Ohio; the next three came in Nauvoo, Illinois; the next two were born at Kanesville (Council Bluffs), Iowa; and the last three were born in Salt Lake City, Utah. Their eldest child was born in 1835; the youngest in 1858. When Elder and Sister Hyde and their family reached Utah, they responded to the order for plural families, gaining a sizable posterity.

Elder Orson Hyde's sojourn in mortality was concluded 28 November 1878, in Spring City, Sanpete County, Utah, at the age of seventy-three.

Summary and Application to Our Day

This chapter could hardly do justice to this great man by way of biography. If it identifies traits of his character, the depths of his testimony, and his tireless power to endure, it will have served its purpose. He proved his faith in many ways, not the least of which was by his willingness to walk in the pathway of the Lord.[36] At age fourteen, this orphan boy walked from Connecticut to Ohio, where he would later find the gospel. Having found it, he walked again some two thousand miles—from Ohio to New York, Massachusetts, Rhode Island, Pennsylvania, and back to Ohio. He helped to open the work in Canada and England, and dedicated the land of Palestine for the gathering of the Jews. Though challenged by periods of physical separation from his family, he applied the principles of the gospel in his private life as a husband and father. He brought temporal competency and spiritual intensity to his many assignments. He proved himself by obedience to the commandments of God. He responded to promptings of the Lord as one who was foreordained from before the foundations of the world to respond to the Spirit of the Lord and to accomplish his work.

He exemplified fulfillment of sacred doctrinal responsibilities given to the Twelve Apostles, applicable both then and now. Consider the fidelity of Elder Orson Hyde in accomplishing these divine commands, as listed in sections 107 and 112 of the Doctrine and Covenants:

- "The twelve traveling councilors are called to be the Twelve Apostles, or special witnesses of the name of Christ in all the world—thus differing from other officers in the church in the duties of their calling" (D&C 107:23).

- "The Twelve are a Traveling Presiding High Council, to offici-ate in the name of the Lord, under the direction of the Presi-dency of the Church, agreeable to the institution of heaven; to build up the church, and regulate all the affairs of the same in all nations, first unto the Gentiles and secondly unto the Jews" (D&C 107:33).

- "The Twelve being sent out, holding the keys, to open the door by the proclamation of the gospel of Jesus Christ, and first unto the Gentiles and then unto the Jews" (D&C 107:35).

- "Wherefore, whithersoever they shall send you, go ye, and I will be with you; and in whatsoever place ye shall proclaim my name an effectual door shall be opened unto you, that they may receive my word" (D&C 112:19).

- "Whosoever ye shall send in my name, by the voice of your brethren, the Twelve, duly recommended and authorized by you, shall have power to open the door of my kingdom unto any nation whithersoever ye shall send them" (D&C 112:21).

The study of Elder Hyde's life has led me to several conclusions:

- He came into the world with an intrinsic love of the Lord.
- The Lord knew and loved Orson Hyde and managed to move him where he needed to be. As once said to Abraham, so the Lord could have said to Orson, "Thou wast chosen before thou wast born" (Abraham 3:23).
- Hard work and the overcoming of incredible challenges were his lot in life.
- Obedience, consecration, and sacrifice were hallmarks of his service.

Surely Elder Orson Hyde, Apostle of the Lord, stands as one of the stalwart heroes of the Restoration.

Appendix
Dedicatory Prayer
Given by Orson Hyde in Jerusalem,
October 24, 1841

O Thou! who art from everlasting to everlasting, eternally and unchangeably the same, even the God who rules in the heavens above, and controls the destinies of men on the earth, wilt Thou not condescend, through thine infinite goodness and royal favor, to listen to the prayer of Thy servant which he this day offers up unto Thee in the name of Thy holy child Jesus, upon this land, where the Sun of Righteousness set in blood, and thine Anointed One expired.

Be pleased, O Lord, to forgive all the follies, weaknesses, vanities, and sins of Thy servant, and strengthen him to resist all future temptations. Give him prudence and discernment that he may avoid the evil, and a heart to choose the good; give him fortitude to bear up under trying and adverse circumstances, and grace to endure all things for Thy name's sake, until the end shall come, when all the Saints shall rest in peace.

Now, O Lord! Thy servant has been obedient to the heavenly vision which Thou gavest him in his native land; and under the shadow of Thine outstretched arm, he has safely arrived in this place to dedicate and consecrate this land unto Thee, for the gathering together of Judah's scattered remnants, according to the predictions of the holy Prophets—for the building up of Jerusalem again after it has been trodden down by the Gentiles so long, and for rearing a Temple in honor of Thy name. Everlasting thanks be ascribed unto Thee, O Father, Lord of heaven and earth, that Thou hast preserved Thy servant from the dangers of the seas, and from the plague and pestilence which have caused the land to mourn. The violence of man has also been restrained, and Thy providential care by night and by day has been exercised over Thine unworthy servant. Accept, therefore, O Lord, the tribute of a grateful heart for all past favors, and be pleased to continue Thy kindness and mercy towards a needy worm of the dust.

O Thou, Who didst covenant with Abraham, Thy friend, and Who didst renew that covenant with Isaac, and confirm the same with Jacob with an oath, that Thou wouldst not only give them this land for an everlasting inheritance, but that Thou wouldst also remember their seed forever. Abraham, Isaac, and Jacob have long since closed their eyes in death, and made the grave their mansion. Their children are scattered and dispersed abroad among the nations of the Gentiles like sheep that have no shepherd, and are still looking forward for the fulfillment of those promises which Thou didst make concerning them; and even this land, which once poured forth nature's richest bounty, and flowed, as it were, with milk and honey, has, to a certain extent, been smitten with barrenness and sterility since it drank from murderous hands the blood of Him who never sinned.

Grant, therefore, O Lord, in the name of Thy well-beloved Son, Jesus Christ, to remove the barrenness and sterility of this land, and let springs of living water break forth to water its thirsty soil. Let the vine and olive produce in their strength, and the fig-tree bloom and flourish. Let the land become abundantly fruitful when possessed by its rightful heirs; let it again flow with plenty to feed the returning prodigals who come home with a spirit of grace and supplication; upon it let the clouds distil virtue and richness, and let the fields smile with plenty. Let the flocks and the herds greatly increase and multiply upon the mountains and the hills; and let Thy great kindness conquer and subdue the unbelief of Thy people. Do Thou take from them their stony heart, and give them a heart of flesh; and may the Sun of Thy favor dispel the cold mists of darkness which have beclouded their atmosphere. Incline them to gather in upon this land according to Thy word. Let them come like clouds and like doves to their windows. Let the large ships of the nations bring them from the distant isles; and let kings become their nursing fathers, and queens with motherly fondness wipe the tear of sorrow from their eye.

Thou, O Lord, did once move upon the heart of Cyrus to show favor unto Jerusalem and her children. Do Thou now also be pleased to inspire the hearts of kings and the powers of the earth to look with a friendly eye towards this place, and with a desire to see Thy righteous purposes executed in relation thereto. Let them know that it is Thy good pleasure to restore the kingdom unto Israel—raise up Jerusalem as its capital, and constitute her people a distinct nation and government, with David Thy servant, even a descendant from the loins of ancient David to be their king.

Let that nation or that people who shall take an active part in behalf of Abraham's children, and in the raising up of Jerusalem, find favor in Thy sight. Let not their enemies prevail against them, neither let pestilence or famine overcome them, but let the glory of Israel overshadow them, and the power of the Highest protect them; while that nation or kingdom that will not serve Thee in this glorious work must perish, according to Thy word—Yea, those nations shall be utterly wasted.

Though Thy servant is now far from his home, and from the land bedewed with his earliest tear, yet he remembers, O Lord, his friends who are there, and family, whom for Thy sake he has left. Though poverty and privation be our earthly lot, yet ah! do Thou richly endow us with an inheritance where moth and rust do not corrupt, and where thieves do not break through and steal.

The hands that have fed, clothed, or shown favor unto the family of Thy servant in his absence, or that shall hereafter do so, let them not lose their reward, but let a special blessing rest upon them, and in Thy kingdom let them have an inheritance when Thou shalt come to be glorified in this society.

Do Thou also look with favor upon all those through whose liberality I have been enabled to come to this land; and in the day when Thou shalt reward all people according to their works, let these also not be passed by or forgotten, but in time let them be in readiness to enjoy the glory of those mansions which Jesus has gone to prepare. Particularly do Thou bless the stranger in Philadelphia, whom I never saw, but who sent me gold, with a request that I should pray for him in Jerusalem. Now, O Lord, let blessings come upon him from an unexpected quarter, and let his basket be filled, and his storehouse abound with plenty, and let not the good things of the earth be his only portion, but let him be found among those to whom it shall be said, "Thou hast been faithful over a few things, and I will make thee ruler over many."

O my Father in heaven! I now ask Thee in the name of Jesus to remember Zion, with all her Stakes, and with all her assemblies. She has been grievously afflicted and smitten; she has mourned; she has wept; her enemies have triumphed, and have said, "Ah, where is thy God?" Her Priests and Prophets have groaned in chains and fetters within the gloomy walls of prisons, while many were slain, and now sleep in the arms of death. How long, O Lord, shall iniquity triumph, and sin go unpunished?

Do Thou arise in the majesty of Thy strength, and make bare Thine arm in behalf of Thy people. Redress their wrongs, and turn their sorrow into joy. Pour the spirit of light and knowledge, grace and wisdom, into the hearts of her Prophets, and clothe her Priests with salvation. Let light and knowledge march forth through the empire of darkness, and may the honest in heart flow to their standard, and join in the march to go forth to meet the Bridegroom.

Let a peculiar blessing rest upon the Presidency of Thy Church, for at them are the arrows of the enemy directed. Be Thou to them a sun and a shield, their strong tower and hiding place; and in the time of distress or danger be Thou near to deliver. Also the quorum of the Twelve, do Thou be pleased to stand by them for Thou knowest the obstacles which they have to encounter, the temptations to which they are exposed, and the privations which they must suffer. Give us, [the Twelve] therefore, strength according to our day, and help us to bear a faithful testimony of Jesus and His Gospel, to finish with fidelity and honor the work which Thou hast given us to do, and then give us a place in Thy glorious kingdom. And let this blessing rest upon every faithful officer and member in Thy Church. And all the glory and honor will we ascribe unto God and the Lamb forever and ever. Amen.[37]

NOTES

1. "History of Orson Hyde," *Millennial Star*, 26 (1864): 742.

2. Ibid., p. 743.

3. Ibid.

4. "History of Orson Hyde," p. 760.

5. Ibid., p. 761.

6. *The Discourses of Wilford Woodruff*, ed. G. Homer Durham (Salt Lake City: Bookcraft, 1969), pp. 38–39.

7. "History of Orson Hyde," p. 776.

8. See *Encyclopedia of Mormonism* 3:1269.

9. In *Journal of Discourses* 7:314–15. Elder Neal A. Maxwell also has quoted Elder Hyde's statement on premortal life. See *But for a Small Moment* (Salt Lake City: Bookcraft, 1986), pp. 99–100; *Deposition of a Disciple* (Salt Lake City: Deseret Book, 1976), p. 27; *Things as They Really Are* (Deseret Book, 1978), p. 27.

10. In *Journal of Discourses* 1:123. Quoted in Harold B. Lee, *Stand Ye in Holy Places* (Deseret Book, 1974), p. 169.

11. "History of Orson Hyde," pp. 790–91.

12. Neal A. Maxwell, *All These Things Shall Give Thee Experience* (Deseret Book, 1979), p. 117.

13. See *Deseret News 1995–1996 Church Almanac* (Salt Lake City: Deseret News, 1994), p. 51.

14. See *Church History in the Fulness of Times* (Salt Lake City: The Church of Jesus Christ of Latter-day Saints, 1989), pp. 174–76; see also "History of Orson Hyde," p. 792.

15. See "History of Orson Hyde," pp. 742–44, 760–61, 774–76, 790–92.

16. In Conference Report, April 1960, p. 110.

17. For additional information, see V. Ben Bloxham, James R. Moss, Larry C. Porter, eds., *Truth Will Prevail—The Rise of The Church of Jesus Christ of Latter-day Saints in the British Isles 1837–1987* (Salt Lake City: The Church of Jesus Christ of Latter-day Saints, 1987).

18. Orson Hyde described that illness as "bilious fever," from which he "did not fully recover until the spring of 1839" ("History of Orson Hyde," p. 792).

19. *Evidences and Reconciliations*, sel. G. Homer Durham (Salt Lake City: Bookcraft, 1960), p. 261.

20. *The Gospel Kingdom*, sel. G. Homer Durham (Salt Lake City: Bookcraft, 1944), pp. 191–92.

21. *Teachings of the Prophet Joseph Smith*, comp. Joseph Fielding Smith (Salt Lake City: Deseret Book, 1976), p. 163.

22. See *Encyclopedia of Mormonism* 1:69.

23. Myrtle Stevens Hyde, "Was Orson Hyde a Jew?" 26 August 1985, pp. 3, 4; typescript, Church Historical Department.

24. Ezra Taft Benson, *This Nation Shall Endure* (Salt Lake City: Deseret Book, 1977), pp. 132–33.

25. Quoted in Joseph Fielding Smith, *Doctrines of Salvation*, comp. Bruce R. McConkie, 3 vols. (Salt Lake City: Bookcraft, 1954–56), 3:154.

26. Ibid., pp. 154–55; see also *Times and Seasons* 5 (15 September 1844): pp. 651, 698.

27. *Times and Seasons* 5 (15 September 1844): 651.

28. *The Teachings of Ezra Taft Benson* (Salt Lake City: Bookcraft, 1988), p. 266.

29. *Doctrines of Salvation* 3:326.

30. As quoted in James R. Clark, comp., *Messages of the First Presidency*, 6 vols. (Salt Lake City: Bookcraft, 1965–75), 1:360.

31. In *Messages of the First Presidency* 2:34.

32. In *Messages of the First Presidency* 2:173; emphasis in original.

33. See *Journal of Discourses* 2:47–49.

34. See William G. Hartley, "The Priesthood Reorganization of 1877: Brigham Young's Last Achievement," *BYU Studies* 20 (Fall 1979): 6.

35. See Andrew Jenson, *Latter-day Saint Biographical Encyclopedia*, 4 vols. (1901–36; reprint, Salt Lake City: Western Epics, 1971), 1:82.

36. Elder Neal A. Maxwell referred to Oliver Cowdery, Martin Harris, and Thomas B. Marsh as having chosen to "vote with their feet" by traveling westward to rejoin, be reconciled, and to sustain God's plan and its enunciating latter-day prophets (see "The Great Plan of the Eternal God," *Ensign*, May 1984, p. 22). For different reasons, Orson Hyde could surely be added to that list of those who would "vote with their feet" in responding to promptings from the Lord.

37. *History of the Church* 4:456–59.

5

Elder Jeffrey R. Holland

Heber C. Kimball
Common Man,
Uncommon Servant

Heber Chase Kimball was, by every standard, one of the greatest of the men raised up by God to establish His work in those early, crucial years of the restoration of the Church of Jesus Christ in these latter days. The third man in this dispensation (after Lyman E. Johnson and Brigham Young) to be ordained to the Quorum of the Twelve Apostles at the hands of the Three Witnesses, Brother Kimball possessed abilities that would soon make him one of the most influential preachers and most successful missionaries the Church would ever know.

Blessed with unusual gifts of the Spirit, Brother Kimball was the recipient of many dreams and visions and enjoyed a particular gift for prophecy—a gift bestowed to such a degree that it was considered second only to that exercised by the Prophet Joseph Smith himself.[1] Heber remained loyal to the Prophet Joseph through all the difficult days of the latter's life, and was then equally loyal to the Church's next president—his dearest friend, Brigham Young, who called Brother Kimball to serve as his First Counselor when the First Presidency was reorganized on December 27, 1847.

Throughout his life Heber was known as one who had "as much integrity . . . as any man who ever lived on the earth."[2] Indeed, in a moment of declaration late in his life, Heber said to those who might impugn his motives or minimize his service, "My name is Faithful—my name is Integrity."[3] Brigham Young himself said of his friend, missionary companion, and counselor, "His knees never trembled, his hands never shook."[4]

Born June 14, 1801, in Sheldon, Franklin County, Vermont, Heber was the fourth child and second son in a family of seven. As with others living the frontier life of those times, his education was limited, coming to a formal end when at age fourteen he went to work for his father as an apprentice blacksmith. Some five years later when the family lost what little property they had as a result of the economic panic of 1819, Heber found himself without employment, without the care his father had previously been able to give him, and uncertain about his future. Something of his unpresupposing, even shy, personality is evident from his own description of those challenging days: "I saw some days of sorrow; my heart was troubled, and I suffered much in consequence of fear, bashfulness and timidity. I found myself cast abroad upon the world, without a friend to console my grief. In these heart-aching hours I suffered much for want of food and the comforts of life, and many times went two or three days without food to eat, being bashful and not daring to ask for it."[5]

Moving to Mendon, New York, where he learned the potter's trade from his brother, Heber met Vilate Murray, whom he married in 1822. Theirs was something of a lifelong storybook romance, even through the tests and trials both of them faithfully faced in receiving the law of polygamy.[6] Throughout their married life they prayed they could die together, and in fact they passed away within one year of each other—Vilate in 1867, Heber in 1868.[7]

But back to the early story. Only three weeks after joining the Baptist Church in 1831, Heber and Vilate met the missionaries of The Church of Jesus Christ of Latter-day Saints. They joined the Church shortly thereafter. Of this experience Heber said: "I was convinced that they [the missionaries] taught the truth, and I was constrained to believe their testimony. I saw that I had only received a part of the ordinances under the Baptist Church. I also saw and heard the gifts of the spirit manifested in them. . . . Brigham Young and myself were constrained, by the Spirit, to bear testimony of the truth, and when we did this, the power of God rested on us."[8]

In 1833 Heber and Vilate moved to join the body of the Saints gathering in Kirtland, Ohio, and from that point on Heber C. Kimball's history and that of the growing Church he had joined would be inter-twined forever. In 1834 he took part in Zion's Camp. In February 1835 he was ordained an Apostle of the Lord Jesus Christ.

Except for those devastating days leading to and following the martyrdom of the Prophet Joseph Smith, perhaps no period of time in the early history of the Church was more perilous for faithful Latter-day Saints than the spring and summer of 1837 in Kirtland, Ohio. It was a time of economic upheaval in which, as one has observed: "The greed of gain, the spirit of speculation was abroad in the land. Mam-mon had reared his altars on consecrated ground. The money-changer was within the temple. The love of the things of earth had usurped, in many hearts, the love of the things of heaven, and comparatively few were free from the soul-destroying influence of idolatry."[9]

In that period the United States experienced a financial panic of staggering proportions. Hundreds of banks failed, one of those being the Kirtland Safety Society, which had been established by the Prophet Joseph and other Church leaders for the use and benefit of the Saints in Ohio. When the society failed there was a terrible out-pouring of hostility and accusation against the Prophet. The poetic Orson F. Whitney described it this way: "The good ship Zion, storm-tossed and tempest-driven, her sails rent, her timbers sprung, a portion of her officers and crew in open mutiny, was drifting with fearful ra-pidity toward the rocks and breakers of destruction."[10]

In that crucible of difficulty for the Church and its thirty-one-year-old prophet, the integrity and loyalty of Heber C. Kimball was being forged and refined. Heber had responded immediately when he heard the gospel preached, and having set his hand to the plow of the restored gospel, he would never look back.

Of that period in Kirtland Heber wrote, "A man's life was in dan-ger the moment he spoke in defense of the Prophet of God."[11] But speak in that defense he did. He said he literally mourned to see the spirit that came upon some of his dearest friends and associates. "The only source of consolation I had," he said, "was in bending my knees continually before my Father in Heaven, and asking Him to sustain me and preserve me from falling into snares, and from betraying my brethren as others had done; for those who apostatized sought every means and opportunity to draw others after them. They also entered into combinations to obtain wealth by fraud and every means that was evil."[12]

It was in this perilous time and difficult circumstance that Heber would be asked by God and His prophet to step forward, to put his gift upon the altar and magnify his calling as an Apostle, a special witness of the name of Christ in all the world (see D&C 107:23). In doing so he would perform a work, as one said, "that would perpetuate his memory, and make his name a household word upon the lips of tens of thousands in both hemispheres."[13] That estimation, used in 1888, would a century later more accurately read "upon the lips of millions in both hemispheres."

It would seem from the circumstances here mentioned that one of the last things the Prophet Joseph Smith would want to do in 1837 would be to send far from his side one of his most loyal and resolute defenders. But in the spring of that year the Prophet said, "God revealed to me that something new must be done for the salvation of His church."[14] That "something new" would be the opening of worldwide missionary work, a labor which would characterize Heber C. Kimball and The Church of Jesus Christ of Latter-day Saints forever more.

"On Sunday, the 4th day of June, 1837," recorded Heber in his journal, "the Prophet Joseph came to me, while I was [in the Kirtland Temple], and whispering to me, said, 'Brother Heber, the Spirit of the Lord has whispered to me: "Let my servant Heber go to England and proclaim my Gospel, and open the door of salvation to that nation." ' "

The thought was staggering to Heber. He had been humbled beyond expression at his call to the holy apostleship just two years earlier, but this seemed an even more lonely and frightening call. He exclaimed: "O, Lord, I am a man of stammering tongue, and altogether unfit for such a work; how can I go to preach in that land, which is so famed throughout Christendom for learning, knowledge and piety; the nursery of religion; and to a people whose intelligence is proverbial!"[15]

Feeling such inadequacy, he immediately asked the Prophet if his fellow Apostle and dearest friend, Brigham Young, could accompany him on the assignment. But although Brigham would go to England later, there was no chance for him to go now. The Prophet Joseph had other things for him to do. Even more distraught in hearing this news, Heber wrote, "The idea of such a mission was almost more than I could bear. . . . I was almost ready to sink under the burden which was placed upon me."

Then comes one of the greatest declarations ever made by an elder of Israel, ancient or modern, a declaration that every contemporary missionary for The Church of Jesus Christ of Latter-day Saints ought to recite and remember. In spite of his sense of weakness, and the forbidding circumstances of his family and his Church, Heber said: "However, all these considerations did not deter me from the path of duty; the moment I understood the will of my Heavenly Father, I felt a determination to go at all hazards, believing that He would support me by his almighty power, and endow me with every qualification that I needed; and although my family was dear to me, and I should have to leave them almost destitute, I felt that the cause of truth, the Gospel of Christ, outweighed every other consideration."[16]

Hyrum Smith, upon hearing that Heber had accepted this mission call in spite of the plight the Kimball family faced, wept like a little child. He gave Heber the utmost encouragement and blessing, and prophesied that he would prosper as almost no other missionary would prosper. The First Presidency of the Church confirmed that prophecy when, laying their hands on Heber and setting him apart to preside over the mission, they conferred great blessings upon him, saying among other things that "God would make me mighty in that nation in winning souls unto Him; angels should accompany me and bear me up, that my feet should never slip; that I should be mightily blessed and prove a source of salvation to thousands, not only in England but America."[17]

Having received his call and been set apart, Heber went daily into the attic of the Kirtland Temple and there poured out his soul to the Lord, asking His protection and power for a successful and honorable mission. The day of his departure came, and Heber, ever a devoted family man, called his wife and young family around him. A contemporary, Elder Robert B. Thompson, records the poignant scene:

> The day appointed for the departure of the Elders to England having arrived, I stepped into the house of Brother Kimball to ascertain when he would start, as I expected to accompany him two or three hundred miles, intending to spend my labors in Canada that season.
>
> The door being partly open, I entered and felt struck with the sight which presented itself to my view. I would have retired, thinking that I was intruding, but I felt riveted to the spot. The father was pouring out his soul to [God] that he would grant him a prosperous

voyage across the mighty ocean, and make him useful wherever his lot should be cast, and that He who "careth for sparrows, and feedeth the young ravens when they cry" would supply the wants of his wife and little ones in his absence. He then, like the patriarchs, and by virtue of his office, laid his hands upon their heads individually, leaving a father's blessing upon them, and commending them to the care and protection of God, while he should be engaged preaching the Gospel in a foreign land.

While thus engaged his voice was almost lost in the sobs of those around, who tried in vain to suppress them. The idea of being separated from their protector and father for so long a time was indeed painful. He proceeded, but his heart was too much affected to do so regularly. His emotions were great, and he was obliged to stop at intervals, while the big tears rolled down his cheeks, an index to the feelings which reigned in his bosom. My heart was not stout enough to refrain; in spite of myself I wept, and mingled my tears with theirs. At the same time I felt thankful that I had the privilege of contemplating such a scene. I realized that nothing could induce that man to tear himself from so affectionate a family group, from his partner and children who were so dear to him—nothing but a sense of duty and love to God and attachment to His cause.[18]

Walking away from his family after such an emotional parting, he was going to what must have seemed like the uttermost reaches of the earth. Heber recorded: "[I] started without purse or scrip on my mission, this being the first foreign mission of the Church of Christ in the last days."[19]

Eager to be the first to set foot on British soil as the new missionaries arrived in England on July 20, 1837, Heber leaped the six or seven feet from the deck of the *Garrick* to the pier at Liverpool. "For the first time," he wrote," I stood on British ground. . . . My feelings at that time were peculiar, particularly when I realized the importance and extent of my mission; the work to which I had been appointed, and in which I was shortly to be engaged. However, I put my trust in God, believing that He would assist me in publishing the truth, give me utterance, and be a present help in time of need."[20]

The rest is of course history—Church history. Starting in Preston, Lancashire, the work of the Lord began to unfold immediately and miraculously. Heber preached his first sermon in the Vauxhall chapel of the Reverend James Fielding on Sunday, July 23. He and his companions had their first baptisms—nine of them—from that congregation one week later. When the Reverend Fielding realized he had made a mistake and was losing his congregation wholesale, he immediately closed the door of his chapel to these missionaries. But by then the spirit of the work had taken hold. Homes and other buildings were opened to the elders and they were soon busy preaching the gospel throughout Preston.

But even as they felt the power of God rest upon them and the people, it was made equally clear to them that the adversary was fully aware of the great beginning of international missionary work that this portended. The missionaries had taken lodgings (in a building which still stands) on the corner of Fox and Wilfred Streets in the heart of Preston. Early in the morning of Sunday, July 30—only ten days after their arrival in England and just hours away from their first scheduled baptisms—Elder Isaac Russell awakened Elder Kimball and Elder Orson Hyde, asking them for a blessing to rebuke the evil spirits that were assailing him. Of this experience, Heber later wrote:

> While thus engaged, I was struck with great force by some invisible power and fell senseless on the floor. The first thing I recollected was being supported by Brothers Hyde and Richards, who were praying for me. [They then] assisted me to get on the bed, but my agony was so great I could not endure it, and I arose, bowed my knees, and prayed. I then . . . sat on the bed. . . . We could distinctly see the evil spirits, who foamed and gnashed their teeth at us. We gazed upon them about an hour and a half (by Willard [Richards's] watch). We were not looking towards the window, but towards the wall. . . .
>
> We saw the devils coming in legions, with their leaders, who came within a few feet of us. They came towards us like armies rushing to battle. They appeared to be men of full stature, possessing every form and feature of men in the flesh, who were angry and desperate; and I shall never forget the vindictive malignity depicted on their countenances as they looked me in the eye; and any attempt to paint the scene which then presented itself, or portray their malice and enmity, would be vain.
>
> I perspired exceedingly, my clothes becoming as wet as if I had been taken out of the river. I felt excessive pain, and was in the great-

est distress for some time. I cannot even look back on the scene without feelings of horror; yet by it I learned the power of the adversary, his enmity against the servants of God and got some understanding of the invisible world. We distinctly heard those spirits talk and express their wrath and hellish designs against us. However, the Lord delivered us from them, and blessed us exceedingly that day.[21]

Weak and exhausted by this confrontation, which went on toward dawn, these missionaries still kept their commitment to their baptismal candidates and met at the River Ribble to perform this saving ordinance for the first time in the British Isles.

Years later, Heber told the Prophet Joseph Smith of the above experience with evil spirits and asked him why it had happened, and did it indicate he was in any way unworthy or otherwise susceptible to the adversary's influence?

"No, Brother Heber," the Prophet Joseph replied, "at that time you were nigh unto the Lord; there was only a veil between you and Him, but you could not see Him. When I heard of it, it gave me great joy, for I then knew that the work of God had taken root in that land. It was this that caused the devil to make a struggle to kill you."

The Prophet Joseph then related some of his own experiences (the most obvious of which would have been the attack of the adversary prior to the First Vision) and said, "The nearer a person approaches the Lord, a greater power will be manifested by the adversary to prevent the accomplishment of His purposes."[22]

Teaching and baptizing at an almost feverish pace, Heber and his companions went on through the fall and winter, frequently breaking ice in the River Ribble for the baptisms or else performing them (depending on the area of their labors) in the frigid waters of the ocean. Heber recorded in his journal that he had never preached in a location that he did not baptize people and build up the Church. He recalled that on some days their clothing was never dry as a result of the repeated visits into the waters of baptism.

As this first mission came to a close after just nine months in England, there were more than 1,500 members in Preston and surrounding villages of the Ribble Valley, with a strong mission presidency remaining to lead the people. As Heber left the village of Downham before his return home, "the hearts of the people appeared to be broken."

People crowded in doorways and leaned out of windows, with scores of others lining the streets, weeping as they said farewell to their missionary. Heber wrote: "While contemplating this scene we were induced to take off our hats, for we felt as if the place was holy ground—the Spirit of the Lord rested down upon us, and I was constrained to bless that whole region of country, we were followed by a great number, a considerable distance from the villages who could hardly separate themselves from us. My heart was like unto theirs, and I thought my head was a fountain of tears, for I wept for several miles after I bid them adieu."[23]

In nearby Chatburn, the people left their fields and shops and ran into the streets to say farewell. Children followed along, singing, weeping, and clinging to the clothing of the elders. One of the missionaries wrote: "Some of them said that if they could but touch us they seem better. They evidently believe that there is Virtue in Brother Kimball's Cloake."[24]

In Barnaldwick the people would not leave after the final testimony meeting with the elders, remaining in conversation nearly until dawn, "weeping like little children" when they finally had to tear themselves away from Heber and his companion.

Historians of this period note that what seemed to set Heber C. Kimball apart was his inherent, almost intuitive spiritual power. Joseph Fielding called him "mighty in Tongues and in Prophesying" and "mighty in Faith and also in Preaching." Orson Hyde wrote to his wife, saying matter of factly of Heber, "The Lord is with him." Brother Kimball himself acknowledged the gifts of heaven in his ministry. He regularly had dreams and visions regarding the work, and he felt directly guided in his travels. These spiritual gifts along with his common, homespun approach made him a very effective speaker and very popular with common folk—the farmer, the workman, the villager. Brigham Young once described the warm, comfortable way Brother Kimball put people at ease so he could teach them.

"Come, my friend, sit down," he would say; "do not be in a hurry." Then he preached the Gospel in "a plain, familiar manner" that made his hearers believe what he said. Some stayed with him all day; some were converted after one sermon. He gently led them: "You see how plain the Gospel is? Come along now," and at the right moment he put his arm around them saying, "Come, let us go down to the water."

"The Lord appointed me to [this] work because I was willing to be the simplest," Heber would say of his unlearned manner.[25]

When Heber arrived back in the United States in May, 1838, conditions in Kirtland were worse than when he had left about eleven months before. The financial situation had worsened, apostasy was more widespread, and most of the strong, faithful Saints had moved to Missouri. Heber and his family promptly followed the latter example, arriving at Far West in July.

But very soon the persecution in that area intensified—the Saints' homes were plundered and burned, fields were laid waste, and families were driven from their homes. By October's end, mob brutalities and Governor Boggs's extermination order had resulted in many Church leaders being taken away to jail—Joseph Smith and others having narrowly escaped a firing squad. Far West had been left swarming with predators who were ostensibly enforcing harsh, militia-imposed conditions. Some of these were directed into the city by apostate members, those who had turned against the Church and its leaders.

One of these turncoats was William E. McLellin. He sought out Heber, who with others was under guard. "Brother Heber," he sneered, "what do you think of the fallen prophet now? . . . Are you satisfied with Joseph?"

The reply was predictably forthright: "Yes, I am more satisfied with him a hundred-fold than I ever was before, for I see you in the very position that [Joseph] foretold you would be in. . . . I tell you Mormonism is true, and Joseph is a true prophet of the living God; and you with all others that turn therefrom will be damned and go to hell."[26]

The major task now was to get the Saints out of Missouri to a new location. Along with his friend Brigham Young, now the President of the Quorum of the Twelve, Heber played a major part in organizing and assisting in this work. Furthermore he traveled nearly forty miles each way almost every week to visit Joseph Smith and the other prisoners in the Liberty Jail.[27] On April 16, 1839, those prisoners, having been allowed to "escape," began to make their way to Quincy, Illinois, where by this time most of the Saints expelled from Missouri had gathered.

By this time too another mission loomed before Heber. A revelation received on July 8, 1838, commanded the twelve Apostles to

hold a meeting at Far West on April 26, 1839, preparatory to embark-
ing on a mission to Britain the following spring (see D&C 118). In
view of the expulsion and the Missouri threats, it took considerable
courage to journey to and attend that meeting. Nevertheless Heber C.
Kimball and the other Apostles were there, and the prophecy requiring their presence was fulfilled. Many of the Apostles, including
Heber, were sick the next year when they left Nauvoo bound for
Britain. Indeed, the scene of Brigham Young and Heber C. Kimball
bidding farewell to their wives Mary Ann and Vilate, respectively, is
one of the most poignant in the early history of the Church. All four
were ill, and so too were several of the children in both families, but
these brethren mustered their famous cry "Hurrah, Hurrah, Hurrah for
Israel!" and went forward in faith. In their one-year mission to England the eight Apostles and their helpers reaped a harvest of several
thousand souls.

When he returned home, Heber was forty years old. Years of service lay ahead, each bringing its own experiences: Church growth in
Nauvoo; temple ceremonies revealed; Joseph's bestowal of priesthood
keys on the Apostles; apostates conspiring against the Prophet's life;
persecution's ugly features being displayed again; and then the ultimate infamy—the martyrdom of Joseph and Hyrum. Soon after that
would come yet another forced and bitter and desolate trek from their
previously hoped-for refuge; and in this too, in both planning and im-
plementation, Heber played a key role.

The rock-like Heber was loyal and true through it all. Naturally
he was one of the 148 souls in the original pioneer trek from Winter
Quarters to the Salt Lake Valley in 1847. At that year's end, in the reorganization of the First Presidency Heber was made the First Counselor to President Brigham Young, a position in which he served faithfully for nearly twenty years.

In the Valley, besides serving in his Church calling, Heber held
office in the provisional government. More important, he would have
said, was his constant charitable concern for the poor and needy. In
time of famine, "President Kimball and his family, especially his noble
and unselfish partner, Vilate, . . . kept an open house, and fed from
twenty-five to one hundred people at their table, daily, besides making
presents innumerable of bread, flour and other necessities."[28] He
threw his support too behind "The Perpetual Emigration Fund, for the
benefit of the poor Saints who were unable to gather to Zion."[29]

Through it all, the love of Heber's life was Vilate. In October 1867 she died. "I shall not be long after her," he sadly prophesied.[30]

In the spring of the following year Heber suffered an accident, being thrown from his buggy when the wheels suddenly went into a ditch. This appears to have been responsible for the malady that took his life a few weeks later, on June 22, 1868.

Elder Orson F. Whitney wrote of Brother Kimball:

> [He was] tall and powerful of frame, with piercing black eyes that seemed to read one through, and before whose searching gaze the guilty could not choose but quail. He moved with a stateliness and majesty all his own. . . . [He] was a humble man, and in his humility, no less than his kingly stature, consisted his dignity, and no small share of his greatness. It was his intelligence, earnestness, simplicity, sublime faith and unwavering integrity to principle that made him great, not the apparel he wore, nor the mortal clay in which his spirit was clothed. Nevertheless, nature had given him a noble presence in the flesh, worthy the godlike statue of his spirit. . . .
>
> [His] temperament was religious and poetical. Sociable as he was, and even bubbling over with mirth, at times, his soul was essentially of a solemn cast. . . .
>
> He was a diamond in the rough, but a diamond nevertheless. . . . Unlettered and untaught, save in nature's school, the university of experience, where he was an apt and profound scholar, he was possessed of marvelous intuition, a genius, God-given, which needed no kindling at a college shrine to prepare it for the work which providence had designed. Not but that education would have polished the gem, causing it to shine with what the natural eye would deem a brighter lustre.

"The fact remains" Elder Whitney added, "that Heber C. Kimball, as he was, not as he might have been, was best adapted for the divine purpose, the career marked out for him by the finger of Deity."[31]

NOTES

1. See George Q. Cannon remarks at the time of Heber C. Kimball's death, quoted in Orson F. Whitney, *Life of Heber C. Kimball* (Salt Lake City: Bookcraft, 1967), p. 454.

2. Brigham Young, speaking at Heber C. Kimball's funeral, quoted in Whitney's *Life*, p. 495.

3. In *Journal of Discourses* 8:276.

4. Quoted by Alice K. Smith in *Improvement Era*, June 1930, p. 558.

5. Quoted in Whitney's *Life*, p. 7.

6. See Whitney's *Life*, pp. 321–28.

7. Whitney, *Life*, p. 476.

8. *Deseret News*, March 31, 1858, quoted by Stanley B. Kimball in *BYU Studies*, Spring, 1978, p. 398.

9. Whitney, *Life*, p. 98.

10. *Life*, p. 103.

11. Quoted in *Life*, p. 101.

12. Quoted in *Life*, p. 101.

13. Quoted in *Life*, p. 102.

14. *History of the Church* 2:489.

15. *Life*, p. 104.

16. Quoted in *Life*, p. 104.

17. Quoted in *Life*, p. 105.

18. Quoted in *Life*, pp. 108–9.

19. *Life*, p. 109. Technically the first "foreign" mission had been that opened by Parley P. Pratt and others sent into Canada. Phineas Young records that "[e]arly in June [1832] I started on a mission to Canada in company with Elders Elias Strong, Eleazer Miller and Enos Curtis. . . . We labored in Canada about six weeks with great success, raised the first branch in British America, and returned home rejoicing" (Elden Jay Watson, comp., *Manuscript History of Brigham Young, 1801–1844* [Salt Lake City: Elder J. Watson, 1968], pp. xxiv–xxv).

20. *Life*, p. 119.

21. *Life*, pp. 130–31.

22. *Life*, pp. 131–32.

23. James B. Allen, Ronald K. Esplin, and David J. Whittaker, *Men with a Mission, 1837–1841* (Salt Lake City: Deseret Book, 1992), pp. 50–51.

24. Joseph Fielding, quoted in *Men with a Mission*, p. 51.

25. Quoted in *Men with a Mission*, pp. 46–47.

26. Quoted in *Life*, p. 218.

27. See *Life*, p. 240.

28. *Life*, pp. 402–3.

29. *Life*, p. 394.

30. *Life*, p. 473.

31. From *Life*, pp. 9–10, 13–14; quoted by Alice K. Smith in *Improvement Era*, June 1930, pp. 558–59.

6

President James E. Faust

Edward Partridge
A Man like unto
Nathaniel of Old

Just a few years ago, I telephoned my aged, beloved aunt Angie Finlinson Lyman as she was nearing death. After discussing a few pleasantries, I said, "Aunt Angie, tell me again what your grand-mother said about the Prophet Joseph." I knew what she was going to say. I had grown up hearing stories about the Prophet Joseph and his associate Edward Partridge. Aunt Angie's grandmother Caroline Ely Partridge Lyman was one of the daughters of Edward Partridge and knew the Prophet Joseph intimately. The Prophet Joseph had been in the home of Bishop Partridge and in turn she, Caroline Ely Partridge Lyman, had lived in the home of the Prophet Joseph. That day Aunt Angie repeated to me for the last time her grandmother's testimony of the prophetic calling of the Prophet Joseph. The Prophet Joseph was very close to Edward Partridge.

His ancestors had emigrated from Scotland in the seventeenth century and settled in Massachusetts where Edward was born in 1793 and spent his formative years. Early in life, he experienced the first stirrings of the Spirit. The Prophet Joseph's history recorded: "he re-members that the Spirit of the Lord strove with him a number of times, insomuch that his heart was made tender, and he went and wept; and that sometimes he went silently and poured the effusions of his soul to God in prayer."[1]

He began his apprenticeship at the age of sixteen and spent four years acquiring a knowledge of the hatter's trade. He continued to

think about religion because by "the age of twenty he had become dis-
gusted with the religious world," and "saw no beauty, comeliness, or
loveliness in the character of the god that was preached up by the
sects."[2] Even so, he did not lose his faith. He still believed in his own
mind that God lived and that the Bible was His word.

In 1818 he left Painesville for Mackinaw on April 25. There he
enjoyed a short time of recreation and kept a journal of the weather
conditions as he went to Lake Michigan, Green Bay, and Fort Howard
at the mouth of Fox River, and then back to Mackinaw, where he
opened a shop but did not enjoy success. He then set sail for home,
anchoring off Grand River on July 31.

He married Lydia Clisbee in 1819 in Painesville, Ohio, and by her
had five daughters: Eliza Maria, Harriet Pamelia, Emily Dow, Caroline
Ely, and Lydia; and two sons: Clisbee, who died in infancy, and Edward Partridge Jr.

The two-story house reputed to be the Edward Partridge home still
stands on the Town Square of Painesville. There in 1830 he met Parley
P. Pratt, Oliver Cowdery, Peter Whitmer Jr., and Ziba Peterson, early
elders of the newly organized Church of Jesus Christ. Certain events
had occurred in his life prior to that time that piqued his interest in
their message.

The incident of Edward Partridge's baptism is enriched in interest
by some particulars related by Lucy Smith. She refers to Edward Partridge as being a man of intelligence and character, only accepting
baptism after making the inquiries she alludes to. Then she recounts:

> In December of the same year, Joseph appointed a meeting at our
> house. While he was preaching, Sidney Rigdon and Edward Partridge
> came in and seated themselves in the congregation. When Joseph
> had finished his discourse, he gave all who had any remarks to make,
> the privilege of speaking. Upon this, Mr. Partridge arose, and stated
> that he had been to Manchester, with the view of obtaining further
> information respecting the doctrine which we preached; but, not
> finding us, he had made some inquiry of our neighbors concerning
> our characters, which they stated had been unimpeachable, until
> Joseph deceived us relative to the Book of Mormon. He also said that
> he had walked over our farm, and observed the good order and indus-
> try which it exhibited; and, having seen what we had sacrificed for
> the sake of our faith, and having heard that our veracity was not

questioned upon any other point than that of our religion, he believed our testimony, and was ready to be baptized, "if," said he, "Brother Joseph will baptize me."

"You are now," replied Joseph, "much fatigued, brother Partridge, and you had better rest today, and be baptized tomorrow."

"Just as brother Joseph thinks best," replied Mr. Partridge, "I am ready at any time."

He was accordingly baptized the next day [11 December 1830 by the Prophet Joseph Smith in the Seneca River].[3]

A few days after his baptism he was ordained an elder by Sidney Rigdon. Soon after that he was commanded by the Lord to preach the gospel (see D&C 36). He and Sidney Rigdon remained in the East until the end of January 1831, when they started back to Kirtland in the company of the Prophet Joseph. In February 1831, at the age of thirty-seven, he was called to serve as the first bishop of the Church:

> And again, I have called my servant Edward Partridge; and I give a commandment, that he should be appointed by the voice of the church, and ordained a bishop unto the church, to leave his merchandise and to spend all his time in the labors of the church;
>
> To see to all things as it shall be appointed unto him in my laws in the day that I shall give them.
>
> And this because his heart is pure before me, for he is like unto Nathanael of old, in whom there is no guile. (D&C 41:9–11.)

He was ordained a high priest 3 June 1831 by Lyman Wight. Bishop Partridge's counselors were Isaac Morley and John Corrill, who later were both called to serve as bishops in Far West, Missouri. Parley P. Pratt and Titus Billings were called to serve as counselors in their place.[4]

As first bishop of the Church, he presided over the affairs of the Church in Jackson County, Missouri.

HIS TRAVELS AND MINISTRY

Edward Partridge, called by revelation on a special mission to Missouri, traveled in company with the Prophet Joseph Smith and others to that state and participated in the festivities connected with the beginning of the Latter-day Saint colony in Jackson County, Missouri.

Edward Partridge labored with Orson Pratt in Clay County, Missouri, according to appointment, visiting the different small branches of the Church. He traveled to Kirtland in April 1835, then labored in the eastern states, where he visited twenty-five branches of the Church, held fifty meetings, and preached thirty-two sermons.[5] On his return from this mission he visited Kirtland in the latter part of October 1835. While he was there, on Saturday, November 7, the word of the Lord came to the Prophet, saying:

> Behold, I am well pleased with my servant Isaac Morley and my servant Edward Partridge, because of the integrity of their hearts in laboring in my vineyard for the salvation of the souls of men. Verily I say unto you their sins are forgiven them, therefore say unto them in my name that it is my will that they should tarry for a little season and attend the school, and also the solemn assembly for a wise purpose in me, even so amen.[6]

Pursuant to this divine instruction, Edward Partridge remained for the dedication of the Kirtland Temple, March 27, 1836.

The dedication period was marked by a rich outpouring of the Spirit that boosted the faith and lifted the spirits of the struggling Saints. For Bishop Partridge this was a great contrast with the cruel persecutions he had suffered in Jackson County, Missouri, only three years earlier.

TARRING AND FEATHERING

With Martin Harris and others of the elders, Edward had been directed by the Lord to move from Ohio to Jackson County, Missouri, in 1831. He took his family to Missouri, purchased land, and built a home near the village of Independence. The Saints had been told that this was the land of their inheritance where the city of Zion should be built. These prophetic announcements inspired Bishop Partridge to write the hymn "Let Zion in Her Beauty Rise."[7]

However, on 20 July 1833, while he was sitting with his frail wife, who had recently given birth, three mobsters burst in on them and forced Edward out of his Zion house into the bedlam of the street.

Men, women, and children were running in all directions. William W. Phelps's house and printing establishment had been razed to the ground, his wife and child thrown out. The Saints feared who would be the next object of the mob's fury. But the mobsters wanted their leaders.

Hiking a red flag to show their bloody intent, they rushed upon Edward Partridge and Charles Allen and dragged them to the public square where a murderous mob of five hundred stood ominously armed with rifles, dirks, pistols, clubs, and whips. Their spokesman demanded that Edward and Charles either renounce their faith in the Book of Mormon or leave the county. Edward quickly responded: "If I must suffer for my religion, it is no more than others have done before me. I am not conscious of having injured any one in the county and therefore will not consent to leave it. I have done nothing to offend anyone. If you abuse me, you injure an innocent man."[8]

His last sentence was all but drowned out by the tumult of the frenzied rabble. "Call upon your God to deliver you!" they yelled. When neither of the two would give in to their demands, the mobsters, determined to wreak vengeance, began to tear off their clothes. Edward knew only too well what they had in mind. He could smell the tar. But he protested against being stripped naked in the street. In the event, they did allow him his shirt and pantaloons but were not deterred from their ultimate infamy. He would later write, "For the want of anything legal against us, they proceeded against us illegally."[9]

The mobsters brought their buckets and daubed Edward and Charles from head to foot in a mixture of tar and pearl-ash which contained a flesh-eating acid. Then they threw a quantity of feathers over the sticky tar. The two men bore this cruel abuse with such restraint and dignity that the crowd stopped their taunting and grew still. The sky was darkening; and as evening descended, the two brethren silently left the ugly scene.

Three days later the armed mob returned to this scene of desolation. Rather than see the Saints endure further ruin, the elders entered into a treaty. Each of the Saints had to pledge to leave the county within a certain time or face whipping and death. Most of them did sign even though it meant leaving their property to the mob militia. However, Bishop Partridge remarked that "all those who did deny the faith were exonerated from signing this deed of trust."[10]

FURTHER PERSECUTIONS

The 1833 cruelty and expulsion from Jackson County was only the beginning of the misery in Missouri. The horror continued, culminating in thousands of people being driven from their homes in 1838, some even being imprisoned, even though they had committed no civil offense. Edward Partridge wrote of these times that he and scores of his brethren in the bleak autumn of that year were driven off like dumb cattle to Richmond, thirty miles away, and there kept as prisoners for three or four weeks, without cause.[11] Said he: "We were confined in a large open room, where the cold northern blast penetrated freely. Our fires were small and our allowance for wood and food was scanty; they gave us not even a blanket to lie upon; our beds were the cold floors. . . . The vilest of the vile did guard us and treat us like dogs; yet we bore our oppressions without murmuring."[12]

During the winter of 1838–39, in conformity with Governor Boggs's exterminating order, the Edward Partridge family moved to Quincy, Illinois, where, after his release from prison, he rejoined them. Soon after, he was appointed as bishop of the Upper Ward in Nauvoo. But the career of Edward Partridge was drawing to a close. His health was broken, and for many months he had been unfit for any manual labor. In the words of Orson F. Whitney: "The persecutions he had passed through, added to the sickly climate in which the Saints were now settling, finally overcame what was left of a healthy, but by no means robust constitution. About ten days prior to his decease, he was taken with pleurisy in his side, as the result of over-lifting, and prostrated upon the bed from which he never again rose. He expired on Wednesday, May 27, 1840, at his home in Nauvoo, in the forty-seventh year of his age."[13] The Prophet Joseph wrote in his journal, under the same date, this closing comment on the death of his friend: "He lost his life in consequence of the Missouri persecutions, and he is one of that number whose blood will be required at their hands."[14]

STATEMENTS OF HIS FAITH AND DEVOTION

In January of 1835, Edward Partridge composed a letter which he addressed to all his dear friends and neighbors, setting forth his testimony in the form of a treatise. The following are some excerpts:

I want you now to . . . carefully and prayerfully compare the book of Mormon with the gospel, as preached on the day of pentecost, and see if the sentiment is not the same; if it is the same, it must be the gospel, and if the gospel, it must be the power of God unto salvation. . . . If you admit John's declaration that the gospel is everlasting, . . . that he saw in the last days an angel flying through the midst of heaven, having the everlasting gospel to preach to all nations, kindreds, tongues and people, it will prove that there is such a thing as the everlasting gospel, and if so, is it not the gospel of God?

If the book of Mormon contains the same gospel that the apostles preached, which it certainly does, and that its whole drift appears to be to make men righteous and happy; and if the men who attest to the truth of the book are men of piety, and men who have sacrificed their property, and even their good name for this cause, which certainly is the case, what does it argue? Does it not argue that this work is true; that the book of Mormon is the fulness of the gospel, sent forth to this generation, that a people may be prepared for the coming of the bridegroom? Surely it does.

At length the Lord saw fit to raise up a standard, even the fulness of his gospel, and give unto his people a prophet, through whom they can have the word of the Lord from time to time. . . . I will rejoice and praise my Father in heaven, that he has permitted me to live in this day and age, when I can see the work of the Lord and know it for myself—that is, I know it, or have no more doubt of it, than I have that there is such places as London, Paris, or Jerusalem.[15]

His Own Statement about Sacrifice

In Edward Partridge's treatise of January 1835, he wrote his feelings on what it is to give up all for Christ:

All the sacrifices that I have made I count as nought, when compared with the hope that I have of one day being enabled to exclaim with Paul, "I have fought a good fight, I have finished by course, I have kept the faith; henceforth there is laid up for me a crown of righteousness, which the Lord, the righteous judge, shall give me at that day: and not to me only, but unto all them also that love his appearing." I now ask, do you love his appearing? Is it your prayer that he may come in this generation? O, think on these things, and not suffer the god of this world to blind your eyes.

Since I have torn my affections from this world's goods; from the vanities and toys of time and sense, and been willing to love and serve God with all my heart, and be led by his holy Spirit, my mind has been as it were continually expanding—receiving the things of God, . . . The testimony that I have borne and now bear to you in favor of the book of Mormon, and the great things that are to take place in these last days, is such that I feel clear in my mind. . . .

O take the advice of one who wishes you well and would rejoice to meet you in the celestial kingdom of God.[16]

OLIVER COWDERY'S STATEMENT

Many of the saints are acquainted with this individual, and none, I presume, will hesitate to say, that the longer the acquaintance the more desirable the society. If this world produces a plain man, it is bishop Partridge. I do not mean particular plainness of dress, though he is truly an ensample of prudence and economy in all his temporal avocations—but of speech, precept, example and doctrine. Neither do I suppose that a commendation from my pen will have the effect to alter one hair "from black to white," but from the knowledge of the persecution and personal abuse which has been heaped upon him, I am prepared to say, that if a man was ever persecuted for righteousness' sake, without casting an anxious look back to the applause of the world and the flattery of the great, it is bishop Partridge.[17]

NOTE IN WILFORD WOODRUFF'S JOURNAL

Wilford Woodruff notes in his journal the death of Bishop Edward Partridge, and makes this comment, "Bishop Partridge was one of the wisest and best men of the last generation. Like Nathaniel of old, in him there was no guile. He had passed through much persecution with the Saints, for the word of God and the testimony of Jesus."[18]

THE PROPHET JOSEPH'S STATEMENTS
ABOUT HIS FAITHFULNESS

The Prophet's January 7, 1838, letter to him begins: "Brother Partridge, Thus saith the Lord, my servant Edward and his house shall be numbered with the blessed and Abraham their father, and his name shall be had in sacred rem[em]brance. . . . Awake my shepherds and warn my people! for behold the wolf cometh to destroy them! receive him not. . . . It is my earnest prayer to God that health, peace, and plenty may crown your board and blessings of Heaven rest upon the head of him in whom the Lord hath said there is no guile."[19]

Isaac Morley, Edward's counselor, friend, and companion in the work, was also kind and gentle in disposition. Speaking of them collectively, the Prophet Joseph wrote in his journal: "Went to meeting at the usual hour Elder [Isaac] Morley preached and Bishop [Edward] Partridge in the afternoon; their discourses were well adapted to the times in which we live, and the circumstances under which we are placed, their words were words of wisdom, like apples of gold in pictures of silver, spoken in the simple accents of a child, yet sublime as the voice of an angel, the saints appeared to be much pleased with the beautiful discourses of these two fathers in Israel."[20]

I wish to bear witness of the nobility, sacrifice, devotion, and example of this humble, great servant of the Lord. There can be no higher praise of this saintly man than that given by the Lord in the 124th section of the Doctrine and Covenants wherein the Lord says:

"When [Lyman Wight] shall finish his work I may receive him unto myself, even as I did my servant David Patten, who is with me at this time, and also my servant Edward Partridge, and also my aged servant Joseph Smith, Sen., who sitteth with Abraham at his right hand, and blessed and holy is he, for he is mine" (D&C 124:19).

NOTES

1. Dean C. Jessee, ed., *The Papers of Joseph Smith*, 2 vols. (Salt Lake City: Deseret Book, 1989), 1:348.

2. Ibid.

3. Lucy Mack Smith, *History of Joseph Smith* (Salt Lake City: Bookcraft, 1956), p. 192.

4. *Times and Seasons*, vol. 6, p. 800.

5. "Comments" no. 71, *Early LDS Member Records*, Susan Black, comp.

6. Dean C. Jessee, ed., *The Personal Writings of Joseph Smith* (Salt Lake City: Deseret Book, 1984), p. 73.

7. *Hymns*, no. 41; J. Spencer Cornwall, *Stories of Our Mormon Hymns*, (Deseret Book, 1961), p. 255.

8. See B. H. Roberts, A Comprehensive History of The Church of Jesus Christ of Latter-day Saints, 6 vols. (Salt Lake City: Deseret News Press, 1930), 1:333.

9. Clark V. Johnson, ed., Mormon Redress Petitions (Provo: BYU Religious Studies Center, 1992), p. 514.

10. Ibid., p. 515.

11. See Mormon Redress Petitions, p. 514.

12. Andrew Jenson, Latter-day Saint Biographical Encyclopedia, 1901, 1:221.

13. Ibid.

14. History of the Church 4:132.

15. Messenger and Advocate, January 1835, pp. 60–61.

16. Ibid., p. 61.

17. Ibid., p. 61.

18. Matthias F. Cowley, Wilford Woodruff, His Life and Labors (Salt Lake City: Bookcraft, 1964), p. 150.

19. Edward Partridge Jr., "Family Record," p. 52, Church Historical Department.

20. The Personal Writings of Joseph Smith, p. 94.

BIBLIOGRAPHY

Backman, Milton V. Jr. The Heavens Resound, A History of the Latter-day Saints in Ohio 1830–1838. Salt Lake City: Deseret Book Company. 1983.

Brown, S. Kent, Cannon, Donald Q., and Jackson, Richard H. Historical Atlas of Mormonism. New York: Simon and Schuster. 1994.

Cannon, Donald Q., and Cook, Lindon W., eds. Far West Record. Salt Lake City: Deseret Book Company. 1983.

Cook, Lindon W. The Revelations of the Prophet Joseph Smith. Salt Lake City: Deseret Book Company. 1981.

History of the Church, vol. 1.

Jessee, Dean C., ed. The Papers of Joseph Smith, vol. 2. Salt Lake City: Deseret Book Company. 1992.

Journal History, 27 May 1840. From History of the Church.

Knight, Newel. Autobiography, in Classic Experiences.

Pratt, Parley P. History of Persecution. 1839.

Whitmer, John. "Book of John Whitmer." Typescript. BYU-A.

Whitney, Orson F. In Collected Discourses Delivered by President Wilford Woodruff. . . . Brian H. Stuy, ed. B. H. S. Publishing. 1987. Pages 354–69.

Woodruff, Wilford. Journal, August 12, 1840.

Young, Emily. "Auto." Woman's Exponent 14 (1885). Page 145.

Young, Emily. Autobiography. Typescript. BYU-S. Pages 5–6.

7

Elder Cecil O. Samuelson

David W. Patten

The valor, gallantry, and other contributions of many who were instrumental in the unfolding of the restoration of the gospel of Jesus Christ in our time, the dispensation of the fulness of times, are wonderfully remarkable and varied. Relatively few, however, are so unique in their contributions and sacrifices as to qualify for the honored designation of *hero*. One who would clearly meet the criteria for such designation is Elder David W. Patten, the first apostolic martyr in modern times.[1]

Much about David Patten seems rather ordinary in the context of his times. He was not particularly wealthy, well educated, widely known, or otherwise prominent in worldly terms. By all accounts he was modest, thoughtful, considerate, and gentle, yet absolutely fearless in defense of the faith and consistently loyal to his duty. He understood deeply the teaching of Jesus Christ, thought to be paradoxical by some, that the safest way to save one's life was to be willing to lose it for the Savior (see JST, Luke 9:24–25).

David Wyman Patten was born November 14, 1799, at Theresa, Jefferson County, New York. While not a great deal is known about his early years, we know he left his birthplace in his youth and made his way to Dundee, Monroe County, Michigan, where he made his home for several years. He married Phoebe Ann Babcock in 1828. Although very happy together, they were not blessed with children.

During his youth and young adult years David had a series of very private but very real spiritual experiences that sustained and enlightened him throughout his life. He gained the assurance that the true church of Jesus Christ would arise in his time and that he could be part of it. It is interesting that these special experiences were roughly contemporaneous with the theophany and the angelic ministrations experienced by the Prophet Joseph Smith.

Elder Patten apparently first became aware of the Book of Mormon in late 1830, but his initial reactions and involvements, if any, are not fully recorded. He was looking for the truth, with confidence that he would find it, but as yet it was not fully made known to him. In the spring of 1832 he received word from his brother John, who was living in Indiana at the time, that he had joined the Church of Jesus Christ and that the restoration David had been awaiting had occurred.

Feeling a sense of urgency about this development, David traveled immediately to his brother's home in Green County, Indiana, and was himself baptized a member of the Church on June 15, 1832, by his brother, John. Because of the strength of his conversion and commitment he was ordained an elder by Elisha H. Groves two days after his baptism and ordained a high priest by Hyrum Smith only weeks later on September 2, 1832. From this time until his seemingly premature death from the wounds he received at Crooked River just over six years later, he was found in almost constant missionary and Church service of one kind or another.

Church history records a number of noteworthy items with respect to Brother Patten:

- Member of Zion's Camp
- Member of the original Quorum of the Twelve Apostles
- Specifically mentioned in Doctrine and Covenants 114 and 124
- First apostolic martyr in this dispensation

Perhaps most helpful to us, however, are the personal characteristics and attitudes of David Patten that likely made the historical record plausible, if not inevitable. While these attributes were not, or are not, necessarily unique or specific to him, they nevertheless are the fabric of his character and personality. These traits contributed to the observation that he was absolutely trustworthy when presented with heavy responsibilities and challenges. They clearly were conducive also to his being so loved and honored by the Lord and His prophet, Joseph.

Among the qualities he exhibited, there are seven so distinctive that they seem to identify themselves readily to us as we study his life and could provoke our careful consideration and emulation.

FEARLESS

During the first decade of the restored Church, persecution was never far away. While David never was one to look for trouble, he also was unable to look away if his principles or his brethren were being attacked. His frequent missions were never easy, but his willingness to teach and testify in any situation and to any group of people was a hallmark of his ministry. Multiple accounts have been preserved that highlight his courage and his capacity to withstand afflictions for the gospel's sake.

In 1838, as persecution became particularly fierce, David W. Patten was always at the forefront in defending the Saints and their property. When appointed a captain in the militia of Caldwell County, he acquired the interesting nickname of "Captain Fearnaught" (fearnothing) because he was described by the Prophet Joseph and others as "fearless."[2] He had frequent experience with mobs, critics, and dissenters, but he consistently acknowledged what he knew to be true and defended it with all of his energies. While not foolhardy, he nevertheless was not dissuaded from his duty. He was known to stand up to armed men, mobs, and even the courts when he felt that inappropriate intrusions or liberties were being taken with the servants of the Lord or His people.

MAN OF FAITH

David Patten had the faith not only to attempt but also to accomplish all that he was asked to do by those in authority over him. Joseph Smith expressed his appreciation for Elder Patten's faith while David lived and again after he died. When Brother Patten told of his hope that he might be found worthy to give his life as a martyr for the kingdom, Joseph said, "[W]hen a man of your faith asks the Lord for anything, he generally gets it."[3] After his tragic death, the Prophet reported, "In the engagement Capt Patten (a man beloved of all who had the pleasure of his acquaintance) was wounded and died shortly after."[4]

Elder Wilford Woodruff recorded the following in his journal: "Brother David Patten was a man of great faith, and performed many miracles in the name of Jesus Christ; he had many visions and dreams, and was very valiant in the testimony of Jesus and the word of God."[5]

Even at the moment of his death his faith was firm and absolute. Elder Heber C. Kimball made these comments about Elder Patten: "The principles of the gospel [that] were so precious to him before, afforded him the support and consolation at the time of his departure, which deprived death of its sting and horror." He went on to add: "Speaking of those who had fallen from their steadfastness, he [David] exclaimed, 'O that they were in my situation! For I feel that I have kept the faith, I have finished my course, henceforth there is laid up for me a crown, which the Lord, the righteous Judge, will give me.'"[6]

STUDENT OF THE DOCTRINE

Elder Patten's epistle to the Saints in July 1838, turned out to be his valedictory message to the Church generally.[7] It presented much of the doctrinal basis for developing an understanding of the dispensations and gave particular insight into the dispensation of the fulness of times. As his treatise and other contributions attest, David Patten knew the scriptures and used them abundantly and distinctly in his writing and teaching. His doctrine was clear and correct and his testimony was a compelling witness that the Restoration had commenced.

MAN OF THE SPIRIT

During the period prior to his baptism into the Church, as well as during his entire mortal ministry, David W. Patten was worthy of and received a number of specific, and sometimes dramatic, spiritual experiences. He prayed with faith from his youth onward and was called to repentance in a spiritual manifestation at age twenty-one. In the following years many significant future events were made known to him by the Spirit. He was convinced that the true Church of Jesus Christ would emerge during his lifetime and he was prepared to receive it when he learned of the glorious events surrounding its organization in the fulness of times. His constant theme seemed to be to cry to Heavenly Father for more faith even when he demonstrated faith to a remarkable degree.

Because he learned early to live by and with the Spirit, he was able to receive help that was sometimes dramatic or even life-saving during his service as a missionary and priesthood leader. Although valiant, he was not foolhardy, and he consistently sought direction from the Spirit when boldness or physical courage might be required, as when he was confronted by mobs and significant opposition of various kinds. Whether it was facing a disruptive opponent of truth in a worship service, defending the rights of his brethren or himself in questionable courts of law, or receiving direction with respect to the bearing of testimony to those he taught, he always was dependent on the Spirit and followed its promptings.

HEALER

From the time he was ordained an elder and received the Melchizedek Priesthood, David's ministry was frequently characterized by the remarkable and frequent healings that resulted from his administrations to those who shared his gifts of faith and worthiness. It was not unusual for him as a missionary to seek out the sick and, after teaching them and hearing their sincere expressions of faith, to command their illnesses to leave them so that they could arise and present themselves for the baptismal ordinance which he then performed.

Many accounts of priesthood healings performed by Elder Patten have been recorded.[8] A Mrs. Lane had been ill for years and had not been able to walk for many months. She heard of the missionaries and begged her husband to send for them. David Patten responded almost immediately and taught this family the gospel. Mrs. Lane believed his testimony and received a priesthood administration from him. He then took her by the hand and commanded her, in the name of Jesus Christ, to rise and be made whole. She was healed and then entered the waters of baptism. In the confirmation that followed, Elder Patten promised that she would continue to increase in strength and within the year she would have a son. Although she had been married for some twelve years without having children, this prophecy was fulfilled and she bore a son whom she named David Patten.

MISSIONARY

In several locations he was able to establish branches of the Church with newly converted but absolutely committed members within days of his arrival and the commencement of his preaching and teaching. While often attended by persecution and opposition, he nevertheless was not distracted from his duty or his obligations to build the kingdom. Many came into the Church through his efforts and gave him great credit for the positive influence he had on them. One of these was Lorenzo Snow, who was later to serve not only as one of the Twelve Apostles but also as the prophet of the Lord. These are his words:

> All the circumstances of my first and last meeting with Apostle David W. Patten are as clear to my mind as if it were an occurrence of but yesterday, and yet it took place some sixty-four years ago. He appeared to me then to be a remarkable man, and that impression has remained with me ever since.
>
> We traveled together on horseback from my father's home, at Mantua, Ohio, to Kirtland, a distance of perhaps twenty-five miles, he on his return from some missionary labor, I to commence a course of studies at Oberlin College.
>
> On the way our conversation fell upon religion and philosophy, and being young and having enjoyed some scholastic advantages, I was at first disposed to treat his opinions lightly, especially so as they were not always clothed in grammatical language; but as he proceeded in his earnest and humble way to open up before my mind the plan of salvation, I seemed unable to resist the knowledge that he was a man of God and that his testimony was true. I felt pricked in my heart.
>
> This he evidently perceived, for almost the last thing he said to me, after bearing his testimony, was that I should go to the Lord before retiring at night and ask him for myself. This I did with the result that from the day I met this great Apostle, all my aspirations have been enlarged and heightened immeasurably. This was the turning point in my life.
>
> What impressed me most was his absolute sincerity, his earnestness and his spiritual power; and I believe I cannot do better in this connection than to commend a careful study of his life to the honest in heart everywhere.[9]

ENDURED TO THE END

During the difficulties in Kirtland and Missouri, many of the seemingly steadfast grew faint in their testimonies, or at least in their resolves to stand by the Prophet and the kingdom. Elder Patten was not one of these. Even as he lay suffering greatly and dying from the horrible wounds inflicted at Crooked River, he bore his testimony of the truth of the work and also proclaimed his loyalty to the faith for which he literally gave his all. One of his last expressions to his wife, as he lay dying, was: "Whatever you do else, O! Do not deny the faith."[10] Shortly thereafter he breathed his last breath, formally becoming an apostolic martyr on October 25, 1838.

After his death and burial in Far West, Missouri, his work was not yet finished. In a revelation received by Joseph Smith the Lord spoke of "David Patten, who is with me at this time," and also said, "David Patten I have taken unto myself; behold, his priesthood no man taketh from him" (D&C 124:19, 130). His priesthood was still clearly necessary because he obviously is one "among the noble and great ones who were chosen in the beginning to be rulers in the Church of God." Likewise, he most certainly is with those "choice spirits who were reserved to come forth in the fulness of times to take part in laying the foundations of the great latter-day work . . . and . . . were also in the spirit world." (D&C 138:53–55.)

CONCLUSION

In all usual ways David W. Patten was an ordinary man who accomplished extraordinary things. His only agenda was to do what was right and to follow the Savior, including following those called in the Church to preside over him. He is known and revered as the first apostolic martyr of the dispensation of the fulness of times but also should be recognized as a man who both lived his life well and died well. A faithful Apostle of the Lord Jesus Christ, he did all that he was asked to do, and as such has become not only an inspiration to those of like mind but also a wonderful example of those who have chosen to risk mortal life, if necessary, to gain the only life that is ultimately worthwhile—eternal life!

NOTES

1. Most biographical details for this piece were taken from Lycurgus A. Wilson, *Life of David W. Patten: The First Apostolic Martyr* (Salt Lake City: Deseret News, 1900) and Andrew Jenson, *Latter-day Saint Biographical Encyclopedia*, vol. 1 (Salt Lake City: Andrew Jenson History Co., 1901), pp. 76–80.

2. B. H. Roberts, *A Comprehensive History of The Church of Jesus Christ of Latter-day Saints*, 6 vols. (1957; reprint, Provo: Brigham Young University Press, 1965), 1:477 n. 27.

3. Wilson, *Life of David W. Patten, The First Apostolic Martyr*, p. 58.

4. Dean C. Jessee, ed., *The Papers of Joseph Smith*, 2 vols. (Salt Lake City: Deseret Book, 1989), 1:217.

5. *Millennial Star* 26 (2 July 1864): 423.

6. *Millennial Star* 26 (16 July 1864): 454–55.

7. See *History of the Church* 3:49–54.

8. See Jenson, *Latter-day Saint Biographical Encyclopedia* 1:76–80.

9. In James R. Clark, ed., *Messages of the First Presidency*, 6 vols., 1965–75 (Salt Lake City: Bookcraft), 3:324–25.

10. *History of the Church* 3:171.

8

Elder Carlos E. Asay

Orson Pratt

In an insightful scriptural account, we learn that the Lord showed Abraham "the intelligences that were organized before the world was; and among all these there were many of the noble and great ones" (Abraham 3:22). These noble and great ones, including Father Abraham, were chosen before they were born and were foreordained to play leading roles in the drama of mortality as the purposes of Almighty God were and still are being fulfilled.

One such noble and great one was Orson Pratt—a notable leader in the early years of The Church of Jesus Christ of Latter-day Saints. Elder Pratt distinguished himself as an Apostle, pioneer, philosopher, scientist, educator, and historian. His accomplishments blend into the landmark events associated with the restoration of the gospel of Jesus Christ and the ushering in of the dispensation of the fulness of times.

Even a casual review of Elder Pratt's life attests that he was "called and prepared from the foundation of the world according to the foreknowledge of God" (Alma 13:3). No one coerced him to accept the gospel, yet from the day of his conversion till the day of his death he seemed driven in his desire to proclaim truth and to establish the kingdom of God on earth. Thus he became deeply involved in historical events such as Zion's Camp, the School of the Prophets, the calling of the original twelve Apostles in this day and age, the first missions to Europe, the western migration, and other momentous happenings that swallowed him up in a fifty-one-year ministry of heroic proportions. In the end it seemed as though he submitted fully to a higher will and became an instrument in the hands of God in doing extraordinary things.

Orson Pratt was an exact man—a man who loved measures and instruments that could be used to unlock the mysteries of the universe. He spoke of and used microscopes, telescopes, sextants, and other devices. If he were living today he would probably carry a calculator in his pocket and spend considerable time at the keyboard extracting data from a personal computer. It is also likely that he would apply his keen intellect in developing software programs, for he loved to organize words and numbers, particularly those related to astronomy, mathematics, and other sciences.

If Elder Pratt were required to conduct a postmortem of his own life and make an assessment of his sojourn in mortality, I believe he would approach the task in a scientific manner. First, he would research and methodically identify the criteria of success. Second, he would prepare a scale of measurement. And third, he would chart his own accomplishments on the scale and compare them with a prescribed ideal. Such an organized approach was typical of his nature and would lead to objective, more than subjective, conclusions.

He once warned a congregation not to judge others through the "devil's looking glass"—a glass that exaggerates the flaws in others and ignores one's own. Rather, he urged his listeners to use "the Lord's microscope" in mirroring their own imperfections.[1]

I have no desire to make use of the "devil's looking glass" or to stand in judgment of a man who labored so diligently and long in the cause of righteousness. I do, however, want to look at Orson Pratt through "the Lord's microscope" so that the true measure of the man might be revealed. In the process the reader will understand why Elder Pratt is regarded as one of the real heroes of the Restoration.

Greatness or heroism may be measured in terms of (1) personal achievements, (2) willingness to sacrifice, (3) noble qualities of character, (4) centralness in a specific period of time, and (5) worthiness to serve as a role model. These criteria seem most appropriate in evaluating the life of one who, like Job, desired to "be weighed in an even balance, that God may know mine integrity" (Job 31:6).

PERSONAL ACHIEVEMENTS

Orson was born to Jared and Charity Pratt in Hartford, New York, on September 19, 1811. He was next to the youngest of six children in a family that scratched out a living by weaving and by tilling the soil. Consequently, Orson's opportunities for schooling were limited to a few months each year until the spring of 1822. Nonetheless, it is said that "at intervals he picked up a knowledge of arithmetic, bookkeeping, geography, grammar, and surveying."[2]

From the beginning, this self-educated man seems to have had an insatiable thirst for truth. Said he: "For about one year before I heard of this Church, I had begun seriously in my own mind to inquire after the Lord. I had sought him diligently—perhaps more so than many others that professed to seek him. I was so earnest and intent upon the subject of seeking the Lord, when I was about eighteen years of age, and from that until I was nineteen, when I heard this Gospel and received it, that I did not give myself the necessary time to rest. Engaged in farming and labouring too by the month, I took the privilege, while others had retired to rest, to go out into the fields and wilderness, and there plead with the Lord, hour after hour, that he would show me what to do—that he would teach me the way of life, and inform and instruct my understanding."[3]

News of the restored gospel was brought to Orson by his older brother, Parley P. Pratt, and on his nineteenth birthday he was baptized. Years later he acknowledged that the Book of Mormon was instrumental in his conversion. He wrote: "Uncertainty and ambiguity have been the principal cause of all the divisions of modern Christendom. The only way to remedy this great evil, is to obtain another revelation of the gospel. . . . Such a revelation is the Book of Mormon; the most infallible certainty characterizes every ordinance and every doctrinal point revealed in that book. In it there is no ambiguity—no room for controversy."[4]

His love for the Book of Mormon is further verified in this statement: "When I was . . . 21 years of age, I had, for the two years during my first acquaintance with the book, read it so much that I could repeat over chapter after chapter, page after page, of many portions . . . and could do it just as well with the Book closed or laid to one side."[5]

In addition to the many accomplishments of Orson Pratt already mentioned were the following:

- He was a mathematician, a surveyor, and an astronomer.
- He was a Greek and Hebrew linguist.
- He was the author of several books, many magazine articles, and missionary tracts.
- He was a powerful preacher-orator.
- He was instrumental in the conversion of thousands at home and abroad and their gathering to Zion.
- He was one of the first two Mormon pioneers to enter the Salt Lake Valley.
- He was a spokesman for the Church on issues such as plural marriage, and was a legislator.
- He was the husband of several wives, the father of forty-five children, thirty of whom survived him.

The list goes on and on—there seemed to be no end to the notable achievements of this tireless and driven man.

WILLINGNESS TO SACRIFICE

President Spencer W. Kimball declared: "We must lay on the altar and sacrifice whatever is required by the Lord. We begin by offering a 'broken heart and a contrite spirit.' We follow this by giving our best effort in our assigned fields of labor and callings. We learn our duty and execute it fully. Finally we consecrate our time, talents, and means as called upon by our file leaders and as prompted by the whisperings of the Spirit. . . . And as we give, we find that 'sacrifice brings forth the blessings of heaven!' (*Hymns*, no. [27].) And in the end, we learn it was no sacrifice at all."[6]

Few, if any, leaders placed more upon the altar than did Orson Pratt. He served mission after mission and surrendered his time and talents to the Lord again and again without a whimper or a word of protest. Note the ring of consecration in this admission: "I am willing to do everything the Lord requires at my hands, so far as I understand His will concerning me. What is property? what is gold? what is silver? what are houses and inheritances, or any of the riches of this world, compared with the riches of eternal life? Have I anything that I have obtained by my own wisdom, or by my own exertions, independent of the hand and providences of the Almighty? No, I have not. The earth is the Lord's, and the fulness thereof is His. I am in His hands, and all that I have is in His hands; and if the servants of God require it, if God desires all that I have, it is on hand, at any moment."[7]

In 1859, Elder Pratt preached: "If any one should ask me where my home has been for the last quarter-of-a-century, I should answer—Among the nations; for that has been my principal abidingplace ever since the year 1830. . . . Should my brethren say to me 'Brother Orson, we wish you to take a mission, now, to China, or to the East Indies, or to any other part of this globe, and tarry there twenty-seven years before you return to your home,' I would go. Yes, I would gladly go, and feel that it was my duty, and that I was pleasing God in obeying the counsel of his servants."[8]

Riches and honors of the world were unimportant in the life of Orson Pratt. What mattered most was the Church and the welfare of the whole human race. So he fulfilled one assignment after another and crossed the Atlantic sixteen times on the Lord's errands, even though he agonized over the fact that sometimes his family was left at home suffering in abject poverty.

Elder Orson F. Whitney of the Quorum of Twelve Apostles penned these stirring words:

> Thank heaven there are some men and some women who bow not down to the god of gold; men and women who are not for sale; men and women with whom the Giver, not the gift, is supreme. Such a man was the Prophet Joseph Smith. Such were his associates and successors. Such men lead us today, and such are all true Latter-day Saints, the world over.
>
> Such a man was Orson Pratt, a true and genuine Apostle. "A rich man," said President John Taylor at his funeral. Yes, for "he that hath eternal life is rich." Eternal riches was his quest. In moderate, even lowly circumstances, so far as this world's wealth was concerned, he was rich in powers of mind and accumulations of knowledge; an intellectual and a spiritual millionaire.[9]

Noble Qualities of Character

Many noble qualities of character are associated with Orson Pratt. He had a brilliant mind; he had a dogged determination; his work ethic was impeccable; and he seemed to enjoy a special closeness to the Spirit. But the quality that impressed me most as I studied his life was the willingness to acknowledge error, confess sins, and try again.

On two occasions he had disputes with the Prophet Joseph Smith—one over a business transaction and one over the Prophet's alleged misconduct (a domestic misunderstanding, fueled by apostate John C. Bennett's slanderous lies, that resulted in Orson's estrangement from the Church for approximately six months). Moreover, more than once President Brigham Young took exception to some of Orson's writings and interpretation of doctrine. Yet in each instance Elder Pratt confessed his sins and weaknesses and manifested deep repentance.[10]

In an address given in 1860 he stated:

> I have sinned; and for this I am willing to make my confession to the Saints. I ought to have yielded to the views of my brethren. I ought to have said, as Jesus did to his Father on a certain occasion, "Father, thy will be done." . . .
>
> God placed Joseph Smith at the head of this Church; God has likewise placed Brigham Young at the head of this Church; and he has required you and me, male and female, to sustain those authorities thus placed over us in their position. . . .
>
> Inasmuch as there may have been any feelings in the hearts of the Latter-day Saints that are now before me, I desire to do all in my power to bring about a complete reconciliation. I wish the whole Territory were here, and all the good people of England, and all the Saints that have ever seen any of my writings or read my views; I would say to them all, Brethren, I make a confession: I have sinned; I have been too stubborn; I have not yielded as I ought; I have done wrong, and I will try to do so no more. And if the whole kingdom of God can be reconciled with me, I shall be very glad. At least, I will do all I can to obtain their reconciliation.[11]

Elder Pratt defined a true believer as one "that receives the ordinances, and not only believes in them but manifests his faith by his works." And he described true charity as the willingness to use "the plain naked truth" in telling people whether they are walking on the right path. When these definitions are applied to Orson, he comes away as a true believer and as one who possessed true charity.[12]

CENTRALNESS TO A PERIOD OF TIME

Orson Pratt was surely raised up for a purpose and was a man for all seasons. One biographer, T. Edgar Lyon, wrote: "Orson Pratt did more to formulate the Mormon idea of God, the religious basis of polygamy, the pre-existence of spirits, the doctrine of the gathering, the resurrection, and eternal salvation than any other person in the Church, with the exception of Joseph Smith."[13]

Orson Pratt has been referred to as "the St. Paul of Mormondom." Such tribute acknowledged not only Orson's missionary zeal and extensive travels but also his willingness to defend the faith he had embraced body and soul. In addition it acknowledged his persuasive power of speech as demonstrated in the famous debate with Dr. John P. Newman on the issue of polygamy—a debate that caused one eastern paper to print, "Some one carrying more guns than Dr. Newman will have to be sent out missionarying among the Mormons."[14]

A modern biographer provides this concise and descriptive summary of Elder Pratt's accomplishments and centricity in the early years of the Church: "Orson Pratt's contributions remain unequaled in volume and scope: his ingenious attempt to bring together a unified theory of nature, God, and humanity, his deeply affirmative vision of man as a noble truthseeker and son of God bring to mind a Mormon Aquinas; a Mormon Aristotle; a 'philosopher apostle'—hence a Mormon Paul."[15]

If doubts still remain concerning the pivotal role played by Orson Pratt as the gospel was restored and as the Church became established, one should note the words of Wilford Woodruff. Said he: "Brother Pratt had lived longer in this Church, traveled more miles and preached more sermons than any man in it. He had baptized thousands, and fulfilled the revelation given to him through the Prophet Joseph Smith, November 4th 1830. . . . [Moreover] he had studied and written more upon the Gospel and upon science than any man in the Church."[16]

WORTHINESS AS A ROLE MODEL

Orson Pratt would be quick to caution others in the selection of role models. He knew much about the frailties of men and the weaknesses of the flesh. So in all probability he would advise "would-be" admirers not to pattern their lives after his; but rather to follow after the Man of Galilee—He who is the ultimate role model.

Elder Pratt often admitted his weaknesses and shortcomings. He knew that some of his sermons became tedious, especially to the young. He felt bad over the fact that he couldn't provide better for his wives and children. And I suppose that he was aware of his tendency to become over-exacting and sometimes even stubborn in holding to his opinions. Nevertheless there is much in Elder Pratt's life that is worthy of emulation. I refer to strengths of character such as an unwillingness to waste time, a desire to become informed on all subjects, a determination to speak under the influence of the Holy Spirit, a love for teaching, a loyalty to the Church and its presiding officers, and, as mentioned previously, a willingness to confess sins. All of these virtues and more set Orson apart from the average man and help to explain why he was able to accomplish so much in one lifetime.

CONCLUSION

Put to the test and carefully examined through the Lord's microscope, Orson Pratt meets every requirement as one of the real heroes of the Restoration. His list of personal achievements is impressive, to say the least. His willingness to sacrifice is indisputable. His noble qualities of character are worthy of emulation by all. His centralness to a period of time is obvious to even the novice historian. And his life and legacy will always serve as a role model to those who desire to serve God with all their might, mind, and strength. For as Brigham Young said, "If you were to chop up Elder Pratt into inch-square pieces, each piece would cry out, 'Mormonism is true.'"[17]

In one of his last public appearances, Elder Orson Pratt preached: "There is nothing so precious to me as the great principles of salvation. They have for the last 51 years of my life—it being 51 years tomorrow since I was baptized—occupied the uppermost place in my mind. Riches, the honors of this world, etc., have been but a very small consideration with me, compared with the riches of eternal salvation, the blessings of the everlasting Gospel, the new covenant which we have embraced, the great work which the Lord our God is performing by his mighty hand in the age in which you and I live."[18]

His dying words, dictated to President Joseph F. Smith (words that later became the epitaph on his tombstone), were: "My body sleeps for a moment, but my testimony lives and shall endure forever."[19]

Thus the fitting tribute which was published in the *Deseret News* at the time of his death:

> Orson Pratt was truly an Apostle of the Lord. Full of integrity, firm as a rock to his convictions, true to his brethren and to his God, earnest and zealous in defense and proclamation of the truth, ever ready to bear testimony to the latter-day work, he had a mind stored with scripture, ancient and modern, was an eloquent speaker, a powerful minister, a logical and convincing writer—an honest man, and a great soul who reached out after eternal things, grasped them with the gift of inspiration, and brought them down to the level and comprehension of the common mind. Thousands have been brought into the Church through his preaching in many lands, thousands more by his writings. He set but little store on the wealth of this world, but he has laid up treasures in heaven which will make him eternally rich.[20]

"The hero of my tale," said Tolstoi, "whom I love with all the power of my soul, whom I have tried to portray in all his beauty, who has been, is, and will be beautiful, is truth."[21]

The hero of this brief essay is Elder Orson Pratt—one who loved truth more than life itself. Truths associated with this great man have outlived him for a century and will never die in the minds and hearts of those who become familiar with the heroes of the Restoration.

NOTES

1. In *Journal of Discourses* 3:305 (hereafter cited as *JD*).

2. Orson F. Whitney, *Improvement Era*, January 1912, p. 196.

3. In *JD* 7:177.

4. Breck England, *The Life and Thought of Orson Pratt* (Salt Lake City: University of Utah Press, 1985), p. 18.

5. In *JD* 21:170–71.

6. Spencer W. Kimball, in Conference Report, April 1978, pp. 123–24.

7. In *JD* 2:260.

8. In *JD* 6:199–200.

9. *Improvement Era*, January 1912, p. 206.

10. See England, chapters 4 and 9.

11. In *JD* 7:374–76.

12. In *JD* 23:166–68.

13. *Orson Pratt—Early Mormon Leader*, M.A. Thesis, University of Chicago, 1932, p. 125.

14. See Orson F. Whitney, *Improvement Era*, January 1912, p. 203.

15. England, p. 299.

16. England, p. 288, quoting Milando Pratt, "Life and Labors of Orson Pratt," *Contributor*, October 1891, p. 460.

17. England, Foreword, p. xi.

18. In *JD* 22:223–24.

19. *Improvement Era*, January 1912, p. 203.

20. Ibid., p. 193, quoting *Deseret News*, October 8, 1881.

21. Leo Nikolaevich Tolstoi, "Sevastopol in May 1855," in Bartlett's *Familiar Quotations*, 16th ed. (Boston: Little, Brown, and Company, 1992), p. 510.

9

Elder John H. Groberg

Parley P. Pratt
Apostle of the Lord

The morning breaks, the shadows flee;
Lo, Zion's standard is unfurled!
The dawning of a brighter day,
Majestic rises on the world.[1]

Parley Parker Pratt not only wrote these words but also helped fulfill them. His life, like the cause he espoused, was remarkable. The poet and the prophet within him created much of beauty and much of progress. His autobiography is one of the great chronicles of the early days of the Church. In the preface to this autobiography, John Taylor, who helped edit it, wrote that Parley P. Pratt

> manifested . . . a true and living faith in God and his religion—an honesty of purpose, an inflexible will, and an unflagging, indefatigable industry and perseverance. He possessed a comprehensive mind, coupled with a sound judgment. He manifested an indomitable fortitude under the most trying circumstances, and in adversity and trials, as well as in prosperity, exhibited an example worthy of praise and emulation. He was indeed a true Latter-day Saint, an honorable Apostle, a good and kind husband, an affectionate father, a true friend, and an honest man.[2]

Parley P. Pratt was truly a latter-day hero.

Parley was born April 12, 1807, in Burlington, New York, the third of five sons of Jared and Charity Pratt. He was born at a time of new beginnings. Just twenty years earlier, George Washington, James Madison, Alexander Hamilton, Benjamin Franklin, and fifty-one others had written the divinely inspired Constitution of the United States. Just prior to Parley's birth Thomas Jefferson had concluded the Louisiana Purchase from France, thus doubling the size of the infant nation.

Enthusiasm, confidence, and faith characterized the men and women who were spreading across the face of the land, taming the wilderness, building homes, establishing churches, and rearing families. No distance was too far to walk, no forest too dense to clear. Nothing seemed impossible—not even new revelations from the Almighty. What an atmosphere for Parley to begin his life in!

Parley's parents instilled in their sons the ethic of hard work, integrity, chastity, reverence for God, and scripture study. In teaching her boys to read, Charity used the Bible for their daily practice. Parley was an apt and eager student. His earliest heroes were Joseph, who was sold into Egypt; David, the shepherd boy; Samuel, the boy prophet; and Jesus the Christ. By age twelve, Parley's most fervent longing was to be among the disciples and martyrs of Jesus who would rise in the first resurrection and reign with Him a thousand years. He never forgot those feelings.

Parley's father was a hard-working farmer who taught his sons to use their minds as well as their muscles, to wring a livelihood from the rocky soil. They had a difficult time making a living despite their hard work.

As with most frontier families, Parley had only occasional opportunities to attend school. During the winter months of his sixteenth year he attended school for a while. His diligence and progress were so exemplary that the teacher admonished the other students, "If you would learn as he does, you would become men of wisdom and talent in the world."[3]

In the autumn of his seventeenth year Parley trekked the width of upstate New York with his older brother William to find and prepare land for a better home for the family. For two seasons, first with his brother and then with his father, he cleared trees, plowed the earth, planted grain, built fences, harvested crops, and hired out to established neighbors.

During the long hours of physical toil, Parley analyzed and pondered the biblical promises of baptism by immersion for the remission of sins and of the laying on of hands for the gift of the Holy Ghost to all who would repent. On Sundays he sought congregations that could offer him the gospel ordinances he believed in from his study of the Bible. He found none, but he kept searching. His mind seemed as tireless as his strong arms and stout legs.

For two years the Pratts made the mortgage payments on the land they worked, but in the third year, despite an abundant harvest, the price for wheat was so low that they could not meet the third payment. Parley and his family watched all their efforts disappear as they lost their improved land.

Disappointed with his seemingly unrewarded efforts in both farming and religion, Parley, with nineteen-year-old idealism, resolved to leave civilization and live among the natives of the western forests, learn their language, and teach them of Jesus by reading them the scriptures.

Alone, he traveled across densely timbered and muddy country until winter winds and drifting snows made further progress impossible. Thirty miles west of Cleveland, Ohio, he built a hut and waited out the winter. It was another type of school for Parley as he studied the Bible, pondered the prophecies contained therein, prayed about their meaning, and rejoiced in the understanding that came from God.

During the long winter he learned it was not good to be alone. Thus when spring arrived he returned to his boyhood home and asked for the hand of this longtime sweetheart, Thankful Halsey. With her at his side he went back to the Ohio woods and turned a newly purchased bit of wilderness into a little Garden of Eden.

When his brother William visited the lovely homestead, he was amazed at Parley's prosperity. He was even more astonished when Parley and Thankful told him they planned to abandon their hand-built home, garden, and orchard, and go to teach the prophecies and commandments of Christ. Parley had been touched by the Spirit. He also had been influenced by Sidney Rigdon, a Campbellite preacher who lived in the area.

When William asked Parley how he would provide for his family, Parley replied: "I see plainly you know but little of . . . how vastly wealthy I have become. . . . I have bank bills enough, on the very best institutions in the world, to sustain myself and family while we live."

In proof, he showed his brother a stack of promissory notes, which were papers with wording such as the following: "And every one that hath forsaken houses, . . . or lands, for my name's sake, shall receive an hundredfold, and shall inherit everlasting life" (Matthew 19:29). "If ye abide in me, and my words abide in you, ye shall ask what ye will, and it shall be done unto you" (John 15:7). "All things are possible to him that believeth" (Mark 9:23).[4]

Parley believed unquestioningly that the signer of these notes, Jesus Christ, would keep His promises—and keep them literally. He and Thankful left their home for good to embark on a self-appointed mission to share with others the light he had received from his search of the scriptures. The Lord was preparing him for a marvelous work.

The couple traveled to Cleveland, took a schooner across Lake Erie to Buffalo, and then boarded a canal boat to Albany. At Rochester, however, Parley felt something. He wrote:

> I informed my wife that, notwithstanding our passage being paid through the whole distance, yet I must leave the boat. . . . Why, I did not know; but so it was plainly manifest by the Spirit to me. I said to her: "we part for a season; go and visit our friends in our native place; I will come soon, but how soon I know not; for I have a work to do in this region of country, and what it is, or how long it will take to perform it, I know not; but I will come when it is performed."[5]

His wife saw the hand of God in this and proceeded alone to Canaan, eastern New York, where she waited at her parents' home. Parley went ashore and walked from village to village, teaching the truths of the Bible as he understood them. He taught the scriptures with power and confidence and had many invitations to speak. Then one day a Baptist deacon showed him a strange book entitled the Book of Mormon. The deacon's explanation of what the book purported to be excited Parley. In Parley's own words:

> I opened it with eagerness, and read its title page. I then read the testimony of several witnesses in relation to the manner of its being found and translated. After this I commenced its contents by course. I read all day; eating was a burden, I had no desire for food; sleep was a burden when the night came, for I preferred reading to sleep.
>
> As I read, the spirit of the Lord was upon me, and I knew and

comprehended that the book was true, as plainly and manifestly as a man comprehends and knows that he exists. My joy was now full, as it were, and I rejoiced sufficiently to more than pay me for all the sorrows, sacrifices and toils of my life. I soon determined to see the young man who had been the instrument of its discovery and translation.[6]

Parley immediately set out for Palmyra to find the translator of this miraculous scripture. Joseph was away, but his brother Hyrum Smith explained to Parley about the coming of angels, the restoration of the gospel, and the organization of the Church of Jesus Christ by divine revelation. Within days Parley was baptized and ordained to the priesthood by Oliver Cowdery. It was five months since the Church had been formally organized. Parley now returned to his wife, duly authorized to preach the gospel and administer the ordinances thereof. He immediately began teaching his family, friends, and neighbors. Many believed.

Parley and Thankful traveled to Manchester, where for the first time they met Joseph Smith Jr., the young latter-day prophet of God. Parley described him as follows:

> President Joseph Smith was in person tall and well built, strong and active; of a light complexion, light hair, blue eyes, very little beard, and of an expression peculiar to himself, on which the eye naturally rested with interest, and was never weary of beholding. His countenance was ever mild, affable, beaming with intelligence and benevolence; mingled with a look of interest and an unconscious smile, or cheerfulness, and entirely free from all restraint or affectation of gravity; and there was something connected with the serene and steady penetrating glance of his eye, as if he would penetrate the deepest abyss of the human heart, gaze into eternity, penetrate the heavens, and comprehend all worlds.[7]

At a conference a revelation (see Doctrine and Covenants 32) was received in which Parley, aged twenty-three, received his first official mission call. He and three other young men, who had recently been baptized and ordained, were assigned to the western frontiers (Missouri) to take the Book of Mormon to the Indians. Parley approached this work with characteristic faith, energy, and good humor. He had a good understanding of the trackless wilds of the western territories.

The missionaries preached in settlements along the way to Missouri. Parley was particularly anxious to get to the Kirtland area and visit with Sidney Rigdon, who had earlier influenced him in his search for truth. Sidney and many others in the Kirtland area received baptism. Parley recorded: "In two or three weeks from our arrival in the neighborhood with the news, we had baptized one hundred and twenty-seven souls, and this number soon increased to one thousand. The disciples were filled with joy and gladness; while rage and lying was abundantly manifested by gainsayers; faith was strong, joy was great, and persecution heavy."[8]

Continuing their journey to Missouri, Parley was at one point arrested on a frivolous charge and dragged before a court of false witnesses and a prejudiced judge in the dark of night. When urged to pay a fine, he sang a hymn, "O How Happy Are They." This infuriated his adversaries. He offered to pray for their forgiveness if they would repent of their lying testimonies and unjust judgments. The court became angrier. Finally, awaiting escort to prison, they locked him up for the night.

The next morning Parley turned to his guard and good-naturedly invited him to a footrace. The man assured him that his bulldog would quickly take him down if he bolted. Parley explained that he had enjoyed the opportunity to preach and sing, but that he now needed to continue his journey, and he walked off, quickening his pace as he rapidly added yards between the immobilized officer and himself.

By the time the guard recovered from his astonishment and began his pursuit, Parley had jumped a fence and was two hundred yards away, making his way through a field. The officer now began clapping his hands and commanding his huge dog, "Stu-boy, Stu-boy—take him—down with him." When the dog got close, Elder Pratt pointed his finger to the forest ahead, clapped his hands, and imitated the officer's command. The dog obeyed and raced into the woods, doubling his speed in response to the urging. Parley eluded his persecutor on backwoods trails and rejoined his companions six miles later.[9]

For the next several years Parley traveled great distances between Maine and western Missouri, on mission after mission, preaching the gospel and gathering the Saints. He endured the perils of winter blizzards, spring flooding, summer heat, sickness, and persecution. He experienced miraculous healings, saw visions and dreams, discerned false spirits, and explained glorious truths to the honest in heart. He established many new branches of the Church and strengthened fledgling congregations. He not only preached but also labored with his own hands to build homes for his wife and parents as they followed him from New York to Ohio to Missouri. Parley and his family were driven with the Saints from place to place in Missouri. He participated in Zion's Camp. He was an eyewitness to the terrible persecutions heaped upon the Saints in Missouri. Despite all this, he knew that the Lord had commanded, "Be not weary in well-doing" (D&C 64:33). Parley Pratt obeyed.

Parley appears to have been one of the hardiest among the early Church leaders. He had a broad, high forehead, square jaw, thick neck, stout chest, and strong shoulders. However, beneath those dark, thick brows his eyes showed the soft and gentle light of a disciple's heart and a poet's soul.

In 1835 Parley was ordained an Apostle. At this time Elder Pratt was blessed "to run and not be weary, to walk and not to faint;" and to bring "many nations to a knowledge of the truth." In a personal charge by President Oliver Cowdery he was told: "Your labor must be incessant, and your toil great; you must go forth and labor till the great work is done. . . . Count well the cost. . . . You will be dragged before the authorities for the religion you profess." Do not "shrink when dangers thicken upon, or appalling death stares you in the face. . . . There are strong dungeons and gloomy prisons for you. . . . All your hopes of deliverance from danger and from death will rest upon your faithfulness to God; in His cause you must necessarily serve Him with a perfect heart and a willing mind."[10] The new Apostle did not forget.

Thus far Parley had proven faithful, but more tests were not long in coming. When asked to go on another mission he hesitated briefly. His wife was ill, he was in debt, his house was only partially finished, and he had no means to sustain himself or his family.

He was administering to a sick friend when he heard the call of "Fire! Fire!!" He ran out and saw his house going up in flames. He felt this was a sign to him to put all worldly concerns aside. His friends rallied around him, forgave him his debts, gave him a coat and hat, donated money for his mission, and agreed to care for his family while he was gone.

He first began preaching near Kirtland and was greeted with anger, prejudice, and an ear-splitting band that drowned out his preaching. He recorded: "At length, finding that no disturbance of this kind would prevent the attempt to discharge my duty, they rushed upon me with one accord at a given signal, every man throwing an egg at my person. My forehead, bosom, and most of my body was completely covered with broken eggs. At this I departed, and walked slowly away, being insulted and followed by this rabble for some distance. I soon arrived in Kirtland, and was assisted by my kind friends in cleansing myself and clothes from the effects of this Christian benevolence."[11]

He resumed his mission along with other Apostles, visiting branches and holding conferences in the East, returning in the fall of 1835. He and his wife now moved to Kirtland, where he stayed that winter and helped with the temple. Heavily in debt, he wondered how he could possibly go on the mission projected for the spring.

April arrived, and he was still undecided. One evening Brother Heber C. Kimball came to his home and said he had a blessing for Parley and his wife. To this point the Pratts had not been able to have children. Elder Kimball blessed Thankful Pratt that she would have a son, and blessed Parley that he would go to Upper Canada and do a great work there that would lead to the opening of missionary work in England.

In Canada Parley was able to baptize John Taylor, the Fielding family, and many others. He returned to Kirtland in time for the birth of his first son, who was named Parley P. Pratt Jr. A few days earlier Thankful had received a personal vision in which she knew her mission in life was finished. About three hours after the birth of baby Parley she passed away.

Parley was deeply affected by the birth of his son and the death of his wife, but had little time to ponder. He was called almost immediately on another mission—to New York City. There he wrote the booklet *Voice of Warning,* which for years was a major proselyting tract for the Church. Thousands trace their conversion to the reading of this booklet.

Returning from his mission in New York, Parley married Mary Ann Frost, who had been widowed and had a young daughter.

Another test for Parley came in the form of the financial panic of 1837, which resulted in the failure of the Kirtland Safety Society.

Satan used every means he could to try to disarm the effectiveness of Parley and other Church leaders. For a moment, Parley's vision became clouded and he wrote a letter critical of some of the Church leaders and their involvement in the failure of the Safety Society.

However, Parley had cast his bread upon the waters in Canada, and now, six months later, part of it returned to him in the form of an admonition from John Taylor. Brother Taylor, who would later become the third President of the Church, went to Parley and reminded him that in bringing the gospel to John he had testified that Joseph was a prophet. He told Parley, "If the work was true six months ago, it is true today; if Joseph Smith was then a prophet, he is now a prophet." In tears, Parley acknowledged his error and received full forgiveness from the Prophet.

Parley was next asked to join and help the beleaguered Saints in Missouri. At first they tried to defend their homes; then, outnumbered, they retreated for their lives. Parley lived through the drivings, the killings, the burnings, and other outrages inflicted on the Saints in Missouri. He was arrested, along with the Prophet and many other priesthood bearers, and the Missouri mobsters marched them through the streets of Independence as a prized trophy. As prophesied, the sentence of death was passed upon him and others, but also as prophesied the Lord came to their rescue and spared them for another season of service. Parley was held in chains for months, along with other Church leaders. We are indebted to Parley for recording the following incident that took place while he was in prison with Joseph and others.

> In one of those tedious nights we had lain as if in sleep till the hour of midnight had passed, and our ears and hearts had been pained, while we had listened for hours to the obscene jests, the horrid oaths, the dreadful blasphemies and filthy language of our guards, Colonel Price at their head, as they recounted to each other their deeds of rapine, murder, robbery, etc., which they had committed among the "Mormons" while at Far West and vicinity. They even boasted of defiling by force wives, daughters and virgins, and of shooting or dashing out the brains of men, women and children.
>
> I had listened till I became so disgusted, shocked, horrified, and so filled with the spirit of indignant justice that I could scarcely refrain from rising upon my feet and rebuking the guards; but had said nothing to Joseph, or any one else, although I lay next to him and

knew he was awake. On a sudden he arose to his feet, and spoke in a voice of thunder, or as the roaring lion, uttering, as near as I can recollect, the following words:

"*SILENCE, ye fiends of the infernal pit. In the name of Jesus Christ I rebuke you, and command you to be still; I will not live another minute and hear such language. Cease such talk, or you or I die THIS INSTANT!*"

He ceased to speak. He stood erect in terrible majesty. Chained, and without a weapon; calm, unruffled and dignified as an angel, he looked upon the quailing guards, whose weapons were lowered or dropped to the ground; whose knees smote together, and who, shrinking into a corner, or crouching at his feet, begged his pardon, and remained quiet till a change of guards.

I have seen the ministers of justice, clothed in magisterial robes, and criminals arraigned before them, while life was suspended on a breath, in the Courts of England; I have witnessed a Congress in solemn session to give laws to nations; I have tried to conceive of kings, of royal courts, of thrones and crowns; and of emperors assembled to decide the fate of kingdoms; but dignity and majesty have I seen but once, as it stood in chains, at midnight, in a dungeon in an obscure village of Missouri.[12]

Joseph remained in Richmond Jail for some time longer, he and others being eventually separated from Parley and sent to a jail in Liberty, Missouri. After eight months of imprisonment Parley finally escaped. After many harrowing experiences he finally made his way to Nauvoo, where he rejoiced in a wonderful reunion with his family, Joseph Smith, and others.

Just as Parley was getting settled in Nauvoo, he was called on another mission—this time to England. For this assignment he was able to take his wife and three children. In England, Parley was appointed to be the first editor and publisher of a new monthly periodical for the Saints in England, to be called *The Millennial Star*. For the cover of the first edition, Parley wrote the words of the hymn "The Morning Breaks."

Parley wrote many other poems and texts of hymns, some of which are: "An Angel from on High," "Come, O Thou King of Kings," "Jesus Once of Humble Birth," and "Truth Eternal."

He published books and pamphlets and periodicals that were ultimately responsible for the gathering of thousands to the restored

Church. He also organized many companies of Saints to sail from England to Nauvoo.

After nearly four years in England, the Pratts returned to Nauvoo. Parley recorded:

> Between the middle of September and my own embarkation in October, I chartered three vessels for New Orleans, and filled them with the emigrating Saints, viz:
>
> The "Sidney," with one hundred and eighty souls; the "Medford," with two hundred and fourteen souls; and the "Henry," with one hundred and fifty-seven.
>
> I next chartered the "Emerald," on which I placed about two hundred and fifty passengers, including myself and family.
>
> Having finished my present mission in England and taken an affectionate leave of the Saints and friends there, I embarked on the "Emerald," and sailed on the 29th of October. We had a tedious passage of ten weeks, and some difficulties, murmurings and rebellions; but the Saints on board were called together, and chastened and reproved sharply, which brought them to repentance. We then humbled ourselves and called on the Lord, and he sent a fair wind, and brought us into port in time to save us from starvation.
>
> We landed in New Orleans early in January, 1843. Here I chartered a steamer called the "Goddess of Liberty," and took passage with the company for St. Louis.[13]

Of his arrival in Nauvoo, Parley recorded: "I was astonished to see so large a city all created during my absence, and I felt to rejoice. I visited my brothers Orson and William and their families, by whom I was hospitably entertained. I also visited President Smith and family, who received me with the usual welcome and "*God bless you, Brother Parley*."[14] Elder Pratt loved Joseph Smith with total devotion.

In the spring of 1844 Parley and many of the Twelve were sent on missions to the eastern United States. While traveling and preaching on this mission, on June 27, 1844, Parley experienced one of the darkest moments of his life. He felt as if the very powers of hell had been unleashed. He put away his missionary tracts and kept a personal vigil of silence, weighed down by a grief he could not explain. Not until several days later did he learn of the assassination of Joseph and his brother Hyrum, at the very hour of this black melancholy.

As soon as he learned of the Martyrdom, Parley returned to Nauvoo.

As I walked along over the plains of Illinois, lonely and solitary, I reflected as follows: I am now drawing near to the beloved city; in a day or two I shall be there. How shall I meet the sorrowing widows and orphans? How shall I meet the aged and widowed mother of these two martyrs? How shall I meet an entire community bowed down with grief and sorrow unutterable? What shall I say? or how console and advise twenty-five thousand people who will throng about me in tears, and in the absence of my President and the older members of the now presiding council, will ask counsel at my hands? Shall I tell them to fly to the wilderness and deserts? Or, shall I tell them to stay at home and take care of themselves, and continue to build the Temple? With these reflections and inquiries, I walked onward, weighed down as it were unto death. When I could endure it no longer, I cried out aloud, saying: O Lord! in the name of Jesus Christ I pray Thee, show me what these things mean, and what I shall say to Thy people? On a sudden the Spirit of God came upon me, and filled my heart with joy and gladness indescribable; and while the spirit of revelation glowed in my bosom with as visible a warmth and gladness as if it were fire. The Spirit said unto me: "Lift up your head and rejoice; for behold! it is well with my servants Joseph and Hyrum. My servant Joseph still holds the keys of my kingdom in this dispensation, and he shall stand in due time on the earth, in the flesh, and fulfil that to which he is appointed. Go and say unto my people in Nauvoo, that they shall continue to pursue their daily duties and take care of themselves, and make no movement in Church government to reorganize or alter anything until the return of the remainder of the Quorum of the Twelve. But exhort them that they continue to build the House of the Lord which I have commanded them to build in Nauvoo."[15]

In obedience to one of the most difficult and refining commandments of the early part of the latter-day dispensation of the gospel, Parley had accepted, under the direction of Joseph, the stewardship of other wives. Over several years he married twelve wives. Before his death thirty children (sixteen sons and fourteen daughters) were born to Parley and nine of his twelve wives (three had no children). Of those children, six sons and one daughter died in infancy or early childhood. The remaining ten sons and thirteen daughters were reared with kindness and tender affection. One of his wives, Ann, wrote:

> In what I have written I have used the expression, "my husband" when sometimes I should have said, "our husband" for I was one of several wives, some of them as noble women as ever lived. The one I traveled and drove team with, Belinda Marden Pratt, was one of my husband's wives. A better, or more noble woman I never knew. In our traveling together we sometimes took turns—she driving one day and I the next. She had a delicate babe and when she drove I took care of it, and through all the vicissitudes of our life together we have loved and respected each other greatly and she has always been very near and dear to me and her children are next to my own.
>
> This principle of marriage if understood and lived rightly does not, as many suppose, develop the baser feelings common to fallen humanity, but rather the higher and nobler attributes. It teaches unselfishness, that the world and all it contains was not made for you alone, but that others have feelings, rights, and privileges as well as you have and are just as worthy of consideration. If lived prayerfully and patiently it tends to purify and ennoble the heart, expand the mind, and helps one to understand and comprehend a higher life which can be learned in no other way.[16]

Many people have wondered about plural marriage. To me there are at least three things we must remember. 1) God gives and rescinds commandments through His prophets. Abraham and others were obedient, and were obviously righteous men. 2) The Savior said: "By their fruits ye shall know them." The fruits of Parley's family (and others) over decades have been good. 3) The Holy Ghost confirmed to Parley and Ann and others the rightness of the principle. The Holy Ghost cannot do that for us today because the principle is not ordained of God for us today. Therefore it is pointless for us to try to feel as they felt, for our time and circumstances are different. The Holy Ghost can only confirm those things that *are* right, which includes *when* they are right, as declared by God through His living prophet.

Persecution continued in Illinois, and Parley led his own family with a company of exiled Saints from Nauvoo to Florence, Nebraska, in 1846. Parley often acted as the scout to find river crossings and build bridges and ferries for the companies that followed.

While the pioneers rested at Winter Quarters, Parley was called by the prophet Brigham Young to return to the British Isles to correct certain abuses of authority and direct the missionary work there. Six months later he returned from England. Along with John Taylor he resumed the leadership of their pioneer company and started west.

They reached the valley of the Great Salt Lake in September 1847, being the second company to arrive. One of his wives recorded:

> One of the first things my husband did was to overhaul our supplies, take out the seed grain, then carefully estimate the probable length of time before harvest, how many were depending upon him for sustenance, and ration them accordingly. He concluded that if we had our wheat ground into unbolted flour we could have from half to three-quarters of a pound a day to each person. This might seem ample but when it is remembered that we had no vegetables, milk, or butter, and hungry winter coming on, it was but short allowance to eke out our bread. A steer—the best one we had was killed, and there was not fat enough in the whole creature to fry the liver. This was put down in salt (we had plenty of that) so you see what our fare was— plenty of lean corned beef and a little graham bread. What little groceries we had left at the end of our journey were reserved for sickness.[17]

Parley again began plowing, planting, irrigating, and building. Over a period of two years he cleared forty-two miles of willow and scrub oak from what is now called Parley's Canyon. This made access to the valley easier and safer for the more than sixty thousand pioneers who would yet make the perilous journey across the plains.

Life was starting to get more stable for Parley and his family. Their first crop matured. His wife Ann records: "Just think what a feast! It was the first time in nine months we had all the bread we could eat. My husband remarked while eating dinner, 'This is the first time since I came into the Church that I have reaped what I have sowed; I have either gone on missions and left my labors for others to reap the benefits, or I have been driven by mobs from my possessions.'"[18]

There was little rest for Parley, however, as he was called to lead an exploration party through what is now southern Utah. He also worked in government positions and helped draft the first constitution for the Provisional State of Deseret. He served several terms as a member of its Legislative Assembly.

In 1851 Parley was called on another mission. This time he was set apart by the First Presidency of the Church to preside over what was called the "Mission of the Pacific." It encompassed the "islands and coasts" of that vast ocean. He began this mission with a three-month horse and wagon trip to Los Angeles. He then took a steamship to San Francisco. He established branches of the Church in these areas and wrote letters of comfort and instruction to the missionaries already serving in the Society Islands (Tahiti) and the Sandwich Islands (Hawaii). He called and sent out additional missionary couples to these and other islands. He then sailed to Valparaiso, Chile, to open the work in South America.

In Chile he labored in Valparaiso and Quillota with discouraging results. His wife Phoebe was with him, and shortly after arriving she gave birth to a son whom they named Omner. The baby died when he was about six weeks old, and was buried in Chile.

Parley studied Spanish diligently and made every type of contact he knew how. After months of effort he felt that because of political turmoil, lack of funds, and other problems, the time for the opening of the work in South America had not yet arrived. Sadly he determined to return to Utah.

Parley and Phoebe left South America and Chile feeling they had not been accepted there. My own experience tells me that their efforts and sacrifices, including the laying of their baby to rest there, had a sanctifying effect on South America, and especially on Chile.

I am certain it is more than coincidence that when the work started to grow rapidly in South America, about one hundred years later, Chile was one of the major growth areas. In fact, in all of Chile the Valparaiso area (Viña del Mar Mission) was one of the top areas for new converts. While living in South America, I along with some of Parley's descendants visited the graveyard where baby Omner Pratt was buried. As we stood at that sacred spot we read some pages from Parley's autobiography, about his mission to Chile and South America. One of the most poignant was written on board ship.

> Just imagine sundown, twilight, the shades of evening, the curtains of the solitary night gathering in silent gloom and lone melancholy around a father who loves his home and its inmates; his fireside and the family altar! Behold him standing leaning over the vessel's side as it glides over the waters of the lone and boundless Pacific,

gazing for hours in succession into the bosom of its dark abyss, or watching its white foam and sparkling spray! What are his thoughts? Can you divine them? Behold, he prays! For what does he pray? For every wife, for every child, for every near and dear friend he has on earth, he prays most earnestly! most fervently! He calls each by name over and over again, before the altar of remembrance. And when this is done for all on earth, he remembers those in Heaven; calls their names; communes with them in spirit; wonders how they are doing; whether they think of him. He calls to mind their acts and sufferings in life, their death, and the grave where sleeps their precious dust.

This done, he prays . . . for earth, and Heaven, and God, angels and men, to be joined forever in the bonds of eternal peace, and love and truth. . . . He commends himself, the vessel and his all on board to God, and to the guardianship of his good angel. . . . Walks the deck a few minutes, examines the sails, the speed of the vessel, the course of the wind, and then retires to rest to dream of home.[19]

As I read these and other passages, a feeling of deep peace came over me. Parley and Phoebe had gone to Chile and worked there with pure intent. They had uncomplainingly given their all—including laying a child to rest in that faraway land. Even though they returned feeling they had been less than successful, in time God took their pure efforts and multiplied them a thousandfold. That tiny grave, unknown to but a few, seemed to be the center around which thousands were now flocking to join the Church.

I looked at the man presiding over this fast-growing area. Who was he? None other than a direct descendant of Parley P. Pratt! I thought of the many mission presidents over many years in Latin America who were descendants of Parley. Truly the Lord had accepted the purity of purpose and the earnest efforts of Parley and Phoebe Pratt. Now, though over a hundred years had passed, that purity and those efforts were bearing abundant fruit. There is no time with God—only purity of purpose and honesty of effort. They alone bear good fruit.

When Parley returned from South America he went to Salt Lake City and worked hard to provide for his family. He continued to serve in the Church and in the legislature. Soon he was called on another mission to California.

When he returned from this mission he enjoyed the company of his family for a short time before being called on another mission (which proved to be his last) to the eastern United States. On this mission he fulfilled many assignments given him by the First Presidency. These included helping John Taylor with some writing, printing, and other concerns in New York.

Parley seemed melancholy when he wrote to his family from his mission in the East:

> I feel for my family and pray for them continually. I hope they with me may have grace to endure to the end, and be saved in the kingdom of God. . . .
>
> My feelings, and the affections of my heart, I will not attempt to describe, but. . . . Should I never return, be assured they are as warm and as tender as ever, and I think a little more so.
>
> I hope you will not be cast down or borrow any trouble about me because I admit an *if*, as to my safe return. . . . I must acknowledge that I do anticipate with a great deal of pleasure the change of worlds.[20]

Parley turned fifty in the mission field and wrote the following poem:

My Fiftieth Year

> I am fifty years old! I have lived to see
> Seven times seven and a Jubilee.
> That period famed in the days of yore
> As a grand release for the humble poor;

Towards the end of the poem he wrote:

> I have lain in a dungeon, bound in chains,
> And been honored in Courts where Justice reigns.
> In a thousand joys, and a thousand fears
> I have struggled on through my fifty years.
> And now, by the law of God, I am free;
> I will seek to enjoy my Jubilee.[21]

In answer to this poem his good friend John Taylor wrote:

A Response to P. P. Pratt's "Fiftieth Year"

Go rest thee, my friend, for weary and long
Thou hast faithfully striven with a wayward throng;
With a world environed with error's chain
Thou hast wrestled and struggled, but not in vain. . . .

With flaming words and a burning pen
Thou has bearded gaunt priestcraft in his den, . . .

May thy sun go down with glory rife,
And dying may'st thou burst into life;
And, when sleeping among the silent dead,
Have the blessings of millions on thy head;
And living with God, may'st thou be free,
And partake of an endless Jubilee.[22]

Just as he was concluding this mission, the innocent wish of Parley P. Pratt's childhood—to be among the martyrs of Jesus Christ—was fulfilled. He died from an assassin's bullet at Van Buren, Arkansas, May 13, 1857.

Elder Taylor later remarked:

From various premonitions which [Parley P. Pratt] had during his last visit with me in New York, I was satisfied that, when I took my last sad leave of him in that city, I should never see his face again in the flesh. These presentiments were but too speedily and sadly fulfilled. He has gone—but has left a name and a fame that will live throughout time and burst forth in eternity; and in the morning of the first resurrection, when the opening heavens shall reveal the Son of God, and he shall proclaim, "I am the resurrection and the life," when Death shall deliver up the dead, I expect to meet Brother Parley in the resurrection of the just.[23]

Notes

1. "The Morning Breaks," *Hymns*, no. 1.

2. Parley P. Pratt [Jr.], ed., *Autobiography of Parley Parker Pratt*, 5th ed. (Salt Lake City: Deseret Book, 1961), pp. 7–8; hereafter cited as *Autobiography*.

3. *Autobiography*, p. 21

4. See *Autobiography*, pp. 33–35.

5. *Autobiography*, p. 36.

6. *Autobiography*, p. 37.

7. *Autobiography*, p. 45.

8. *Autobiography*, p. 48.

9. See *Autobiography*, pp. 49–51.

10. *Autobiography*, pp. 120–21.

11. *Autobiography*, pp. 128–29.

12. *Autobiography*, pp. 210–11.

13. *Autobiography*, p. 325.

14. *Autobiography*, p. 328.

15. *Autobiography*, p. 333.

16. In Kate B. Carter, comp., *Our Pioneer Heritage* (Salt Lake City: Daughters of Utah Pioneers, 1974), 17:231.

17. Ibid., p. 227.

18. Ibid., p. 229.

19. *Autobiography*, pp. 389–90.

20. *Autobiography*, pp. 444–45.

21. *Autobiography*, pp. 445–47.

22. *Autobiography*, pp. 447–49.

23. *Autobiography*, p. 8.

10

Elder Merrill J. Bateman

Willard Richards
Integrity to the Trust

Willard Richards is one of the great pioneer examples of the servant who, having put his hand to the plow, never looked back. From the moment he was converted in 1836 to his last breath in 1854, he was consumed by the restored gospel and gave his all to build the kingdom. Within three months of his baptism, he was in the mission field serving in the eastern United States for a short time and then in England for four years. Upon his return in 1841, he was called to be Joseph Smith's private secretary, Church historian and recorder, Nauvoo temple recorder, and recorder and clerk of the Nauvoo municipal court. He kept Joseph's private journal from 1842 until Joseph's death. His last entry occurred in Carthage Jail a few minutes before the Prophet's martyrdom.

Willard was so devoted to the gospel, the Prophet, and the assignments he received that he did not sleep in his own bed for seven years following his first call to serve. Four years as a missionary (1837–41) were followed by three in Nauvoo (1841–1844) where Willard lived with the Prophet's family.[1] During the Nauvoo period, Willard spent considerable time writing Joseph's history and recording Church events. This required almost daily association with the Prophet.

At the time of the Martyrdom, John Taylor and Willard were the only Apostles in Illinois—the others were on missions outside the state. With Elder Taylor wounded, Willard's leadership kept the Nauvoo Saints together until President Brigham Young and other members of the Twelve returned. He worked day and night for six weeks consoling the Saints, accelerating the work on the Nauvoo Temple, and countering the demands of Sidney Rigdon and various local leaders regarding the appointment of a guardian or trustee-in-trust for the Church.

Three years later, Willard was a member of the first pioneer company to the Great Salt Lake Valley as President Brigham Young laid out the route for the Saints to follow. Returning to Winter Quarters in the fall of 1847, he was called as Second Counselor to Brigham Young in the new First Presidency. He served in that capacity until his death seven years later, when he became the first modern Apostle and prophet to die a natural death.

THE EARLY YEARS

Willard was born in Hopkinton, Massachusetts, on June 24, 1804, the eleventh child and sixth son of Joseph and Rhoda Howe Richards. An accident in his early youth had long-term effects on his health. At four years of age Willard fell from a high scaffold attached to a barn and landed on his head. Later in life he experienced attacks of the palsy (muscle tremors) which he believed were traceable to the accident. Not long after the fall, he tumbled into a stream of water and would have drowned if his brother Levi had not been nearby and pulled him out.[2]

A chief characteristic of Willard was his keen mind. As a youth he loved to study and had a strong aptitude for learning. On occasion he read late into the night and was late for chores the next morning, incurring his father's displeasure.[3] He attended school into his mid-teens, unusual for the day, and then became a teacher at sixteen years of age. He taught school in Chatham and Nassau, New York, plus various communities in Massachusetts during the 1820s. He constantly devoted his leisure time to the acquisition of knowledge. By 1827 he had begun lecturing on electricity and other scientific subjects. He traveled throughout New England presenting scientific lectures during the late '20s and early '30s.[4] On one of the tours he purchased a copy of a book called *Practice of Medicine* by Dr. Samuel Thomson, which persuaded him to become a doctor of botanic medicine. His interest in medicine was stimulated by the frailties in his family plus the death of a sister, Susan, who died of a strange ailment. In 1834 he entered the Thomsonian Infirmary in Boston, where he studied and practiced under the direction of Dr. Thomson. Within a short time Willard received his diploma and began practicing medicine and lecturing in the surrounding towns.[5] His brother Levi, also interested in medicine, studied with Thomson at the same time. Whereas Willard's service as a doctor was limited by Church activity following baptism, Levi gave great service to Church members and became highly regarded for his medical skills.[6]

One of Willard's main interests was religion. As a teenager, during the revivals of 1819–21 he listened intently to the ministers. Given his serious nature, he became impressed with the importance of his relationship with Deity. He became concerned about his deportment, and fear for his soul gripped him for a period of time. At age seventeen he decided to join his parents' Congregational Church in Richmond, Massachusetts. His application for admission was denied, which was terribly upsetting and caused some skepticism on his part with regard to organized religion.[7] The "History of Willard Richards," published in the *Millennial Star*, sets forth the following about this experience: "How easy it would have been for Peter, or any other man with authority from God, to have said, 'Willard, repent and be baptized in the name of Jesus Christ for the remission of sins, and you shall receive the gift of the Holy Ghost, the Comforter, which shall lead you into all truth;' but instead of such a comforting declaration saluting [his] ears from a servant of God, [he] was left to believe [he] had committed the unpardonable sin."[8]

CONVERSION

On one of Willard's lecture tours in the summer of 1835, he providentially came across a Book of Mormon that his cousin Brigham Young had left with another cousin, Lucius Parker. Except for derisive newspaper articles concerning "a boy named Jo Smith" finding a gold Bible, Willard knew little about the Latter-day Saints. Knowing nothing of the book, he let it fall open and began reading. After half a page, he exclaimed, "God or the devil has had a hand in that book, for man never wrote it."[9] He read the book twice through in a period of ten days and became convinced of its truth. When Willard believed in something, he did not wait to act. Immediately he began settling his personal affairs in preparation for a trip to Kirtland, Ohio, a distance of seven hundred miles. His intent was to meet with the Saints, thoroughly investigate the new religion, and become a member. He also felt that God had a greater work for him to do than the practice of medicine.

As he began settling his affairs, a severe attack of the palsy set in that rendered him incapable of making the trip. He suffered considerably for more than a year. Finally he was able to leave for Kirtland in the fall of 1836 in company with his brother Levi.[10] Willard and Levi were pleasantly received by Brigham Young and spent the next month learning about the events of the Restoration and studying the doctrine. On December 31, 1836, Willard Richards was baptized a member by his cousin Brigham. On January 8, 1837, he was confirmed by Reynolds Cahoon and partook of the sacrament. His confirmation was a spiritual feast in that he was blessed to understand a song sung in tongues by Elder Lyman Sherman concerning the coming of Christ.[11]

MISSION AND MARRIAGE

Willard was still a bachelor when he joined the Church at age thirty-two. Not having a wife or family, he was soon called to accompany Brigham Young on a mission to the eastern part of the United States. Under the hands of Joseph Smith and Sidney Rigdon, Willard received a blessing of health and was set apart as a missionary on March 13, 1837. He and Elder Young left Kirtland the following day for New York and Boston. After preaching in Massachusetts, Connecticut, and New York in March and April, Brigham departed for Kirtland and Willard spent most of May visiting family and friends in Massachusetts and bearing testimony of the gospel. On June 5 Willard suddenly had a strong desire to return to Kirtland and received a manifestation of the Spirit that he should do so. Shortly after his baptism, Willard had told Heber C. Kimball that he wanted to be among the first to carry the gospel overseas. Arriving in Kirtland on June 11, Willard learned of the setting apart of Heber C. Kimball, Orson Hyde, and Joseph Fielding to serve a mission in England. Willard wrote the following concerning this: "I felt my heart burn within me, strongly desiring that I might be one of the number." The next day he met

Brother Kimball on the street, who told him, "I start for England to-morrow, and you may go with me, so get ready."[12] With almost no time to prepare and little money with which to cover the costs, he was set apart that evening by Sidney Rigdon and Hyrum Smith and left the next day in company with Elders Kimball, Hyde, and Fielding. Con-tributions from faithful Saints paved the way.[13]

Willard, Heber C. Kimball, and Orson Hyde were the first Mor-mon missionaries to set foot on English soil—on July 20, 1837. Two days later they traveled to Preston, where Joseph Fielding's brother, Reverend James Fielding, allowed them to preach their first sermon in his meetinghouse. It was not long before James Fielding realized the consequences of his decision to allow the missionaries to teach his congregation. Within one week nineteen parishioners were baptized, and others were not far behind.[14] The first baptisms in England took place on July 30, 1837. On July 31, the missionaries decided to split into pairs and begin working in different parts of England. Willard and Elder John Goodson were assigned Bedford and its environs, where the two served for seven months.

On August 1, 1837, the day of Willard's departure for Bedford, Elder Kimball introduced the gospel to a young woman who would change Willard's life. Jennetta Richards, a daughter of a minister from a village near Preston and no relation to Willard, met Elder Kimball at a friend's home. He invited her to attend a meeting that evening at which he would preach. She was so impressed that she attended a sec-ond meeting the next evening and was baptized two days later. Be-cause she was leaving for home the next day, she was confirmed im-mediately—the first confirmation in England. On Friday, August 4, the day of Jennetta's baptism and confirmation, Heber wrote Willard saying, "I baptized your wife today."[15]

It is quite likely that Heber continued to impress both Willard and Jennetta regarding their future relationship during the ensuing months. Willard did not meet Jennetta until March 22, 1838, after re-turning to Preston. On that date he was visiting at the home of Brother James Mercer in Thornley when Jennetta walked into the room. Accompanied by other Saints, they set out to attend a meeting. Along the way Willard remarked to Jennetta that Richards was a good name. "I never want to change it," he said. "Do you?" "No, I do not," was her reply, and Willard's journal records, "I think she never will."[16]

Jennetta and Willard were married six months later on September 24, 1838, after much opposition on both sides. Jennetta's parents were displeased with the marriage because her father had experienced the same trauma as Reverend James Fielding. Following Jennetta's baptism the previous year, Reverend John Richards, Jennetta's father, had allowed Heber C. Kimball to preach in his independent congregation. A number in the congregation, especially young people, accepted the gospel. Reverend Richards, fearing the loss of additional members plus his income, closed his chapel to the American missionaries. When Reverend and Mrs. Richards learned of Jennetta's fondness for Willard, they became severe critics of the relationship. Rumors spread suggesting that Willard already had a wife and family in America and that he was taking advantage of Jennetta. Jennetta's brother insisted on investigating Willard's marital status. Jennetta never doubted. She wrote Willard, "I can as soon believe that the gospel you preach is false . . . for if you will deceive in one thing you will in another."[17]

Not all of the opposition came from Jennetta's family. English members of the Church, helping to support the American missionaries, were upset that the daughter of a relatively well-off minister was marrying a missionary who should be giving himself wholly to the ministry. On one occasion during the courtship, the Preston Saints expressed their displeasure by refusing to give Jennetta a place to stay while she was visiting Willard, who was ill.

CALL TO APOSTLESHIP AND OPPOSITION

Shortly after Willard and Jennetta met, and in the midst of the Missouri persecutions, Joseph Smith received a revelation in Far West, Missouri, on July 8, 1838, instructing him to reorganize the Quorum of the Twelve following the Kirtland disaffections. Four new brethren were called: John Taylor, John E. Page, Wilford Woodruff, and Willard Richards. In addition, members of the Quorum of the Twelve who were not serving overseas were to leave the next spring for the British Isles to proselyte. Although Willard's call to the apostleship occurred in the summer of 1838, his ordination awaited the arrival of Brigham Young and other members of the Twelve. They arrived in the spring of 1840, and Willard was ordained on April 14 of that year.

From the time of his call to his ordination, Willard was tried by the adversary. Not only was Jennetta's family opposed to him, but others began to criticize his work. A few years later while writing the *History of the Church*, Elder Richards described in third person the events of 1838–40:

> From the time that Elder Willard Richards was called to the apostleship, in July, 1838, the devil seemed to take a great dislike to him, and strove to stir up the minds of many against him. Elder Richards was afflicted with sickness, and several times was brought to the borders of the grave, and many were tempted to believe that he was under transgression, or he would not be thus afflicted. Some were tried and tempted because Elder Richards took to himself a wife; they thought he should have given himself wholly to the ministry, and followed Paul's advice to the letter. Some were tried because his wife wore a veil, and others because she carried a muff to keep herself warm when she walked out in cold weather; and even the President of the Church [Joseph Fielding][18] there, thought "she had better done without it;" she had nothing ever purchased by the Church; and to gratify their feelings, wore the poorest clothes she had, and they were too good, so hard was it to buffet the storm of feeling that arose from such foolish causes. Sister Richards was very sick for some time, and some were dissatisfied because her husband did not neglect her entirely and go out preaching; and others, that she did not go to meeting when she was not able to go so far.[19]

The period from July 1838 to April 1840 was a trial by fire for Willard. One set of authors indicates that this period "tested his mettle as much as Zion's Camp had tested that of his future colleagues in the Quorum of the Twelve Apostles."[20] On March 9, 1839, one of the members in Preston, an Elder Halsal, "came out openly in council against Elder Richards"[21] stating a number of charges, none of which he could substantiate. The record states, "Most of the Elders in Preston were against Elder Richards for a season, except James Whitehead, who proved himself true in the hour of trial."[22] Sister Alice Hodgin died at Preston on September 2, 1838—the first Latter-day Saint to die in England. Willard was accused of killing her with a "black stick." He was arraigned before the Mayor's Court in Preston on October 3, 1838, but was dismissed when the accusers could provide no evidence.[23] In addition, Willard and Jennetta were weakened physically by frequent bouts of sickness and by the death of their firstborn son. Jennetta was ill throughout the pregnancy. She gave birth to Heber John on 17 July 1839.[24] He died five months later of the smallpox.

During the first quarter of 1840 the thirty-five-year-old counselor in the British Mission presidency continued to find adversity in his path. Jennetta was constantly ill with her second pregnancy. The branch in Preston had a number of problems which required his attention. When he visited the members in Burnley in February he discovered that they had not been meeting for several weeks because of differences among them. On Sunday, February 23, he called a meeting of the Burnley Saints and was able to resolve the differences sufficiently for them to resume their meetings. Jennetta's parents still rejected him although they finally received him for a visit in February 1840 and then allowed Jennetta to move in with them because of her weak condition.

Jealousy, covetousness, and rebellion among the Saints; parental rejection; and sickness and death—these were the elements of the fiery test. In retrospect, the outcome clearly reflects the depth of character and testimony of Willard and Jennetta. He had been a member for only one and one-half years and Jennetta for one year when the trials began. With so much opposition inside the Church, it must have been tempting to withdraw and at least receive the approbation of Jennetta's family. And yet these two new members were faithful to the witnesses received and the trust given them.

On one occasion Willard announced from the pulpit that if any had aught against him or his wife, Jennetta, the individuals should state their grievances and allow him to acknowledge his faults if there were errors on his part. Only one person spoke, and he acknowledged that the faults were his own and not those of Elder Richards.[25]

This fiery period prepared Willard for a future time of turmoil when he again would be called on to provide leadership. Following the Martyrdom, a number of important members were more interested in their own purposes than in the welfare of the Saints. They did not want to follow the leadership of the Twelve, and for a period of six weeks Elder Richards's strength kept the Saints together until the Twelve could gather and thwart the designs of Sidney Rigdon, William Marks, and others.

By April 6, 1840, all members of the Quorum of the Twelve had arrived in England. On April 9 Willard, returning to his apartment in Preston, was almost overwhelmed to find Brigham Young and Heber C. Kimball waiting for him. The Quorum was ready to begin its work. The Quorum held its first official council meeting in England on April 14, at which Willard was ordained an Apostle and Brigham Young was formally sustained as their President. The Twelve also approved the publication of the *Millennial Star* in pamphlet form with Parley P. Pratt as editor. For a time Willard served as assistant editor.[26] Following the conference, Willard was assigned to work in Herefordshire with Wilford Woodruff and Brigham Young. Thus began, as one historian has noted, the "most spectacular harvest of souls since [John] Wesley's time." Between 1837 and 1852, the number of conversions in England totaled 57,000.[27]

Private Secretary, Historian, and Recorder

Willard completed his mission in April 1841 and arrived in Nauvoo in August after visiting family and friends in Massachusetts and leaving Jennetta and his son there until he could establish a home for them. Initially he stayed at the home of Brigham Young. In October he was elected to the Nauvoo City Council and was appointed editor of the *Times and Seasons*. By December 1841 Joseph Smith had asked Willard to be his private secretary, general clerk, and temple recorder. He shared the office on the second floor of Joseph's red brick store. Because of the nature of the work, Willard was given a room in the Prophet's home. Later, when Jennetta and Heber arrived, they established their own home in Nauvoo. In 1842 a number of additional assignments were given to Willard, including recorder for the Nauvoo City Council, clerk for the Nauvoo Municipal Court, Church Historian, and finally, in mid-1843, Church Recorder. All of these responsibilities led to a close association with the Prophet Joseph during the 1841–44 period.[28]

Record keeping in the Church was emphasized by the Lord from the day the Church was organized. On April 6, 1830, Joseph Smith received a revelation stating that "there shall be a record kept" (D&C

21:1). Less than one year later the Lord stipulated that a historian should "write and keep a regular history" (D&C 47:1). A few short statements were kept in the early years by some of the brethren, but it was not until 1839 that Joseph Smith, with the help of some associates, began preparing a record called the "History of Joseph Smith."[29] From 1839 to the time of Willard's appointment as Church Historian in December 1842, a total of 157 pages had been written covering the period 1805 to 1831. The work had gone slowly. During 1842 Willard served Joseph as his private secretary. Seeing the efficiency with which Willard worked, Joseph realized that the solution was to enlist him to the cause, which led to his appointment as Church Historian. Between December 1842 and August 1843, Willard completed the first volume as he added almost four hundred pages in an eight-month period, which brought the historical narrative from 1831 to 1834.

At the time of Joseph's death Willard had completed more than 650 pages and the narrative had been extended to August 1838. In addition, he had compiled much of the source material which supported the uncompleted history. Elder Richards continued as Church Historian under Brigham Young, and by February 1846, with the help of W. W. Phelps and others, had completed 1,485 pages—essentially five of the seven volumes that now comprise the *History of The Church of Jesus Christ of Latter-day Saints*.

The historical record provided by Willard Richards was the result of thousands of hours of labor and reflected his faithfulness, his constancy and dedication, his integrity to the trust. No one could question his industriousness, his scholarly abilities, the diligence with which he worked, or his devotion. Willard was a special man prepared for a critical time in Church history as he preserved the story of those early years. Willard's accomplishment becomes even more incredible when one considers that Jennetta was ill most of the time and that he suffered recurring bouts of palsy and malaria. Moreover, Jennetta and a baby died on July 9, 1845, after he had labored day and night for weeks trying to save them.[30]

In addition to the multivolume Church history, Willard maintained the daily diary of Joseph Smith. As noted earlier, the last entry in that document occurred in Carthage Jail a few minutes before Joseph and Hyrum were killed.

THE MARTYRDOM AND THE AFTERMATH

With the exception of a short trip to Massachusetts to bring his family to Nauvoo, Willard was with the Prophet Joseph from the time he began work in the upper room of the brick store in late 1841 until the Martyrdom three years later. He was with Joseph and Hyrum when they crossed the Mississippi to Iowa in June 1844 with the expectation of going to the Rockies. He returned with them the next day when they were pressured by family and friends who felt abandoned. Willard and John Taylor voluntarily accompanied the Prophet and the Patriarch to Carthage in late June and were incarcerated with them. The two Apostles were the only ones in the jail with Joseph and Hyrum on that fateful afternoon of June 27, 1844. On many previous occasions when the Prophet had been surrounded by potential assassins, he had felt no alarm as his time had not come. But from the moment the party decided to recross the Mississippi and return to Nauvoo and Carthage, Joseph knew that the end was near.

Near 5:00 P.M. on June 27, the jailor became alarmed at the conduct of the mob and suggested to the party of four that they go into the cell room for safety. Joseph turned to Willard and said, "If we go into the cell, will you go in with us?" Willard answered, "Brother Joseph, you did not ask me to cross the river with you—you did not ask me to come to Carthage—you did not ask me to come to jail with you—and do you think I would forsake you now? But I tell you what I will do; if you are condemned to be hung for treason, I will be hung in your stead, and you shall go free." Joseph answered, "You cannot." The reply: "I will."[31]

The most complete record of the Martyrdom is Elder Richards's version entitled "Two Minutes in Jail."[32] Another excellent description is found in a letter Jennetta wrote her parents eleven days after the event.[33] Obviously Jennetta obtained her story from Willard upon his return to Nauvoo. Following the discharge of three or four firearms outside the jail, Willard noticed a large number of armed men with painted faces approaching the door of the jail. Soon musket balls were coming up the stairway against the door of the prison and the prisoners could hear rapid footsteps coming up the stairs. Joseph, Hyrum, John, and Willard were in the jailor's living quarters and quickly shut the door to the stairs and then leaned against it because the latch would not hold. Shortly a shot was fired and a ball came through the door, just missing one of the men. All four jumped back, with Joseph, John, and Willard moving a short distance and Hyrum moving two-thirds of the way across the room. A shot then came from outside the building through the window, hitting Hyrum in the back, while at the same time another shot was fired through the door hitting Hyrum in the face and knocking him to the floor a dead man. Joseph, seeing his dead brother, opened the door a few inches and fired a small revolver at random in the entry while Willard and John, with walking sticks, knocked down the bayonets and muskets constantly firing through the doorway. Finally John Taylor rushed to the window, where a ball from outside smashed his vest pocket watch at the same time a bullet from the door pierced his leg, knocking him to the floor. While Willard continued near the doorway to knock down the mob's muzzles with his stick, two more bullets struck Elder Taylor. As a last resort, Joseph leaped to the window, where two bullets hit him in the back knocking him out the window. Willard records, "As his feet went out of the window my head went in [the window], the balls whistling all around. He fell on his left side a dead man."[34]

After withdrawing from the window, Willard was not satisfied and leaned out the window again to see what had happened to the Prophet. Seeing the lifeless body with a hundred men near it and more coming around the corner of the building, he returned to the room. Finding another room in which to hide John Taylor, he placed him under a bed and then returned, expecting to be shot by the mob. Instead the members of the mob dispersed, realizing they had accomplished their foul deed and wanting to escape the vicinity of the jail.[35] Of the four, only Willard was unharmed, although a bullet had passed under his left ear removing a little of the tip of the ear and searing his neck.[36]

During the next fifteen hours Willard cared for John Taylor and the two bodies and made arrangements for the journey home. The next morning Dr. Richards left for Nauvoo with the bodies of Joseph and Hyrum on two wagons, the bodies being covered with bushes to keep them from the sun.

One can imagine the scene in Nauvoo with almost ten thousand people waiting for the small party to appear. Upon his return, Willard addressed the large congregation, telling them to keep the peace as he had pledged his honor and his life for their good conduct. The following day the Saints were allowed to view the remains.

The next six weeks were hectic as the two Apostles (Richards and Taylor) undertook the leadership of the Saints until the other members of the Twelve returned. With Elder Taylor wounded, the heavy responsibility to counsel and direct the Saints fell to Willard. The Lord had qualified him during the dark days of his mission five years earlier. He proved equal to the task, a man of considerable wisdom, spiritual strength, and good judgment. By the time Parley P. Pratt arrived, the Saints had renewed their labors on the temple and calm prevailed. Shortly after Elder Pratt's arrival, Sidney Rigdon appeared from Pittsburgh. He was a Counselor in the First Presidency and claimed the right to be President and Guardian. Emma Smith was fearful that she would lose the properties that were in Joseph's name. She wanted a trustee-in-trust appointed to protect the assets. Meetings were called by William Marks, the local president of the Nauvoo Stake, for the purpose of appointing a new leader of the Church. In one of the meetings Marks supported Rigdon and in the others he favored Emma's plan. The three members of the Quorum told him that such meetings should not be held in the absence of the General Authorities of the Church. The three Apostles also forbade Marks from conducting any general business of the Church.

Although warned by the Apostles, William Marks and Emma called meetings in which they tried to appoint a new president. At one of the meetings Parley P. Pratt arose and told them the business of the whole Church could only be conducted by its General Authorities and not by the local authority of any one stake. The meeting finally broke up without accomplishing its purpose. A few days later Marks called another meeting. This time Willard and Bishop Whitney objected and the meeting was adjourned.[37]

Finally all of the Twelve were in Nauvoo on August 6, 1844. "From the death of Joseph until the arrival of President Brigham Young and the Twelve, Elder Willard Richards was the principal counselor to the saints in Nauvoo, and had scarcely a moment's rest."[38] He answered questions and gave direction to literally hundreds of families as the Saints moved through a critical transition.

THE FIRST PRESIDENCY

Upon the return of President Brigham Young and the decision by the large majority of Saints to support the Twelve, Willard returned to Joseph's history. At the time of the Prophet's death, the narrative covered the period up to 1838. During the next year and one-half, Willard with the help of others brought the record up to 1843. In February 1846 the records were boxed for the trip west. Willard finally opened the boxes in 1853 in order for the record to be completed.

Willard was chosen as part of the first pioneer company into the Great Salt Lake Valley. Upon his return to Winter Quarters in the fall of 1847, he was called as Second Counselor to President Brigham Young, with Heber C. Kimball as the other Counselor. He served in this capacity for the next seven years, until his death on March 11, 1854.

In the spring of 1848 Willard led one of the large companies of Saints from Winter Quarters to the Valley. During the years that followed, he became postmaster general for the intermountain territories and editor of the *Deseret News*, continued as Church Historian and Recorder, and was appointed secretary of the Provisional State of Deseret and secretary pro tem of the legislature. He also organized the first council on health in the Territory. He served in these various capacities at the same time that he was a much-needed member of the First Presidency. His writing skills were particularly helpful to Presidents Young and Kimball, who depended on him for drafting letters, reports, and other documents.[39]

Willard Richards's death was a great loss to the Church and was especially felt by Presidents Young and Kimball, who had labored closely with him for almost two decades. President Young was responsible for his conversion and baptism. President Kimball had been a close friend. Three weeks after Willard's death, President Young eulogized Willard at a general conference of the Church:

> Bro. Willard Richards I have known from before he became a member of the Church of Jesus Christ of Latter Day Saints. He lived at my house for many years,—boarded with me. From our first acquaintance to his death, in the gospel and out of it, as far as I knew him, in his integrity and friendship, he was as true and unwavering in his course as the sun is to the earth, or as the earth is in revolving upon its axis. There was not a shade of deviation upon his mind, or wavering in his

actions, in his feelings, or in his faith from the principles of righteousness. He was true to his God, to his religion, and to his brethren, and
in administering blessings to all, to whom he had power to administer.
He was careful not to injure any person, and lived and died a Latter
Day Saint.[40]

From the day Willard first read the half-page of the Book of Mormon, he was captured by the Restoration. The Book of Mormon was
the converting tool in his life. His testimony ran deep. Preparation for
his life's mission included the rejection by the Congregational Church
in Richmond, Massachusetts, which forced him to think more deeply
about his relationship with God and strengthen his desire to be clean.
He was grateful for baptism and the Holy Spirit when offered to him
by one with authority. He did not waver in England when the Saints
turned on him nor did he faint when bullets flew around his head in
Carthage. His resolve and mettle showed when he appealed for calm
upon his return to Nauvoo and when he objected to the meetings
called by William Marks and others. He knew the order of the kingdom and was determined to follow it. Finally, he was a key leader for
the trek west and helped the Saints begin the process of redeeming
the waste places of Zion. Willard, a man of integrity to the trust.

NOTES

1. Dean C. Jessee, "The Writing of Joseph Smith's History," *Mormon
Miscellaneous*, Reprint Series, no. 2, September 1984, p. 28.

2. "History of Willard Richards," *The Latter-day Saints Millennial Star*, 25
February 1865, vol. 27, p. 118.

3. Clair Noall, *Intimate Disciple: A Portrait of Willard Richards, Apostle to
Joseph Smith—Cousin of Brigham Young* (Salt Lake City: University of Utah
Press, 1957), pp. 40–41.

4. *Millennial Star*, p. 119.

5. Ibid., p. 120; Davis Bitton and Leonard J. Arrington, "Willard
Richards, 'The Intimate Disciple,'" *Mormons and Their Historians* (Salt Lake
City: University of Utah Press, 1988), p. 5.

6. Blanche E. Rose, "Early Utah Medical Practice," *Utah Historical
Quarterly*, 1942, 10:16–17.

7. *Millennial Star*, p. 119; Bitton and Arrington, p. 5.

8. *Millennial Star*, p. 119.

9. Andrew Jenson, *LDS Biographical Encyclopedia* (*Deseret News*, Salt Lake City, 1901), 1:54.

10. Ibid.

11. *Millennial Star*, p. 133.

12. *Millennial Star*, p. 134.

13. James B. Allen, Ronald K. Esplin, and David J. Whittaker, *Men with a Mission, 1837–1841, The Quorum of the Twelve Apostles in the British Isles* (Salt Lake City: Deseret Book, 1992), p. 25.

14. *Men with a Mission*, p. 37.

15. Ibid., p. 61.

16. Ibid., pp. 61–62.

17. Ibid., p. 63.

18. On 1 April 1838 Willard Richards and Isaac Russell attended a conference in Preston, having been instructed to prepare for their return to America. At the meeting the instructions were changed and Joseph Fielding, Willard Richards, and William Clayton were ordained high priests and set apart as the new mission presidency in the British Isles. Elder Richards was to continue as a missionary, and Elders Kimball and Hyde were to return to America (see *History of the Church* 3:20–21).

19. *History of the Church* 3:276–77.

20. *Men with a Mission*, p. 61.

21. *History of the Church* 3:277.

22. Ibid.

23. *History of the Church* 3:149.

24. Heber John was named after Heber C. Kimball and John Richards, Jennetta's father. He was called John in hopes that this would cause Jennetta's parents to feel more kindly toward her and Willard. (See *Men with a Mission*, pp. 65–66.)

25. *History of the Church* 3:277.

26. *Men with a Mission*, p. 252.

27. Ibid., p. 323.

28. *Willard Richards: The Intimate Disciple*, pp. 6–7; Howard C. Searle, "Willard Richards as Historian," *BYU Studies*, vol. 31, no. 2 (Spring 1991), p. 42.

29. *Mormons and Their Historians*, pp. 7–8.

30. "Willard Richards as Historian," p. 52.

31. *History of the Church* 6:616.

32. William E. Berrett and Alma P. Burton, *Readings in LDS Church History* (Salt Lake City: Deseret Book, 1953), 1:502–4.

33. Daughters of Utah Pioneers, "Historical Letters of the Past," *Our Pioneer Heritage* (1960), 3:130–32.

34. "Two Minutes in Jail."

35. Ibid.

36. "Historic Letters of the Past," 3:131.

37. *Readings in LDS Church History*, 2:2–4.
38. Ibid., 2:6.
39. *Mormons and Their Historians*, p. 13.
40. "Minutes of the General Conference . . . ," *Deseret News*, 13 April 1854.

BIBLIOGRAPHY

Allen, James B. & Esplin, Ronald K. & Whittaker, David J. *Men with a Mission, 1837–1841, The Quorum of the Twelve Apostles in the British Isles*. Salt Lake City: Deseret Book Company. 1992.

Berrett, William E. & Burton, Alma P. *Readings in L.D.S. Church History*. Salt Lake City, Utah: Deseret Book Company. Vols. I & II. 1953–55.

Bitton, Davis & Arrington, Leonard J. "Willard Richards, 'The Intimate Disciple.'" *Mormons and Their Historians*. Salt Lake City: University of Utah Press. 1988.

Daughters of the Utah Pioneers, "Historic Letters of the Past." *Our Pioneer Heritage*. Vol. 3. 1960.

History of the Church. Vol. III.

Hinckley, Bryant S. *The Faith of Our Pioneer Fathers*. Salt Lake City, Utah: Deseret Book Company. 1956.

Jenson, Andrew. *Latter-Day Saint Biographical Encyclopedia*. Salt Lake City: Deseret News. Vol. I. 1901.

Jessee, Dean C. "The Writing of Joseph Smith's History." *Mormon Miscellaneous*, Reprint Series No. 2. September 1984.

Noall, Claire. *Intimate Disciple: A Portrait of Willard Richards, Apostle to Joseph Smith—Cousin of Brigham Young*. Salt Lake City, Utah: University of Utah Press. 1957.

Richards, Preston D. "Willard Richards—The Martyrdom of Joseph and Hyrum Smith." *Improvement Era*. June, 1907.

Richards, Willard. "History of Willard Richards." *The Latter-day Saints' Millennial Star*. Vol. XXVII. February 25, 1865.

Rose, Blanche E. "Early Utah Medical Practice." *Utah Historical Quarterly*. Vol. 10. 1942.

Searle, Howard C. "Willard Richards as Historian." *Brigham Young University Studies*, Spring 1991.

11

Elder John K. Carmack

George A. Smith
Chronicler of Church History

He was there,
Remembered,
and Wrote

Although George A. Smith bore superficial similarities to Shakespeare's fictional Falstaff—corpulence, wittiness, and the capacity to good-naturedly poke fun at himself—we would miss the mark entirely if we characterized him in that manner. His extensive contributions to the Restoration and its history reveal a tremendous commitment and versatility.

Overestimating him and his impact on the restored Church is unlikely. His physical disabilities, which he largely ignored and dismissed with characteristic selflessness and good humor, only add to the luster of his character and his remarkable achievements. His size and wit helped make him a unique character among the Saints, adding pleasure and liveliness to his contemporaries—including outsiders who came to observe and sometimes debunk the early Saints of the Restoration.

Choosing among his many accomplishments, I have placed primary emphasis on his work as chronicler of Church history. The tremendous feat of tenacity, dedication, observation, and memory in finishing and publishing a chronicle of early Church history not only fulfilled an assignment and goal of his beloved cousin Joseph Smith

Jr., but also it may well have been his most important and enduring
contribution to the movement he early espoused.

In completing Joseph Smith's history, correcting and filling in the
work of earlier historians and clerks, and capturing the essence and
spirit of the formational and revelatory first era of the restored Church,
George A. assured himself a heroic place in the hearts of Latter-day
Saints. To place that achievement in context, however, we also need a
brief summary of his life.

WHO WAS HE?

An awkward, overgrown farm boy whom his Potsdam, New York,
classmates loved to bully and taunt hardly seemed the stuff of which
heroes are made. Poor eyesight resulting in a nearly unreadable scrawl
added to the inauspicious beginning.

Sometimes, however, early disabilities and trials such as George
A. experienced during his youth forge steel in one's character. His
classmates' taunting contributed to self-reliance, self-deprecating
humor, humility, and a deep desire to know, remember, and achieve
that characterized his mature years. Necessity and family needs taught
him to work long hours. The bullying, incidentally, stopped when
George A. successfully defended himself against every aggressive class-
mate. These bullies learned that George A. was a force to be reckoned
with. That awkwardness and size belied an inner strength that made
him formidable.

George A. first learned about Joseph Smith's remarkable visions
in a letter to his family from Joseph Smith Sr. (George A.'s father,
John Smith, was a brother to Joseph Smith Sr.). A letter from Joseph
Smith Jr. followed with a declaration concerning his visions and their
portent. Even though the letter deeply impressed George A., and despite his father's observation that "Joseph wrote like a prophet,"[1]
George A. was at first skeptical of his cousin's claims to visions, new
religious insight, and a new gospel dispensation. He sought answers to
his questions in his own Congregational Church. At length he found
his answers, not in his church but in the new Church of Christ organized on April 6, 1830, in Fayette, New York.[2] Following George A.'s
decision to join the restored Church, Reverend Fred E. Cannon, his

minister in the Congregational Church, sealed him up to eternal damnation nine times in the name of Jesus Christ.[3]

A few months after his baptism on September 10, 1832, at fifteen years of age, he and his family joined the Saints in Kirtland, Ohio. There he met his famous cousin Joseph, with whom he became an intimate friend for the rest of Joseph's brief and tumultuous life. As that mutual love and respect ripened, their families often shared dinner, quiet conversation, and always complete confidence and unity of purpose.

When George A. stopped at Joseph's home for advice prior to his mission to the eastern United States, Joseph told him to preach short sermons, give short prayers, and deliver his words with a prayerful heart. This advice, followed by seventeen-year-old George A., became the hallmark of his ministry.

One wealthy member of his Congregational Church had offered George A. a fine education if he would reject the restored Church. This must have been momentarily tempting to a boy who thirsted for education, but following his conscience and convictions brought him travel, responsibility, and practical education. He added to those educational opportunities voracious reading habits, developing unusual powers of observation and memory. He was destined to be the Church Historian, and his preparation included the gifts of direct participation in momentous events, wide acquaintance with the world of ideas and books, together with great powers of observation and feats of memory. He was destined to participate in almost all of the great early events of the Restoration. These experiences and gifts carried the day, as we shall see.

Of his fabulous memory, in typical modesty he once stated that this was less a natural endowment than the habit he developed as a missionary "of sticking to a subject" until he "had learned it so that it would stay learned."[4] About George A., Franklin D. Richards said that he had "a very tenacious and powerfully retentive memory [of] any person, or thing, he ever saw, or heard, once committed to memory, or even carefully read, he seemed never to forget. He was a man of great versatility of thought and idea and seemed peculiarly adapted to that labor and responsibility."[5]

Because it came at such a young age, George A.'s missionary work shaped his character, adding gospel knowledge and missionary skills and attributes that never left him. Those experiences educated and tutored him for his unique ministry, including valuable and intimate association with other great men and women of the new gospel dispensation. He learned to overcome every obstacle, including temporary blindness that accompanied an illness during one of his missions, and he experienced the character-building fire of ridicule and opposition.

In 1839, while serving as a member of the First Quorum of the Seventy, at the tender age of twenty-one he was called by revelation to be a member of the Quorum of the Twelve Apostles. He was ordained at that impressive meeting held at Far West, Missouri, on April 26, 1839, which launched the mission of the Twelve to Great Britain. He replaced Elder Thomas B. Marsh, who had apostatized. George A. has the distinction of being the youngest man ever called to that high and holy station.

When the Saints sustained George A. in Quincy, Illinois, prior to his apostolic ordination, noting his youth and the sad record of loyalty by some of his predecessors, Reynolds Cahoon remarked that he hoped the Saints would exercise sufficient faith "to keep this one from flying [off] the track."[6] Reynolds needn't have worried. Apostasy and quitting were no part of George A.'s character. Much could be written of that memorable mission to Great Britain where he grew in wisdom, stature, and favor with God and men, serving and growing with the great men of the Quorum under the leadership of Brigham Young.

During his mission with the Twelve to the British Isles, he was not only young but was also single and therefore an object of much interest among the English sisters. He had, however, met a young convert during one of his three missions in the United States. He and Bathsheba Bigler had an understanding that in time, as she and he matured, they would marry. Neither were of a nature to forget a commitment. They corresponded regularly while he was in Britain, George A. exhibiting in that correspondence some of the wit and poetic power for which he later became known. After three and one-half years of long-distance courtship, George A. and Bathsheba married about two weeks after his return from Great Britain to Nauvoo.

Perhaps the Zion's Camp march with Joseph that preceded his call as an Apostle was the capstone of George A.'s preparation for high leadership in the Church. During that two-thousand-mile march from Kirtland to and from Missouri, he proved his loyalty, dedication, and faithfulness to the cause of Zion, serving during part of the march as

Joseph's armor bearer and bodyguard. Most of what we know and understand about that interesting period of history is due to his remarkable memory of those days. He had also helped build the Kirtland Temple, quarrying rock and participating in the trials and testing in Kirtland. He was with the Saints through the terrible days of persecution in Missouri, and even visited Joseph and his brethren in Liberty Jail, entering the cell and observing firsthand the conditions that so depressed the brethren who, nevertheless, produced some of the Restoration's finest literature. Surely he was well prepared, even at age twenty-one, for the apostleship.

Along the way George A. learned to observe and remember what he saw and experienced. He began to keep a record of important events. Little of importance happened without his being there. He stood guard at Sidney Rigdon's home to protect him from danger at the hands of mobs; slept in the Prophet Joseph's tent during much of the long Zion's Camp march to and from Missouri; and, as proved valuable when called as Church Historian, learned to write and teach English grammar. The Lord was preparing him for his most important service.

Although he was away on a mission at the time, he learned from eyewitnesses details of the martyrdom of his cousins Hyrum and Joseph in Carthage Jail, and experienced firsthand the persecution in and around Nauvoo following the Martyrdom. Schooled under Joseph, reproved and corrected by Brigham Young, George A. also heard and remembered many of the sermons of the leading brethren. He and Bathsheba participated in building the first two temples of the new dispensation, Kirtland and Nauvoo, and enjoyed the affection and confidence of the Saints. On one occasion Joseph took him into his arms and exclaimed, "[George A.], I love you as I do my own life."[7] He certainly reciprocated that deep love. Few had the unique opportunities and perspectives George A. enjoyed.

He also served as member of the governmental Council of Fifty that, among other responsibilities, looked for a place of retreat in the West for the embattled Saints. Early he accepted the principle of plural marriage and had taken additional family responsibility in exercise of that principle with the full acceptance and support of his beloved Bathsheba.

His journal chronicled the attempt by Sidney Rigdon to take control of the Church after Joseph's death. He joined in the joyful

Hosannah Shout during dedicatory services for the Nauvoo Temple. In that temple his family was sealed for time and eternity.

Without hesitation, experiencing the thrill of anticipation, he joined with Brigham Young and the body of the Saints as they departed their Nauvoo homes across the Mississippi River into Iowa in the freezing cold of the winter of 1846, facing an unknown future with his people. His faith was such that he did not require knowledge of what lay ahead as a condition of acting on his righteous impulses. Before leaving Nauvoo he helped extinguish the blaze in the Nauvoo Temple, which had been built with intense labor and sacrifice. There was no time to sorrow at the loss of their newly completed temple. It was sufficient that they had their endowments and sealings. They could build other temples in the West.

Ahead was Mount Pisgah, Winter Quarters, and participation in the first company across the plains to the Great Salt Lake Valley. In common with many of the Saints, he lost children in the cold and difficult conditions of migration.

We can picture him with the 143 men, three women, and two children in their seventy-two wagons crossing the plains, reading as he went—a large, humble man thirsting for knowledge, seeing and remembering almost everything. Brigham called him a "cabinet of history."[8] He kept his journal as he traveled. When the advance party entered the Salt Lake Valley on July 22, 1847, he was there. His potatoes were the first in the ground. He accompanied Brigham and others to the top of Ensign Peak on Monday the 26th. Brigham Young named George A.'s father, affectionately known as Uncle John Smith, as president of the newly created Salt Lake Stake of Zion. John had also served as stake president at Adam-ondi-Ahman, with George A. serving on that stake high council.

That fall George A. traveled back to Winter Quarters, where he was when Oliver Cowdery rejoined the Saints bearing a powerful witness of the glorious visions and events of the Restoration.

All of these experiences and many more came to that farm boy with poor eyesight and little to predict his illustrious future. With the Saints established in Utah, George A. was destined to play new and important roles in the valleys of his new territory. These included leadership in establishing Parowan and other communities in southern Utah. His service in the south was of such importance that Brigham Young named the town of St. George after him.

Later he served Brigham Young as a Counselor in the First Presidency, filled a mission to Washington, D.C., in search of statehood for Utah, strategized as a colonel in the militia, shouldered responsibility in the so-called Utah War, and upon the death of Willard Richards replaced him as Church Historian and General Recorder. He studied law in the new Territory of Utah, becoming a member of the Utah Bar and in that capacity a powerful advocate for vital community issues and causes. His work as Church Historian was always interspersed with heavy ecclesiastical and community duties.

George A. became a popular leader and folk-hero among his people. With his deep, rumbling voice, his remarkable storytelling ability, his sense of humor, and his refusal either to take himself too seriously or be self-conscious because of his size, he was a favorite among the people. A nonmember visitor to Utah from New York observed that George A. "had had no quarrel with his cook."[9] He was about 5 feet 10 inches in height, weighing 250 pounds and upward. When he was about to leave for his assigned task in Washington, D.C., in 1856, he quipped that he "was about the only person in the Territory but what had plenty to eat, and that people had thought best to send me away, for fear I would get too lean."[10]

The Indians, astounded when he removed his wig, false teeth, and glasses, called him *Non-choko-wicher*, meaning "takes himself apart."[11] In short, he was a colorful character among the Saints. And he continued to read everything in sight, subscribing to many of the leading newspapers, magazines, and journals from the East.

CHRONICLING THE RESTORATION

Saints will remember that the Lord commanded Joseph Smith, a man with little formal English language training, to keep a record of the rise of the restored Church and his part in it (see D&C 21:1). That command worried him for the rest of his life.

After several abortive attempts to write his own and the Church's history, Joseph discovered a method of fulfilling this command that would work for him. This was to have clerks attend him, keep his journal, and write the Church's history. A number of brethren assisted him. James Mulholland actually commenced taking dictation and writing his official history on June 11, 1839. Willard Richards lived with the Prophet and worked with him intimately, writing journals and compiling more of that history started by Mulholland. Joseph "lamented his 'lack of fluency in address,' his 'writing imperfections,' and his 'inability' to convey his ideas in writing. Communication seemed to him to present an insurmountable barrier. He wrote of the almost 'total darkness of paper pen and ink,' and the 'crooked broken scattered and imperfect language.'"[12]

Joseph explained that during his last years he had kept several clerks busy recording and gathering his history and diary. Usually a clerk, often Willard Richards, wrote his journal entries. Reading the entries he personally made, we sense his tender and compassionate nature as compared to the more formal entries made by his clerks.

Joseph felt strongly that the history must be recorded. He said, "There are but few subjects that I have felt a greater anxiety about than my history."[13] He also had a dream in which he was told that "the history must go ahead before anything else."[14]

Just before his martyrdom, he wrote with some satisfaction: "For the last three years I have a record of all my acts and proceedings, for I have kept several good, faithful, and efficient clerks in constant employ: they have accompanied me everywhere, and carefully kept my history, and they have written down what I have done, where I have been, and what I have said."[15]

In the beginning of Joseph's ministry Oliver Cowdery acted as scribe, writing most of Joseph's Book of Mormon dictation and keeping copies of letters and diaries. John Whitmer reluctantly took Oliver's place, keeping a short history, although he withheld it after his apostasy.

Sidney Rigdon acted as scribe, and a succession of others followed. As noted, Mulholland wrote Joseph's early personal history under Joseph's dictation and watchful eye. This extraordinary document is now canonized as scripture in the Pearl of Great Price. The original is still in the Church archives. Joseph also kept a letter book into which scribes copied letters. He was trying to be faithful to the solemn commandment from the Lord.

With that sketchy background we arrive at the point at which Willard Richards undertook the task of writing the history of the Church with the help of other clerks. When he returned from his four-year mission in England in 1841, during which he had edited the *Millennial Star* for a time, Willard was appointed Church Historian, then private secretary and historian, and General Church Recorder. With Joseph constantly, even sleeping in his home, he accompanied Joseph, Hyrum, and John Taylor to Carthage Jail. Thus it was that he was there when the mob burst into their cell shooting Joseph and Hyrum.

Thomas Bullock acted as Willard's chief scribe. In that capacity Bullock wrote under Willard's direction about seven hundred pages of the original manuscript of Joseph Smith's history. George A. Smith spent about seventy days assisting Willard in collecting and compiling the history, absorbing his careful methods in the process. Bullock helped Willard bring the history up to the date of February 1, 1843, wrote a duplicate of it, and, when mobs drove the Saints from Nauvoo, assisted Willard in boxing up the history and the most important documents and records. They placed them in two boxes weighing 381 and 205 pounds respectively. These boxes they placed in Joseph Horn's wagon, and Henry Fairbanks transported them to Winter Quarters, from whence Bullock took them to the Great Salt Lake Valley.

With survival taking priority, the boxes were not even opened until June 7, 1853. Willard dictated one line to Bullock on December 1, 1853, never to write again because of an illness that took his life on March 11, 1854.

George A. replaced Willard as the new Church Historian and General Recorder. We pick up his summary of what he and his clerks did to complete Joseph's history as follows:

> On the 10th April 1854 [a month after Richards's death], I commenced to perform the duties of Historian by taking up the History of Joseph Smith where Dr. Willard Richards had left it when driven from Nauvoo on the 4th day of February 1846. I had to revise and compare two years of back history which he had compiled, filling up numerous spaces which had been marked as omissions on memoranda by Dr. Richards.
>
> I commenced compiling the History of Joseph Smith from April 1st 1840 to his death on June 27th 1844. I have filled up all the reports of sermons by President Joseph Smith and others from minutes or sketches taken at the time in long hand by Dr. Willard Richards, Wilford Woodruff, Thomas Bullock, William Clayton, Miss Eliza R. Snow, &c. which was an immense labor, requiring the deepest thought and the closest application, as there were mostly only two or

three words (about half written) to a sentence. The greatest care has been taken to convey the ideas in the prophets style as near as possible; and in no case has the sentiment been varied that I know of; as I heard the most of his discourses myself, was on the most intimate terms with him, have retained a most vivid recollection of his teachings, and was well acquainted with his principles and motives. . . .

The severe application of thought to the principles of the History, the exercise of memory &c., have caused me to suffer much from a nervous headache or inflammation of the brain; and my application of mind being in exercise both day and night, deprived me of a great portion of necessary sleep.[16]

Completing his intense and harrowing labors, arguably the most important of his life, George A. prepared to publish them for the Church. His methods seem to have been these:

1. Assemble all available materials.
2. Study them carefully.
3. Dictate or write the history in rough draft.
4. Revise his draft.
5. Read it all to Brigham Young, correcting and amplifying it accordingly.
6. Gain Brigham's approval.
7. Write a final copy.[17]

His tenacity comes through in these words—"I am determined to do justice to Jos. Smith's History cost what it will."[18]

Unlike accounts by many other observers, his history (or annals) was heroic in treatment, favorable in tone, and authoritative in that the President of the Church read, corrected, and approved it. George A. had heard most of the recorded sermons contained in it and had participated in most of the events. He called on his considerable talents of observation and memory to make it as accurate as possible, rejecting material he considered inaccurate and untrustworthy. He had access to and used journals of other participants, including the accounts in Wilford Woodruff's marvelous journals. He also conferred with eyewitnesses to events described in the history.

George A. Smith and Wilford Woodruff said this about the history on the occasion of its publication in the *Deseret News*:

The *History of Joseph Smith* is now before the world, and we are satisfied that a history more correct in its details than this was never published. To have it strictly correct, the greatest possible pains have
been taken by the historians and clerks engaged in the work. They
were eye and ear witnesses of nearly all the transactions recorded in
this history, most of which were reported as they transpired, and,
where they were not personally present, they have had access to
those who were. Moreover, since the death of the Prophet Joseph,
the history has been carefully revised under the strict inspection of
President Brigham Young, and approved by him. We, therefore,
hereby bear our testimony to all the world, unto whom these words
shall come, that the *History of Joseph Smith* is true, and is one of the
most authentic histories ever written.[19]

These were serious and sincere statements from those who had
given their full strength to the task. What new religious movement
has taken such pains to present an authoritative history to the world?
Who did more than George A. Smith to bring about its publication to
the Church and to the world?

It is true, as some of our historians point out, that this history is
not scientific, unbiased, professional, and analytical history. Arguably
it is much more than that. It is a passionate and painstakingly accurate account of the restoration of the gospel. Given the circumstances
of its production it is little short of amazing and certainly unprecedented in scope. The authors wrote for Church members and sincere
researchers who desired to know the truth about Joseph Smith and
the restored Church, not for professional colleagues. It is the authoritative source of information about countless events that occurred during the formative and revelatory period of the Restoration. Thank the
Lord it was done. Without it, subsequent analytical and scientific histories would have had much less grain for their historical mill.

The heroic and faith-promoting tone of the history, so motivating
and inspiring, would perhaps have been lost and preempted by later
historians dedicated more to a craft than to a passionate spiritual
cause. In the history we see a partial fulfillment of Isaiah's great
prophecy that the Lord would proceed to do a marvelous work and a
wonder in the last days wherein the wisdom of the wise men and the

understanding of the prudent would be hidden (see Isaiah 29:14). Without the history we would not have access to the pure veins of gold chronicled by a hero of the Restoration whose purpose was to inspire, inform, and guide the faithful in fulfilling their destiny. In this respect it has become a part of the fabric of the Restoration tapestry.

This rotund, awkward, humble, self-taught man of faith is a hero of the Restoration. He died on September 1, 1875, at the age of fifty-eight, but his legacy of Church history survives.

NOTES

1. Manuscript history of Brigham Young, 1844–46, "Sketch of the Autobiography of George Albert Smith," p. 288, Church Historical Department.

2. The Church of Christ was the accepted name of the Church in 1830 (see D&C 20:1). The full name as we know it was not revealed until 1838 (see D&C 115:4).

3. "Sketch of the Autobiography of George Albert Smith," pp. 289, 290.

4. "George A. Smith" *The Contributor*, 4 January 1883, p. 121.

5. Franklin D. Richards, "Bibliography, in answer to questions put by Mr. Herbert [sic] H. Bancroft . . . 1884," pp. 2–3, Church Historical Department.

6. George Albert Smith, Papers, 1834–1875, "History of George A. Smith by Himself," p. 81, Church Historical Department.

7. "Sketch of the Autobiography of George Albert Smith," p. 297.

8. Andrew Jenson, *Latter-day Saint Biographical Encyclopedia*, vol. 7 (Salt Lake City: Andrew Jenson History Co., 1901), p. 442.

9. Fitz Hugh Ludlow, *The Heart of the Continent: A Record of Travel Across the Plains and in Oregon, with an Examination of the Mormon Principle* (New York: Hurd and Houghton, 1870), p. 514.

10. *Deseret News*, 16 April 1856, p. 45.

11. William R. Palmer, "Pioneers of Southern Utah," *The Instructor*, January 1944, p. 24.

12. *The Personal Writings of Joseph Smith*, Dean C. Jessee, ed. (Salt Lake City: Deseret Book, 1984), p. xv.

13. Joseph Smith, *History of The Church of Jesus Christ of Latter-day Saints*, 7 vols. (Salt Lake City: Deseret News, 1950), 6:66, hereafter cited as *History of the Church*.

14. *History of the Church* 5:394.

15. *History of the Church* 6:409.

16. George A. Smith to Wilford Woodruff, 21 April 1856, copy in Docket of the Municipal Court of the City of Nauvoo . . . , p. 218, Church Historical Department.

17. See C. Kent Dunford, "The Contributions of George A. Smith to the Establishment of the Mormon Society in the Territory of Utah" (Ph.D. diss., Brigham Young University, 1970), p. 137.

18. George A. Smith to R. Benson, 30 January 1855, George A. Smith, Papers, Outgoing Correspondence, Church Historical Department.

19. *History of the Church* 1:v–vi.

12

Elder M. Russell Ballard

Hyrum Smith

Hyrum Smith, the second son of Joseph and Lucy Mack Smith, was born February 9, 1800, almost six years before his younger brother Joseph. As he grew to adulthood, Hyrum had a healthy body of work-hardened muscles, a seemingly endless reservoir of energy, and a litheness of movement. A handsome man, it is generally believed he stood about six feet tall, much the same size as the Prophet Joseph. One of Hyrum's sons, John Smith, described them as follows: "The Prophet Joseph stood even six feet high in his stocking feet and weighed 212 pounds. . . . Hyrum Smith stood five feet eleven and a half inches high and they weighed in the same notch, varying from 210 to 212 pounds."[1]

The general membership of the Church has never really known this great-great-grandfather of mine. It was his nature to keep a low profile, but without him the Prophet could never have achieved all that he did. Hyrum's wisdom seemed never to be doubted by Joseph, who would often write or say "What shall we do, Hyrum?" After Hyrum's reply to the query, Joseph would respond, "That is good enough." There is much in Hyrum's noble character that is worthy of emulation.

Perhaps we can best understand Hyrum and the attributes that commend him to us as a hero through those who knew him best. Consider the following tributes given to Hyrum Smith by the Lord and by the first three Presidents of the Church in this dispensation:

I, the Lord, love [Hyrum Smith] because of the integrity of his heart, and because he loveth that which is right before me (D&C 124:15).

I could pray in my heart that all my brethren were like unto my beloved brother Hyrum, for truly he possesses the mildness of a lamb, and the integrity of a Job, and in short the meekness and the quiet spirit of Christ; and I love him with that love that is stronger than death.[2]

Hyrum was as good a man as ever lived. . . . His integrity was of the highest order, . . . I used to think and think now that an angel dwelling in the presence of the Father and the Son possessed no more integrity in their hearts than did Hyrum Smith.[3]

He was a great and good man, and my soul was cemented to his. If ever there was an exemplary, honest, and virtuous man, an embodiment of all that is noble in the human form, Hyrum Smith was its representative.[4]

Love, integrity, and humility were the attributes that guaranteed his greatness as one of the firm pillars of the Restoration, greatness that was cemented by a martyr's death in Carthage at the side of his prophet-brother.

LOVE OF AND SERVICE TO FAMILY AND CHURCH

The highest levels of love and service are epitomized in Hyrum's faithful service to his family and to his church. That service became evident when Joseph was only seven years old and Hyrum just thirteen. Joseph contracted typhoid fever. This resulted in pain in his leg and an eventual excruciating operation without benefit of anesthetics. Lucy Mack Smith carried Joseph in her arms much of the time in an effort to relieve his suffering. She thus became fatigued and very ill. Hyrum stepped in and relieved her of the task, sitting beside Joseph almost day and night for over a week helping Joseph to endure severe pain. Hyrum even held the affected part of the leg, pressing it with his hands to relieve the suffering.[5] This forged a bond between the brothers that was never broken. In fact, during their entire lives they were never apart longer than six months.

From the time Joseph first recounted to his family the wondrous happenings of that early spring day in 1820 when he saw the Father and the Son in vision, Hyrum knew his brother would need his help. He became confidant, companion, and a constant source of strength to his younger brother. Of that brotherly relationship, President Heber J. Grant stated:

> There is no better example of an older brother's love than that exhibited in the life of Hyrum Smith for the Prophet Joseph Smith. . . . They were as united and as affectionate and as loving as mortal men could be. . . . There never was one particle of the jealousy that ofttimes fills the hearts of older brothers toward younger brothers who seem to be preferred ahead of them. There was no place for jealousy in the heart of Hyrum Smith. No mortal man could have been more loyal, more true, more faithful in life or in death than was Hyrum Smith to the Prophet of the living God.[6]

As his father, Joseph Smith Sr., and his prophet-brother Joseph must have received their callings as part of the premortal plan (see 2 Nephi 3:15), Hyrum must also have been divinely called into this family. The Lord himself declared this eternal mission early to Hyrum as he said in 1830, "Thy duty is unto the church forever, and this because of thy family" (D&C 23:3).

Hyrum assisted Joseph during the translating and printing of the Book of Mormon. He provided his tool chest to Joseph to store the gold plates, under hardship made trips to visit the Prophet, and during the printing of the Book of Mormon guarded the manuscript and made frequent trips to the printer. It was in mid-August of 1829 that Hyrum took "the first installment of the manuscript," numbering twenty-four pages, to Egbert G. Grandin's Print Shop, Palmyra, New York. "He had it under his vest, and vest and coat closely buttoned over it" for security.[7] Joseph often entrusted Hyrum with the care of Emma and the children while he was away from home.

While marching with Zion's Camp, Hyrum and Joseph were stricken with cholera and were literally at death's door. As each, with the other, prayed to be healed, Hyrum comforted Joseph as the Spirit testified to him through a vision that they would be spared. Hyrum sprang to his feet and exclaimed, "Joseph, we shall return to our families."[8]

His protective care of and service to his brother often subjected Hyrum to severe affliction. Hyrum was imprisoned with Joseph several times. On one occasion all the testimony that could be produced against him was that he was one of the Presidency of the Church and "a firm friend to my brother Joseph."[9] They were arrested in Far West, Missouri, and sentenced to be shot. They then sustained and supported each other through the cruelty to which they were subjected in jail at Richmond and the inhumane treatment in the dungeons of Liberty Jail. Joseph wrote to Emma from Richmond that Hyrum was chained near him and declared, "thus we are bound together in chains as well as the cords of everlasting love, we are in good spirits and rejoice that we are counted worthy to be [persecuted] for Christ's sake."[10]

Hyrum Smith was baptized by Joseph Smith Jr. in Seneca Lake in June 1829. He was chosen to be one of the original six to formally organize the Church on April 6, 1830. He was ordained a high priest by Joseph Smith the Prophet June 3, 1831. He served faithfully and well in a variety of missionary callings, as a member of the committee to oversee the building of the Kirtland Temple and later the Nauvoo Temple, as a member of the Kirtland High Council, and as Second Counselor in the First Presidency. On 24 January 1841 Hyrum was ordained Patriarch to the Church and Assistant President of the Church by President Joseph Smith. He was given all the priesthood formerly held by Oliver Cowdery.[11] Hyrum Smith then stood next to the Prophet Joseph Smith as the second witness of the Restoration.

Of this later calling, Elder Joseph Fielding Smith stated:

> It is, no doubt, because of this love and integrity, that the Lord conferred upon Hyrum Smith—in addition to the honor of the Patriarchal Priesthood held by his father—the following everlasting blessing: "And from this time forth I appoint unto him that he may be a prophet, and a seer, and a revelator unto my church, as well as my servant Joseph; that he may act in concert also with my servant Joseph; and that he shall receive counsel from my servant Joseph, who shall show unto him the keys whereby he may ask and receive, and be crowned with the same blessing, and glory, and honor, and priesthood, and gifts of the priesthood, that once were put upon him that was my servant Oliver Cowdery. That my servant Hyrum may bear record of the things which I shall show unto him, that his name

may be had in honorable remembrance from generation to generation forever and ever." (D&C 124:94–95.)

Elder Joseph Fielding Smith further declared:

> It is very evident from this promise given by the Lord to Hyrum
> Smith that he had opened to his vision the wonders of eternity. . . .
> This was necessary in the great plan of the Lord that his work might
> be fully accomplished. Hyrum Smith was not fully qualified as the
> special witness for Christ with his younger brother until this vision
> and these keys and powers had been given to him.[12]

INTEGRITY

Integrity is a word that describes Hyrum. Throughout his life he
courageously stood by his convictions in spite of even the vilest of
threats. On one of his missions, Daniel Tyler's sister desired baptism.
Her father threatened Hyrum that "the Elder who baptized her would
do so at his peril." Hyrum responded: "'Mr. Tyler, we shall not baptize
your daughter against your wishes. If our doctrine be true, which we
testify it is, if you prevent your daughter from embracing it, the sin will
be on your head, not on ours or your daughter's.' This remark pricked
him to the heart. He began to think that possibly the 'Mormons' were
right and he was wrong. He therefore decided to counsel his daughter
in the matter and then permit her to exercise her free agency. He
would thus relieve himself of any responsibility." He told his daughter
that "if this new religion was true, it was the best religion in the world,
but, if false, it was the worst. 'These men,' said he, 'know whether it is
true or false, but I do not.' He wished her to reflect upon all these
things before making a move in the matter. She replied that she had
weighed them long ago and believed it to be her duty to be baptized.
He took her on an ox-sled to Lake Erie, a distance of two miles, where,
after a hole was cut through three feet of solid ice, she was baptized and
confirmed into the Church by Elder Hyrum Smith."[13]

Hyrum lived as he believed, and he believed in a gospel of peace.
He was a peacemaker even though the violent winds of tribulation
and persecution constantly raged around him. In one instance he in-
terceded to resolve a conflict on a boat in Lake Erie in 1831. He was

accompanying his mother, Lucy Mack Smith, to Michigan. In her characteristic missionary zeal, Lucy Mack spoke plainly what she felt. Some of the brethren complained about her outspokenness. Hyrum proposed "that Mother Smith should say just what she pleased, and if she got into difficulty, the Elders should help her out of it."[14]

Personal tragedy was a part of Hyrum's life, yet he never faltered in his convictions. He lost a son, a daughter, and a wife. In 1832 Mary, his three-year-old daughter, died in his arms. Grief-stricken, he wrote that this was a scene of "sorrow and mourning" such as "I never before experienced."[15] His wife, Jerusha, died in 1838 shortly after giving birth to their sixth child. Then in 1842, he watched Hyrum, his namesake, die at age seven, probably of malaria or typhoid.

Through these and other trials, Hyrum's testimony remained firm. His faithfulness is manifest in the testimonies he bore even in the face of death. Perhaps this one quotation shows his faith and devotion best. Said Hyrum:

> I had been abused and thrust into a dungeon, and confined for months on account of my faith, and the "testimony of Jesus Christ." However I thank God that I felt a determination to die, rather than deny the things which my eyes had seen, which my hands had handled, and which I had borne testimony to, wherever my lot had been cast; and I can assure my beloved brethren that I was enabled to bear as strong a testimony, when nothing but death presented itself, as ever I did in my life.[16]

While we will never fully understand this hero's suffering for the cause of truth, we can rejoice in the depth of his integrity. Following his confinement in the Liberty Jail, he wrote:

> I . . . suffered much for want of proper food, and from the nauseous cell in which I was confined: but still more so on account of my anxiety for my family, whom I had left without any protector, and who were unable to help themselves: my wife was confined while I was away from home, and had to suffer more than tongue can tell; she was not able to sit up for several weeks, and to heighten my affliction, and the sufferings of my helpless family, my goods were unlawfully seized upon and carried off, until my family had to suffer in consequence thereof. . . .

How inadequate is language to express the feelings of my mind.
. . . I had been dragged from my family at a time, when my assistance
was most needed . . .

From my close and long confinement, as well as from the sufferings of my mind, I feel my body greatly broke[n] down and debili-
tated, my frame has received a shock from which it will take a long
time to recover.[17]

In responding to such terrible trials, Hyrum reaffirmed his testimony: "Yet, I am happy to say that my zeal for the cause of God, and
my courage in defence of the truth, are as great as ever. 'My heart is
fixed,' and I yet feel a determination to do the will of God, in spite of
persecutions, imprisonments, or death."[18]

Part of Hyrum's great legacy of faith and integrity can be found in
the teachings he gave the Church. Hyrum always believed in teaching
basics and leaving the mysteries alone. Addressing the Church in
April of 1844, he instructed: "The Elders are sent into the world to
preach faith, repentance, baptism for the remission of sins, and the
laying on of hands for the reception of the Holy Ghost and they
should let the mysteries alone . . . and if this generation will not receive the first principles of the Gospel and the Book of Mormon, they
will receive nothing greater. . . . It is the power of God that is going to
convert. . . . It is the honest and pure in heart that will h[e]arken to
the everlasting covenant."[19]

The next day he continued: "Preach the first principles of the
Gospel—preach them over again: you will find that day after day new
ideas and additional light concerning them will be revealed to you.
You can enlarge upon them so as to comprehend them clearly. You
will then be able to make them more plainly understood."[20]

Hyrum also taught the Word of Wisdom boldly to leaders and
members alike. The Word of Wisdom was not fully lived in 1842 and
many did not consider it a commandment. Hyrum's commitment led
him to address the Saints and forthrightly tell them: "Listen not to the
teaching of any man, or any elder who says the word of wisdom is of
no moment. . . . These are principles that I have always acted upon;
that I have always practiced; and they are what my family practices;
they are what Brother Hyrum has always contended for, and what I
now contend for; and I know that nothing but an unwavering, undeviating course can save a man in the kingdom of God."[21]

In this same talk to the Saints, Hyrum clarified that "hot drinks" in the Word of Wisdom referred to tea and coffee:

> There are many who wonder what this can mean; whether it refers to tea, or coffee, or not. I say it does refer to tea, and coffee. Why is it that we are frequently so dull and languid? It is because we break the word of wisdom, disease preys upon our system, our understandings are darkened, and we do not comprehend the things of God; the devil takes advantage of us, and we fall into temptation.[22]

Since he led efforts to build both the Kirtland and the Nauvoo Temples, Hyrum understood temple work and the importance of the covenants and endowments in the temple. He promised that there would be a "great and mighty power grow out of" the temple. Additionally he indicated "much depends upon [this temple] for our endowments and sealing powers; and many blessings depend upon it."[23]

Receptive to the promptings of the Spirit, Hyrum also gave inspired blessings and advice. In January 1836 Joseph sent for Hyrum to administer to and heal Lorenzo Young, who had become ill with a severe lung ailment while working on the Kirtland Temple in bitterly cold weather. Lorenzo "had been pronounced by the best physicians in the country past all human aid." The Lord spoke through Hyrum and he said things he couldn't have known himself. Lorenzo described his miraculous healing and a prophecy Hyrum uttered as the Spirit rested mightily upon him:

> He was full of blessing and prophecy. Among other things, he said that I should live to go with the Saints into the bosom of the Rocky Mountains, to build up a place there, and that my cellar should overflow with wine and fatness.

Remember, this was 1836 in Kirtland. Brother Young continued:

> At that time, I had not heard about the Saints going to the Rocky Mountains; possibly Brother Smith had. After he had finished he seemed surprised at some things he had said, and wondered at the manifestations of the Spirit. I coughed no more after that administration, and rapidly recovered.[24]

HUMILITY

There is no greater evidence of Hyrum's humility than his willingness to submit to the will of the Lord, even to the extent of giving up his own life. In a blessing from the First Presidency that Hyrum received in 1835, he was promised: "Thou shalt have power to escape the hand of thine enemies. Thy life shall be sought with untiring zeal, but thou shalt escape. *If it please thee, and thou desirest, thou shalt have the power voluntarily to lay down thy life to glorify God.*"[25]

With perfect faith in the Lord's promise, Hyrum was able to face mobs and persecutions, always knowing that he would eventually escape and return to his family. But at Carthage the time had come to "voluntarily" lay down his life "to glorify God" and to "seal his testimony with his blood" (D&C 136:39)—together with his beloved brother Joseph. As Elder Joseph Fielding Smith noted:

> No honor came to Joseph Smith that was not shared by Hyrum who rejoiced with his brother in all the blessings the Lord bestowed upon him. . . . They passed through the same sorrows and joys together. The same persecutions descended upon them both. They shared the same dungeons for the Gospel's sake, and when the time came for the sealing of their testimony, they shared together the crown of martyrdom. "In life they were not divided, and in death they were not separated." Together they held the keys of the dispensation of the Fulness of Times, and the sealing of the testimony would not have been complete had Joseph died alone. They filled the measure of divine law requiring two witnesses for truth, in their martyrdom, and they died that they "might be honored, and the wicked might be condemned."[26]

There is no doubt that Hyrum made a conscious decision to join his brother in martyrdom at Carthage. He was warned several times not to go to Carthage. A week before the Martyrdom Joseph recorded that "I advised my brother Hyrum to take his family on the next steamboat and go to Cincinnati. Hyrum replied, 'Joseph, I can't leave you.' Whereupon I said to the company present, 'I wish I could get Hyrum out of the way so that he may live to avenge my blood.'"[27]

Three days later Hyrum reaffirmed his determination. Because of threats, Joseph and Hyrum had crossed to the Iowa side of the Mississippi River. Joseph believed that the Saints in Nauvoo would be safe from hostility because it was the Smith brothers that the mobs wanted. But then word came that some of the faint-hearted Saints had called for Joseph's return, some even accusing him of cowardice. Fittingly, Joseph turned to Hyrum and said, "Brother Hyrum, you are the oldest, what shall we do?" Hyrum responded, "Let us go back and give ourselves up, and see the thing out." After a moment to assess the situation Joseph indicated, "If you go back I will go with you, but we shall be butchered." Hyrum's answer showed his great faith in the Lord and his humble willingness to die for His cause: "Let us go back and put our trust in God, and we shall not be harmed. The Lord is in it. If we live or have to die, we will be reconciled to our fate."[28]

On June 24, three days before the Martyrdom, Joseph and Hyrum left Nauvoo for Carthage. As they rode to the edge of the woods near Nauvoo, a messenger arrived from Carthage and reported: "Brother Hyrum, you are now clear, and if it was my duty to counsel you, I would say, do not go another foot, for they say they will kill you, if you go to Carthage."[29]

And so Joseph and Hyrum spent the last few days of their mortal lives together as prisoners in Carthage, brothers to the very end. On June 26 Joseph told his brethren, "Could my brother, Hyrum but be liberated, it would not matter so much about me."[30] Later that evening, as they both prepared for what they must have known was ahead, Hyrum "read . . . copious extracts from the Book of Mormon" and commented upon them. "Joseph bore a powerful testimony to the guards of the divine authenticity of the Book of Mormon . . . and that the Kingdom of God was again upon the earth."[31]

Late in the afternoon of June 27, 1844, a hate-driven mob burst up the stairs and into the room where Hyrum, ever the older brother, was holding the door in an attempt to protect the others. He became the first martyr that dark day, falling to the floor when he was shot and declaring, "I am a dead man." Joseph's thoughts went immediately to his brother. He exclaimed, "Oh dear brother Hyrum!"[32] John Taylor was the next prisoner to be shot, after which Joseph leapt to the window to draw the mob's attention. As soon as he was shot and fell to the ground below, the mob rushed outside, leaving the wounded John Taylor to survey the gruesome scene in the room. He later recorded: "I had a full view of our beloved and now murdered brother, Hyrum. There he lay as I had left him; he had not moved a limb; he lay placid and calm, a monument of greatness even in death; but his noble spirit had left its tenement, and was gone to dwell in regions more congenial to its exalted nature."[33]

I think we can all understand the horrible shock and grief members of the Church must have felt as news of the Martyrdom spread to Nauvoo. Dan Jones, who spent the night before the Martyrdom with the prisoners but who was not present at the time of the murders, gave this poignant description of what he encountered in Nauvoo upon the return of the bodies of Joseph and Hyrum:

> Oh, the sorrowful scene to be seen in Nauvoo that day! There has never been nor will there ever be anything like it; everyone sad along the streets, all the shops closed and every business forgotten. Onward I quickened my pace until I reached the house of the late Joseph Smith. I pushed my way through the sorrowful crowd until I reached the room where his body and that of his brother had been placed. . . . There they lay in their coffins side by side, majestic men as they suffered side by side from prison to prison for years, and they labored together, shoulder to shoulder, to build the kingdom of Immanuel; eternal love bound them steadfastly to each other and to their God until death; and now, my eyes beheld the blood of the two godly martyrs mingling in one pool in the middle of the floor, their elderly mother, godly and sorrowful, . . . a hand on each one of her sons . . . her heart nearly broken by the excruciating agony and the indescribable grief. At the head of the deceased sat the dear wife of each one and around their father stood four of Joseph's little children and six of Hyrum's children crying out intermittently, "My dear father" . . . "Oh, my father." And from the hearts of the mothers, "My husband killed," and the grey-haired mother groaning pitifully, "Oh, my sons, my sons."[34]

Still, Mother Lucy Mack Smith reported that even in the midst of so much grief and despair, there was comfort, and even peace. As she cried in agony, "My God, my God, why hast thou forsaken this family?" she reported hearing a voice reply. "I have taken them to myself, that they might have rest." Then as she looked upon the mortal remains of her two sons, she said:

I seemed almost to hear them say, "Mother, weep not for us, we have overcome the world by love; we carried to them the gospel, that their souls might be saved; they slew us for our testimony, and thus placed us beyond their power; their ascendancy is for a moment, ours is an eternal triumph."[35]

As Elder Joseph Fielding Smith declared: "All honor, praise and glory to these great men, martyrs for the truth! They laid down their lives in the vigor of their manhood in defense of the everlasting gospel. They will take them up again crowned with everlasting glory to sit down in the mansions which are prepared for the righteous in the celestial kingdom of God."[36]

The *American Heritage Dictionary* defines a hero as "a person noted for feats of courage or nobility of purpose, especially one who has risked or sacrificed his or her life." Hyrum Smith truly is a hero of our dispensation. Having given all, his life and testimony now stand as a hero's monument. "I thank God that I [Hyrum] felt a determination to die, rather than deny the things which my eyes had seen, which my hands had handled, and which I had borne testimony to."[37]

NOTES

1. Summary of remarks by Patriarch John Smith, 23 December 1894, in *Salt Lake Herald,* 12 January 1895.

2. Dean C. Jessee, ed., *The Papers of Joseph Smith,* 2 vols. (Salt Lake City: Deseret Book, 1989), 1:168.

3. Brigham Young address, 8 October 1866, 1–2, Church Historical Department.

4. John Taylor, *History of the Church* 7:107.

5. See Lucy Mack Smith, *History of Joseph Smith* (Salt Lake City: Bookcraft, 1956), p. 55.

6. "The Hyrum Smith Monument," *Improvement Era* 21 (August 1918), pp. 854–55.

7. John H. Gilbert Memorandum, 8 September 1892, typescript, Church Historical Department.

8. *History of Joseph Smith,* p. 229.

9. *Times and Seasons* 1:23.

10. Letter dated 12 November 1838, quoted in *The Personal Writings of Joseph Smith*, ed. Dean C. Jessee (Salt Lake City: Deseret Book, 1984), p. 368.

11. See *Encyclopedia of Mormonism* 4:1646; *History of the Church* 4:286.

12. Joseph Fielding Smith, "Hyrum Smith, A Tribute," *Improvement Era* 36 (February 1933), p. 201.

13. Daniel Tyler, "Incidents of Experience," in *Scraps of Biography* (Salt Lake City: Juvenile Instructor Office, 1883), p. 26.

14. *History of Joseph Smith*, p. 211.

15. Hyrum Smith Diary, 2 May 1832, Church Historical Department.

16. *Times and Seasons* 1:23.

17. Ibid., 1:22–23.

18. Ibid., 1:23.

19. *History of the Church* 6:320.

20. *History of the Church* 6:323.

21. *Times and Seasons* 3:800.

22. Ibid.

23. *History of the Church* 6:237, 299.

24. Lorenzo Dow Young, "Lorenzo Dow Young's Narrative," in *Fragments of Experience* (Salt Lake City: Juvenile Instructor Office, 1882), pp. 43–45.

25. Blessing to Hyrum Smith, Kirtland Council Minutes Book, no. 25, February 21, 1835, p. 186.

26. "Hyrum Smith: A Tribute," *Improvement Era* 36 (February 1933), p. 201.

27. *History of the Church* 6:520.

28. *History of the Church* 6:549–50.

29. *History of the Church* 6:558.

30. *History of the Church* 6:592.

31. Dan Jones, "The Martyrdom of Joseph and Hyrum Smith," 1855, p. 9, Church Historical Department.

32. *History of the Church* 6:617–18.

33. *History of the Church* 7:107.

34. "The Martyrdom of Joseph Smith and His Brother Hyrum, by Dan Jones," *Brigham Young University Studies*, vol. 24, (Winter 1984): 93–94.

35. *History of Joseph Smith*, pp. 324–25.

36. "The Martyrs," *Improvement Era* 47 (June 1944): 415.

37. *Times and Seasons* 1:23.

13

Elder Joe J. Christensen

Samuel Harrison Smith
He Was There

Samuel Harrison Smith, the next younger brother of the Prophet Joseph, is truly one of my heroes of the Restoration.

I first remember being impressed in learning about Samuel Smith when we were studying Church history in seminary—actually, more than fifty years ago. Although we didn't spend a lot of time discussing him, I was impressed, and Samuel's example has made a positive impact on me since then in a variety of ways—especially while serving in the mission field in Mexico and Central America.

As a young nineteen-year-old elder, fresh into the mission, I discovered that door-to-door contacting—or tracting, as we used to call it—was not my favorite activity. By nature I was somewhat shy. I had to push myself to get out and knock on those doors.

I suppose it was difficult for a variety of reasons. I was not particularly enthusiastic about intruding into the lives of complete strangers. Also, when someone would come to the door it was not easy for me to stand there feeling somewhat embarrassed and as I attempted to share the message in a language I was just beginning to learn. The anxiety of being rejected—and sometimes hostilely—was not appealing to me. Nevertheless I persisted, and in this I owe much to the example of Samuel H. Smith. He too had left his comfort zone and as a missionary had confronted much greater odds than I was ever called to face. And in addition, on that first mission he didn't even have the benefit of a companion at his side.

With that kind of exemplary incentive, then, I would push myself to make the effort. In time the task became easier; and in fact, before long, contacting those strangers even came to be an enjoyable stimulus and challenge.

Now, years later, I am continually thankful for having had the privilege of facing those missionary difficulties and receiving the opportunity to play even a small part in the lives of several who were converted and came to be faithful members—and some of them even leaders—in the Church in Mexico. I owe an immense debt of gratitude to such as Samuel H. Smith.

Samuel had many other remarkable qualities worthy of our emulation. They began to be evident early in his life's experiences. He was born March 13, 1808. That means that in 1820, when his next older brother, Joseph, told the family of some of his remarkable spiritual experiences in connection with the First Vision, Samuel had just turned twelve years of age.

Soon after Joseph had the remarkable and life-changing experiences in the Sacred Grove, he apparently confided to his family, to ministers, and perhaps to others outside the family some of what he had experienced (see Joseph Smith—History 1:21). Family discussions took on a new excitement. His mother, Lucy, recounted the family's delighted response to the heaven-sent knowledge shared by their eighteen-year-old son and brother:

> From this time forth, Joseph continued to receive instructions from the Lord, and we continued to get the children together every evening for the purpose of listening while he gave us a relation of the same. . . .
>
> During our evening conversations, Joseph would occasionally give us some of the most amusing recitals that could be imagined. He would describe the ancient inhabitants of this continent, their dress, mode of traveling, and the animals upon which they rode; their cities, their buildings, with every particular; their mode of warfare; and also their religious worship. This he would do with as much ease, seemingly, as if he had spent his whole life among them.[1]

I can picture in my imagination, during such occasions of sharing, a younger brother Samuel—wide-eyed, mentally and spiritually tuned in—as he listened to his next older brother. Samuel's entire life following that time proved that he was not merely a passive listener, not just a believer only—he was a doer of the first order. For Samuel, those early years of the Restoration must have been a time of immense spiritual growth and commitment.

Like so many scriptural and historical figures, Samuel Harrison Smith has taught me a great deal. I see in him a rare blend of commitment and constancy. Someone said that just showing up—being where we ought to be—has to be one of the most important characteristics of a good Church member. Samuel was one who "showed up." He was there. In fact, his name is associated with many of the important "firsts" in the history of the Restoration.

Some time in May 1829, Samuel went to Harmony, Pennsylvania, to see his brother Joseph and Oliver Cowdery, who at that time were in the process of translating and transcribing the Book of Mormon. While there, he learned of that monumental visit of the resurrected John the Baptist to Joseph and Oliver on the banks of the Susquehanna River. Samuel was made aware that his brother Joseph and his scribe Oliver had received the Aaronic Priesthood and had been baptized.

Earlier, in the religious excitement that existed in the area of upstate New York, Samuel and others in the family had formally joined one of the Protestant churches. Subsequently, as Samuel learned more about what his brother Joseph was learning and doing, he had the challenge of considering giving up his newfound church and identifying with this new movement. Like many converts today, considering leaving one's faith was trying for him.

> [Joseph and Oliver] informed him what the Lord was about to do for the children of men, and began to reason with him out of the Bible. We also showed him that part of the work which had been translated, and labored to persuade him concerning the Gospel of Jesus Christ, which was now about to be revealed in its fulness. He was not, however, very easily persuaded of these things, but after much inquiry and explanation he retired to the woods, in order that by secret and fervent prayer he might obtain of a merciful God, wisdom to enable him to judge for himself. The result was that he obtained revelation for himself.[2]

After Joseph and Oliver had led the way, on May 25, 1829, Samuel was the first person to be baptized for the remission of his sins in this dispensation. Following the baptism "Samuel was filled with the spirit of prophecy and praise. He uttered many sublime truths of which his mind up to that moment had never conceived."[3]

Samuel was not gullible. He did not rush into his conversion. He wanted to make sure that he knew enough about the restored gospel before he would agree to be baptized; but once he did, there was no retention problem with Samuel—there was no looking back.

A short time later, Samuel's name appeared as one of the Eight Witnesses of the Book of Mormon. He saw the plates. He touched them. He noted the careful workmanship on them. He knew and testified to his dying day that the plates were real—just as his brother Joseph had told him. He signed his name along with the seven others and testified to the world:

> Be it known unto all nations, kindreds, tongues, and people, unto whom this work shall come: That Joseph Smith, Jun., the translator of this work, has shown unto us the plates of which hath both been spoken, which have the appearance of gold; and as many of the leaves as the said Smith has translated we did handle with our hands; and we also saw the engravings thereon, all of which has the appearance of ancient work, and of curious workmanship. And this we bear record with words of soberness that the said Smith has shown unto us, for we have seen and hefted, and know of a surety that the said Smith has got the plates of which we have spoken. And we give our names unto the world, to witness unto the world that which we have seen. And we lie not, God bearing witness of it. (Book of Mormon, The Testimony of Eight Witnesses.)

On the historic date of April 6, 1830, about sixty people gathered at the Peter Whitmer home in Fayette, New York, to witness the formal organization of the Church of Jesus Christ in this dispensation. Samuel was again selected to be another "first" as he was designated one of the six charter members of the Church.

Presumably these six men signed a document required by state law. In Spanish, the word for signature is *firma*. I like that word even better in Spanish than its English equivalent because it comes from the Latin root *firmus*, which means "to strengthen, not yielding under pressure, solid, hard, not moved or shaken easily, fixed, stable, unchanging, resolute, constant, showing determination and steadfast in conviction."[4]

All these definitions characterize Samuel well because when he participated and voted in that sacred inaugural meeting as one of the first members of this newly organized Church, he took it very seriously. His word was literally as good as his bond. Similarly, when he signed the document testifying to the world that he, along with those seven others, had actually seen the plates from which the Book of Mormon had been translated, he was honor-bound by that *firma*, or signature, and he did not waver. He never sought to hide behind the "small print" or seek legal escape from obligation. He was not one ever to go back on that signature, which manifested what he actually had seen and that which he had committed himself to support. His life became a living testament and should be a faith-producing example to all of us.

Samuel Smith set an example of a missionary spirit we could all well follow as committed Latter-day Saints. The Church of Jesus Christ in ancient times was a missionary church, so it follows that in the restoration of that church in our day it too was to be a missionary church. The final commandment the resurrected Savior gave to his disciples just before ascending to His Father in Heaven was related to this missionary responsibility: "And he said unto them, Go ye into all the world, and preach the gospel to every creature. He that believeth and is baptized shall be saved; but he that believeth not shall be damned." (Mark 16:15–16.) That same basic charge has been given to the Church in this dispensation (see D&C 68:8).

Samuel knew that the message of the Restoration needed to be shared. I remember seeing years ago a painting by William H. Whitaker that made a significant impression on me. The painting pictured a solitary figure with a satchel in one hand and a book in the other trudging down what appears to be a muddy road. The painting represents Samuel, all alone, courageously leaving home, family, and loved ones to open this dispensation's missionary efforts.

It is significant that Samuel achieved another "first" in the history of the Church when he was called and set apart as a missionary. He began his mission in June of 1830.

There wasn't much of a temporal nature that Samuel took with him on this mission. He didn't have much money, if any, nor likely any more in his satchel than a few personal items, the rest of the space being occupied by as many copies of the newly published—and publicly boycotted—Book of Mormon as he could carry. As to spiritual things, Samuel carried with him all that was most necessary—a deep faith and an abiding testimony that Jesus was the Christ and that the Book of Mormon was literally another testament of this reality. In this lonely venture Samuel carved his place in history as he fulfilled his responsibility as the first formally called missionary in this dispensation of the fulness of times.

It was not merely a matter of stuffing a few copies of the Book of Mormon into a satchel and going out to share it with others who were anxious to accept it. Residents of the area around Palmyra—ministers of religion and a good share of the parishioners—had been encouraged, and many had agreed, to boycott the book in an effort to prevent it from selling. Thus it was not a benign atmosphere into which Samuel went. His brother Joseph had had his life threatened, and the entire Smith family had been vilified by the wagging tongues and scurrilous reports that spewed from the presses in the vicinity. Thus Samuel was entering a largely hostile world.

Nevertheless, he was willing to sacrifice his time and effort. He went, he began the appointed task of "opening his mouth" and proclaiming the good news that God really does live, and that the claims that Jesus is the resurrected Christ have been verified in modern times through actual revelation from God to a modern prophet.

Samuel's example can be a help to all of us in the area of overcoming "the fear of man" and in "opening our mouths" as we have been commanded. Note the following verses of scripture: "Open your mouths and they shall be filled, and you shall become even as Nephi of old, who journeyed from Jerusalem in the wilderness. Yea, open your mouths and spare not, and you shall be laden with sheaves upon your backs, for lo, I am with you. Yea, open your mouths and they shall be filled, saying: Repent, repent and prepare ye the way of the Lord." (D&C 33:8–10.)

For four years I had the privilege of serving as president of the Missionary Training Center in Provo, Utah. During that time I thought often of Samuel Harrison Smith as I saw the more than 58,000 missionaries who were beginning their preparation for their missions to carry the same message to the world. Now it is taught in more than thirty languages. They, the modern-day missionaries, like this younger brother of the Prophet Joseph, are willing to leave the comfort of their homes and families and go into what occasionally proves to be a somewhat inhospitable world. Like Samuel, they are willing to "open their mouths" and share the precious truths of the Book of Mormon and the restoration of the gospel.

In principle, the nature of a missionary call hasn't changed dramatically over all these years since Samuel's, other than the fact that there are now tens of thousands of companions sharing the same message. In Samuel's time he had to muster the courage and rise to the responsibility to start his mission alone, setting a precedent for all who would follow.

Samuel's valiant example helped me while I was serving as a missionary in Mexico and Central America during a time when the dominant church had great hold on the minds of people and many made us feel that we were not welcome among them. I remember the discouraging feeling of returning to our missionary apartment after a long day of rejections only to find a note attached to our door letting us know that we were not appreciated in the country and telling us that we should go home.

Samuel had experienced such feelings of discouragement long before any of us arrived in the mission field, and his experience, determination, and example were a great help to me. He may have felt disheartened because of the very few people who were willing to accept the book or his account of how it had been received and translated. However, most members of the Church have learned of the remarkable outcome of that first mission in terms of future leaders of the Church who were directly or indirectly influenced by its message— leaders such as President-to-be Brigham Young and Heber C. Kimball.

The record indicates that Samuel left a copy of the Book of Mormon with the Reverend John P. Greene who, at first, was not personally interested. As an evidence of his persistence, Samuel didn't give up easily. He called back three times. At the insistence of his wife, Reverend Greene finally read the Book of Mormon. Later both he and his wife were baptized.

Meanwhile Mrs. Greene's brother, Phineas Young, had earlier obtained a copy of the Book of Mormon from Samuel. He gave it to his brother Brigham, who later passed it along to his sister, Mrs. Murray, the mother of the wife of Heber C. Kimball. Thus we see the serial impact of just one copy of the Book of Mormon in bringing into the Church some of its most influential early leaders.

Have you ever wondered how the history of the Church may have been significantly altered had Samuel not had the courage and fortitude to launch out on that first missionary effort?

Someone said that the Lord is not as much concerned with our ability as with our *availability*. Samuel Smith strikes me as one of those good, solid, committed, regular members of the Church. One of his daughters wrote of her father: "His sisters and his mother have always been loud in their praise of him, his honesty and his good qualities in general. While not as brilliant as some of the rest of his brothers he had a logical turn of mind and many excellent qualities that lay hidden under the stress of circumstances."[5] He may not have had the talent or ability of his brothers Joseph or Hyrum, but he was there—he was available—and willing to serve when so many tasks of significance needed to be done.

I identify with such a man as Samuel Harrison Smith. He has been a great model to me personally. Because of such as he, it has been easier for me to "open my mouth" and come a little closer to being the kind of member missionary I know that I ought to be.

Samuel had other important personal traits and characteristics that I would like to emulate in my own life. Some of them have been described by his contemporaries. It would be marvelous if statements such as these could be made about each of us:

- Orson Hyde, a missionary companion, described Samuel as "a man of good faith and extreme integrity."[6]
- Don Carlos, Samuel's brother, described him as "faithful as the sun."[7]
- Samuel's mother also recorded that "Samuel was never censured by revelation, to my knowledge, for he always performed his missions faithfully, and his work was well approved."[8]
- Samuel's spirituality is made evident by a statement made by his mother, Lucy Mack Smith, when she alleged that "none of her sons had a greater gift of healing than Samuel."[9]
- President George Q. Cannon described Samuel as "a man of integrity and singleness and fixity of purpose."[10]
- George A. Smith, a cousin of Samuel H. Smith, said, "He possessed great strength and wonderful powers of endurance, and was very exemplary in all his habits."[11]

As another one of his "firsts," Samuel was a member of the initial high council called in 1834. Samuel's faithfulness and the integrity of his commitment are illustrated by the fact that during the time of apostasy in Kirtland, when some of the most prominent leaders were falling away, only three of that original high council remained faithful and were sustained. Samuel was one of them. Samuel later became its presiding officer.

Samuel's attributes of faithfulness, integrity, constancy, courage, and missionary zeal are all qualities we should strive to incorporate into our own lives.

We commemorate with love and admiration the martyrdom of the Prophet Joseph and his faithful brother Hyrum on 27 June 1844. We also thrill at the dedication of Elders John Taylor and Willard Richards, who risked their lives to be with the brothers at Carthage. One fact we may tend to overlook is that Samuel was also one of the early martyrs of the Church.

When Samuel heard that his brothers were imprisoned in Carthage, he knew that they were in extreme danger. One of his daughters later recorded that Samuel took a young fourteen-year-old boy and set out in a wagon from Nauvoo to Carthage but was turned back by members of the mob, who anticipated that some help might be coming to Joseph and Hyrum from Nauvoo. Samuel was prevented from continuing. His daughter described subsequent events as follows:

> He then returned home as quickly as possible, purchased a horse noted for its speed, and determined to reach his brothers in time to be of assistance to them, altho the hope seemed a forlorn one. He went unarmed, and as he again neared Carthage he met several people coming from there in great haste, among them a man and a woman in a buggy, of whom he asked what had happened, and received answer that the two Smiths had been killed by the mob. The terrible shock was too much for him, and for an instant he reeled in his saddle and they expected him to fall. Then as the necessity of immediate action flashed across his mind, he steadied himself, saying, "God help me! I must go to them," and he again pressed forward. The mob, expecting his return, and intent upon murder, were secreted in a thicket, and two men on horseback with rifles gave chase. As they emerged from the thicket, the man in the buggy gave a warning shout; my father, turning his head quickly, took in the situation at a

glance, and put his horse to its utmost speed, still keeping his course straight toward Carthage. His splendid horsemanship kept him somewhat out of the range of the bullets sent after him, the one passed thru the top of his hat. The chase was a long and exciting one, but he finally out-distanced them and rode into Carthage.[12]

Again, Samuel was there. Samuel's daughter mentions that her father was the first (another of those "firsts") to arrive at the jail following the Martyrdom.[13]

Along with a Mr. Hamilton, Samuel performed the gruesome task of removing his brothers' bodies to the hotel. The next day was hot and humid. With green branches covering his two brothers' bodies to help protect them from the heat, the grief-stricken Samuel, accompanied by Willard Richards and Mr. Hamilton, escorted the sad caravan back to Nauvoo. Upon arrival, the responsibility fell to Samuel as the first family member to attempt to console the others.

His mother, Lucy, records that after she had retired to her room following viewing the bodies of her murdered sons, Samuel said, "Mother, I have had a dreadful distress in my side ever since I was chased by the mob, and I think I have received some injury which is going to make me sick."[14] Greatly weakened due to fatigue, shock, and apparently some internal injuries he had suffered from the chase, he never recovered. Samuel Harrison Smith, at the young age of thirty-six, passed away on July 30, 1844, just over a month after the death of his brothers. Thus Samuel was a third victim of the Martyrdom. He was willing to sacrifice his all for his convictions.

In these tragic events, again Samuel was there at the very heart of the most important happenings of the time. Samuel's reliability, constancy, unwavering faith, commitment, and courage make him one of the truly outstanding heroes of the Restoration.

NOTES

1. Lucy Mack Smith, *History of Joseph Smith* (Salt Lake City: Bookcraft, 1956), pp. 82–83.

2. *History of the Church* 1:44.

3. George Q. Cannon, *Life of Joseph Smith the Prophet* (Salt Lake City: Deseret Book, 1986), p. 63.

4. See *Webster's New World Dictionary of the English Language*.

5. Mary B. Norman to Sue Beattie, quoted in Dean Jarman, "The Life and Contributions of Samuel Harrison Smith" (master's thesis, Brigham Young University, 1961, p. 108; punctuation altered).

6. *Millennial Star,* December 3, 1864, p. 774.

7. Ruby K. Smith, *Mary Bailey* (Salt Lake City: Deseret Book, 1954), p. 56.

8. *History of Joseph Smith,* p. 210.

9. Ruby K. Smith, *Mary Bailey,* p. 96.

10. George Q. Cannon, *Life of Joseph Smith the Prophet,* p. 63.

11. Journal History, May 11, 1870, Church Historical Department.

12. Mary B. S. Norman, "Samuel Harrison Smith," Church Historical Department.

13. See letter written to Wm. Smith from H. Herringshaw, August 28, 1844, published in *The Prophet,* September 21, 1844.

14. *History of Joseph Smith,* p. 325.

14

Elder Spencer J. Condie

Lorenzo Snow

Lorenzo Snow was born on April 3, 1814, in the rugged frontier of eastern Ohio. Just as Joseph Smith's parents had been influenced by various circumstances to settle near the Hill Cumorah, Lorenzo's parents had moved from Massachusetts to Mantua, less than twenty-five miles from Kirtland. The Snows, like the Smiths, were very religious people, and though they were Baptists they were very open-minded in entertaining divergent views of the various religions of the day. Thus it was not surprising that in 1831 the Snow family learned of the truths of the restored gospel and that Lorenzo's mother and sister Leonora responded positively and were baptized. In 1835 Lorenzo's sister Eliza R. was baptized, but Lorenzo was not quite ready.[1]

At age twenty-one he decided to attend the Oberlin Collegiate Institute, and while en route to the college he met David W. Patten, a young Apostle who was proselyting in the area and who planted the seeds of conversion in Lorenzo's heart and mind. After a brief stint at Oberlin, Lorenzo accepted Eliza's invitation for him to study at the Hebrew school in Kirtland, where one of his classmates would be Joseph Smith.

In June of 1836 Lorenzo was baptized, but he was somewhat disconcerted that after his baptism he felt no particular change in himself. A few weeks later he secreted himself in the woods surrounding Kirtland and began to pray. Immediately he felt an undeniable manifestation of the Spirit of God, which was repeated on many subsequent occasions and served to fortify an unshakable testimony throughout his life.

In the spring of 1837 Lorenzo was called to serve his first mission, traveling without purse or scrip throughout Ohio. Returning to Mantua, he baptized many of his friends of early youth. After going home to Kirtland for a short time, the next year he embarked on another mission, to southern Missouri and part of Kentucky. He humbly confessed that his ability to expound the gospel had been richly aided by the Holy Ghost on many occasions. At the conclusion of this mission in 1839 Lorenzo obtained employment as a schoolteacher in Shalersville, Ohio, where he demonstrated his skills as a very able teacher.

About two weeks before Lorenzo's baptism in 1836 he had attended a very inspirational meeting in Kirtland in which Joseph Smith Sr., as Patriarch to the Church, had pronounced several impressive blessings upon various members of the Church. After the meeting Lorenzo was introduced to Father Smith, who predicted that Lorenzo would soon join the Church and that "you will become as great as you can possibly wish—EVEN AS GREAT AS GOD, and you cannot wish to be greater."[2]

This lofty thought was mulled about in Lorenzo's heart and mind for nearly four years. Then, in the spring of 1840, while Lorenzo was listening to Elder H. G. Sherwood expound upon the Lord's parable of the husbandman who hired servants at various hours of the day to labor in his vineyard, an inspired couplet was revealed to him:

> As man now is, God once was:
> As God now is, man may be.[3]

After the passage of considerable time, Lorenzo eventually discussed this profound spiritual insight with Brigham Young, President of the Twelve, who said: "Brother Snow, that is a new doctrine; if true, it has been revealed to you for your own private information, and will be taught in due time by the Prophet to the Church; till then I advise you to lay it upon the shelf and say no more about it."[4] Three years later the Prophet Joseph Smith confirmed that this doctrine was true.[5]

In May of 1840 Elder Snow was on his way to serve another mission, this time to England. In Manchester, aided by the Spirit,

Lorenzo discussed the gospel freely and several people were converted and baptized. In February of 1841 he was called by President Heber C. Kimball to oversee the work of the Church in London.

While in England Lorenzo wrote and published a pamphlet entitled "The Only Way to Be Saved," with an edition of five thousand copies. He was later called to serve as a counselor to the president of the British Mission, Thomas Ward. In January of 1843 he left Liverpool for home. During the homeward voyage Lorenzo exercised the priesthood in restoring a critically ill young ship's steward to full health. Subsequently several of the ship's crew members were baptized into the Church.

After returning home to Nauvoo, Lorenzo was appointed to be a captain in the Nauvoo Legion, and he also renewed his career as a schoolteacher in the tiny community of Lima just south of Nauvoo.

In 1843 the Prophet introduced the principle of plural marriage to Lorenzo after he returned home from England, but it was almost two years before Lorenzo, at age thirty-one, summoned the courage to marry four women the same day in the Nauvoo Temple in 1845. These first four wives were Mary Adaline Goddard, Charlotte Squires, Harriet Amelia Squires, and Sarah Ann Prichard.

Lorenzo had survived the tumultuous times in Kirtland during the early days of his conversion, and now he was called upon to weather the persecution in Nauvoo and the ultimate martyrdom of his beloved friends Joseph and Hyrum. In February 1846 his family crossed the Mississippi River, and by the end of April they had traveled a mere 145 miles. In May they reached a newly established settlement that became known as Mount Pisgah. Here Lorenzo became extremely ill, but through the power of the priesthood he was once again restored to complete health. It was at Pisgah that his wives Charlotte, Adaline, and Sarah Ann each gave birth to a baby girl, but, alas, Charlotte's baby died in early infancy. Thus the Snow family, notwithstanding their righteous devotion, shared the hardships and heartbreaks that became the refining fire to all the pioneers.

In the early spring of 1848 Brigham Young called the Snow family to come to the Salt Lake Valley. On February 12, 1849, Lorenzo was called to become a member of the Quorum of the Twelve Apostles, and in October of that same year he was called to serve a fourth mission, this time to Italy. Joseph Toronto, of Italian ancestry, was assigned to be his companion.

Elder Snow was prompted by the Spirit to commence his labors in the northern Alpine region of Italy. It was there that he wrote his second pamphlet, "The Voice of Joseph." Lorenzo grew somewhat impatient at the lack of apparent progress he and his companion had experienced during the early weeks of their mission, but on September 7, 1850, an opportunity presented itself for them to manifest the power of the Lord. The three-year-old son of their landlord became gravely ill, and his father solemnly whispered, "He dies! he dies!"

The next day Elder Snow and his companion Elder Stenhouse spent the day fasting and then retired to a nearby mountain to implore the Lord's help. Lorenzo recorded, "I know not of any sacrifice which I can possibly make, that I am not willing to offer, that the Lord might grant our requests."[6]

Upon returning to their place of lodging they administered to the dying little boy, and within a few hours he was much better. The next day the young lad needed no more special care, and after his mother expressed her joy and gratitude to the elders Lorenzo responded, "The God of heaven has done this for you."

On September 18 Elder Jabez Woodward joined the other elders in Italy, and the following day Elders Snow, Stenhouse, Toronto, and Woodward ascended a mountain near LaTour, expressed their gratitude for their many blessings, and prayed for the Lord to honor the sacrifices they had made in leaving their loved ones to proclaim the gospel. In that lofty setting these four brethren organized the Church in Italy, and Lorenzo subsequently recorded that "from that day opportunities began to occur for proclaiming our message."[7]

Somewhat later Elder Snow left Italy for London to assist in the translation and publication of the Book of Mormon in Italian. After eleven months in England he returned to Italy, taking with him four hundred pages of the Book of Mormon that had been translated. A Professor Reta, a man of letters, reviewed the Italian translation and certified it to be bona fide.

Upon Lorenzo's returning home from his mission in the summer of 1852 his lovely wife Charlotte was missing, having died during his long absence. His sister Eliza recorded that as Lorenzo was expressing his willingness to make any sacrifice in order to further the cause of truth in far-off Italy, "the Lord removed, by the hand of death, from my brother's family circle, one of the loveliest of women."[8]

After his lengthy absence, Lorenzo set about building a two-story adobe home. Shortly thereafter he was elected a member of the territorial legislature and was also appointed to the board of regents of the University of Deseret, the forerunner of the University of Utah. It was also during this period that he organized "The Polysophical Society," whose members met in his new home to discuss a wide variety of intellectual subjects, to share great literature, and to be entertained and inspired by good music. This humble effort became the seedbed of the Mutual Improvement Association several years later.

In April of 1853 the cornerstones of the Salt Lake Temple were laid, and in the fall of that year Elder Snow was called to preside over the Saints in Box Elder County. Again it was necessary to build another home, and not long afterward he once again initiated discussions, lectures, and dramatic presentations in his home in Brigham City. During those early days Elder Snow served not only as a member of the Twelve but also as the stake president. He gained the love, respect, and confidence of the Saints with his assertive, visionary leadership.

In 1864 Elder Snow and Elder Ezra T. Benson were sent by the First Presidency to the Sandwich Islands (Hawaii) to resolve some local concerns within the Church. On March 31 several of the elders attempted a landing at Lahaina's beach in the wake of an extremely turbulent surf that capsized their boat, throwing its passengers into the sea. One by one the other passengers bobbed to the surface and were rescued by boats launched by natives who had watched the disaster from the shore. After being brought to shore Lorenzo's body remained lifeless for several minutes until the elders felt impressed to use mouth-to-mouth resuscitation to revive him, a practice which did not become widely known until a century later.

Upon returning from the Sandwich Islands to Brigham City, Elder Snow demonstrated his extraordinary gifts and abilities as a leader in organizing about three dozen varying cooperative ventures that eventually became known as the Brigham City Mercantile and Manufacturing Association. These cooperative ventures included a tannery, a wool factory, sawmills, a furniture factory, an adobe brick factory, several farms with dairy herds, sheep and pigs, orchards, vineyards, greenhouses, and nurseries, and even the planting of mulberry trees to provide food for silkworms for the manufacture of silk. President Brigham Young shared the observation that "up there in Brigham City Brother Snow has led the people along, and got them into the United Order without their knowing it."[9]

In 1872 Elder Snow was invited to accompany President George A. Smith, a Counselor to President Brigham Young, on a pilgrimage to the Holy Land. Walking where Jesus had walked had a profound and lasting influence on the remainder of Elder Snow's ministry.

Upon returning home Elder Snow learned that he had been sustained as a member of the First Presidency on April 4, 1873 to be a Counselor to President Brigham Young and that he would continue to serve as the president of the Box Elder Stake in Brigham City. In June of 1874 President Young officially organized the Brigham City cooperatives into a branch of the united order. In 1876 President Snow started the construction of the handsome Box Elder Tabernacle, which stands today as a beautiful monument to the devotion of the faithful Saints of that area.

In the spring of 1877 President Snow was invited to St. George to attend the dedication of the St. George Temple on April 6. Four months later, on August 18, 1877, President Brigham Young traveled to Brigham City, where he extended an honorable release to President Snow as stake president. Lorenzo's son, Oliver G. Snow, was sustained to replace him. Less than two weeks later President Young passed away and Lorenzo was automatically released as a Counselor in the First Presidency. This release allowed Elder Snow an opportunity to initiate missionary work among the Nez Perce Indians of northern Idaho, the Umatilla of eastern Washington, the Blackfoot and Shoshones of eastern Idaho, and the Arapahos of Wyoming.[10]

By 1885 U.S. marshals, intent on arresting any man involved in a polygamous marriage, disrupted the quiet family lives within many a Latter-day Saint community. Brigham City was no exception. In November of 1885 Lorenzo was arrested for unlawful cohabitation, and after three trials he was convicted and began his imprisonment on March 12, 1886, at seventy-two years of age. Prison cells were only five by seven feet and were each occupied by two men. Eleven months later, after surviving the meager food and crowded conditions, Elder Snow was released from prison on February 8, 1887.

On his first Sunday home he addressed a congregation in the Salt Lake Tabernacle, selecting for his text the words of the Apostle Paul:

"Who shall separate us from the love of Christ? shall tribulation, or distress, or persecution, or famine, or nakedness, or peril, or sword?" (Romans 8:35.)

Because Elder Snow was immune to further prosecution for polygamy, President John Taylor assigned him to preside at the general conference of the Church scheduled to take place in Provo on April 6, 1887. President Taylor passed away four months later, on July 25, 1887, and President Wilford Woodruff became the President of the Church. President Woodruff was not immune to prosecution, as was President Snow, thus President Snow, as President of the Quorum of the Twelve, officiated at many public functions, such as the dedication of the Manti Temple on May 21, 1888.

Throughout his life it was apparent that President Snow had the spiritual gift to heal and to be healed. In March of 1891 his adolescent niece, Ella Jensen, became very seriously ill for a period of several weeks. One day, as her condition worsened, and sensing that death was near, young Ella bade her loved ones farewell, and then suddenly her pulse stopped. Her father left to inform President Snow of his niece's passing, and about two hours later President Snow entered the home where Ella's body was being prepared for burial. President Snow requested some consecrated oil and anointed and administered to Ella, commanding her to come back to complete her mission on earth. He then left the house. About an hour later Ella revived. She lived to the ripe old age of eighty-six.[11]

On April 6, 1893, the majestic Salt Lake Temple was dedicated, and Lorenzo Snow was called to serve as the first temple president. A few years later this loving father wrote the following to his missionary son, LeRoi, in Germany: "I knew it to be the will of the Lord that I should set my household in order; unite the members of my family that they may be a worthy example to the families of Israel." President Snow's love and affection extended to each and every one of his forty-one children born to his nine wives.[12]

Throughout the 1890s the Church was faced with seemingly insurmountable financial challenges, largely resulting from the earlier confiscation and discorporation of Church-owned properties by the U.S. government in compliance with the provisions of the Edmunds-Tucker Act, which sought to eradicate the practice of polygamy. Following the Manifesto of 1890, the Church's personal property was returned, but it was not until 1896 that the Church received title to real property that had been previously impounded.[13] These internal troubles were compounded by an economic depression during the 1890s. Worn weary by the increasing indebtedness of the Church, President Wilford Woodruff passed away on September 2, 1898.

After receiving word of President Woodruff's death, President Snow retired to the Salt Lake Temple, where he pleaded with the Lord to reveal His divine will. Upon concluding his prayer he waited for an immediate answer, but none seemed to be forthcoming. Some time later his granddaughter Allie Young Pond gave the following account:

> One evening while I was visiting Grandpa Snow in his room in the Salt Lake Temple, I remained until the door-keepers had gone and the night-watchmen had not yet come in, so grand-pa said he would take me to the main front entrance and let me out that way. He got his bunch of keys from his dresser. After we left his room and while we were still in the large corridor leading into the celestial room, I was walking several steps ahead of grand-pa when he stopped me and said: "Wait a moment, Allie, I want to tell you something. It was right here that the Lord Jesus Christ appeared to me at the time of the death of President Woodruff. He instructed me to go right ahead and reorganize the First Presidency of the Church at once and not wait as had been done after the death of the previous presidents, and that I was to succeed President Woodruff."
>
> Then grand-pa came a step nearer and held out his left hand and said: "He stood right here, about three feet above the floor. It looked as though He stood on a plate of solid gold."
>
> Grand-pa told me what a glorious personage the Savior is and described His hands, feet, countenance and beautiful white robes, all of which were of such a glory of whiteness and brightness that he could hardly gaze upon Him.[14]

On September 13 President Snow was sustained as the President of the Church with George Q. Cannon and Joseph F. Smith as Counselors. The most critical challenge facing the new presidency was the Church's financial crisis. Shortly after April conference in 1899, President Snow felt strongly impressed to meet with the Saints in St. George, although the specific purpose for such a meeting was not clear to him. The next month he left for southern Utah by train on May 15 with an entourage including his Second Counselor President Joseph F. Smith and a few other General Authorities and their wives.

The Saints who met in the St. George Tabernacle on May 17 had come with great anticipation of listening to their beloved prophet's voice. President Snow's son LeRoi served as a scribe for the meeting and reported the following:

> Complete stillness filled the room. I shall never forget the thrill as long as I live. When he commenced to speak again his voice strengthened and the inspiration of God seemed to come over him, as well as over the entire assembly. His eyes seemed to brighten and his countenance to shine. He was filled with unusual power. Then he revealed to the Latter-day Saints the vision that was before him.
>   . . . He told them that he could see, as he had never realized before, how the law of tithing had been neglected by the people. . . . President Snow said: "The word of the Lord is: The time has now come for every Latter-day Saint, who calculates to be prepared for the future and to hold his feet strong upon a proper foundation, to do the will of the Lord and to pay his tithing in full. That is the word of the Lord to you, and it will be the word of the Lord to every settlement throughout the land of Zion."[15]

On the trip home, President Snow met with the Saints in two dozen special meetings in sixteen different communities along the way emphasizing anew the importance of the law of tithing.[16] On July 2, 1899, a special solemn assembly was held in the Salt Lake Temple with all twenty-six of the General Authorities present and with representatives from all the stakes of the Church. Once again, in that spiritual setting, the law of tithing was the focal point of the addresses and instruction given to priesthood leaders.[17]

President Snow, though in his eighty-sixth year, continued attending stake conferences throughout Utah and southern Idaho inviting the Saints to keep the commandments of God and to pay an honest tithe. By the turn of the century the Church was attaining financial security, and the vistas of this great prophet turned ever outward. In 1901 Elder Heber J. Grant was called to preside over a new mission in Japan. President Snow indicated that the Apostles and the Seventies were to "warn the nations of the earth and prepare the world for the coming of the Savior."[18]

Anticipating the needs of a growing church, he counseled stake presidencies that "the time is coming when you will not have to call and depend so much upon the Twelve Apostles. They will be directed in other channels, and I want you to distinctly understand it; and do not seek to throw responsibilities that belong to you upon these Twelve Apostles and upon the Seventies. . . .[19] The presidents of these fifty stakes . . . should regard [the Saints] as their own family, as their sons and daughters; and take as deep an interest in them as they ought to take in their own wives and children."[20]

Shortly after October conference, the evening of October 8, eighty-eight-year-old President Snow became critically ill, and his condition worsened the following day. On the afternoon of October 10, 1901, this gentle spiritual giant passed on to his eternal reward. At his funeral three days later the Tabernacle was filled to capacity with Saints of the Most High who came to pay their last respects and to show their tender love for a prophet who challenged them to learn to sacrifice that they might become more like Him who sacrificed His Only Begotten Son. On the podium of the Tabernacle was a particularly beautiful floral tribute with the words: "As God Is Man May Be."[21]

NOTES

1. See Eliza R. Snow Smith, *Biography and Family Record of Lorenzo Snow* (Salt Lake City: Deseret News Co., 1884), pp. 4–6.

2. Smith, p. 10.

3. Smith, p. 46.

4. Orson F. Whitney, "Lives of our Leaders—The Apostles: Lorenzo Snow," *Juvenile Instructor,* January 1, 1900, p. 4.

5. Thomas C. Romney, *The Life of Lorenzo Snow* (Salt Lake City: Deseret News Press, 1955), p. 47.

6. Lorenzo Snow to Brigham Young, November 1, 1850, as quoted in Smith, p. 129.

7. Ibid., p. 133.

8. Ibid., p. 233.

9. In *Journal of Discourses* 19:347.

10. Francis M. Gibbons, *Lorenzo Snow: Spiritual Giant, Prophet of God* (Salt Lake City: Deseret Book, 1982), pp. 168–69.

11. See LeRoi C. Snow, "Raised from the Dead," *Improvement Era,* September, 1929, pp. 881–86; October 1929, pp. 972–80.

12. Gibbons, pp. 204–9.

13. See Leonard J. Arrington, *Great Basin Kingdom: An Economic History*

of the Latter-day Saints, 1830–1900. (Cambridge: Harvard University Press, 1958), pp. 245–51, 400–401.

14. LeRoi C. Snow, "An Experience of My Father's," *Improvement Era,* September 1933, p. 677.

15. LeRoi C. Snow, "The Lord's Way Out of Bondage," *Improvement Era,* July 1938, p. 439.

16. E. J. Bell, "The Windows of Heaven Revisited: The 1899 Tithing Reformation," *Journal of Mormon History,* vol. 20, no. 1, Spring 1994, p. 75.

17. Bell, p. 77.

18. Joseph F. Smith, "The Last Days of President Snow," *Juvenile Instructor,* November 15, 1901, p. 690.

19. Lorenzo Snow, Conference Report, October 6, 1901, p. 61.

20. Snow, pp. 60–61.

21. "Funeral of President Lorenzo Snow," Conference Report, October 13, 1901, p. 86.

15

Elder L. Tom Perry

John Taylor
A Man of Eloquence

John Taylor was the third President of The Church of Jesus Christ of Latter-day Saints. "By birth, President Taylor was an Englishman, and he possessed all the finest characteristics of that people; honest, industrious, loving liberty within truth and right living."[1]

He was born on the first day of November 1808 in Milnthorpe, Westmorland, England. His father was James Taylor and his mother's maiden name was Agnes Taylor. (As far as we know, they were not related.) The Taylors had ten children—eight sons and two daughters. Three children died while young. When Edward, the eldest son, died at age twenty-two, John, the second son, stood next to the head of the family, his father.

"When John was eleven years of age his parents settled on a small estate which they had inherited, near the town of Hale, England. At fourteen there was some discussion in the family as to what trade the boy should learn now that he was approaching young manhood." They decided he should learn the trade of cooper. Later he went to Penrith and added the trade of wood turning. "Here he remained from his fifteenth to his twentieth year, laboring diligently with his hands until he had mastered his task."[2] A Bible reader who prayed frequently, at the age of seventeen he became a Methodist preacher.

In the year 1830, . . . the parents of John Taylor, together with his brothers and sisters, took a ship at Liverpool and sailed for Upper

Canada. John . . . was left in England to settle affairs and dispose of some of his father's property. In about two years he completed the business entrusted to him and followed them.[3]

While crossing the British channel the ship he sailed in encountered severe storms, which lasted a number of days. He saw several ships wrecked in that storm, and the captain and officers of his own ship expected hourly that she would go down. But not so with our young immigrant. The voice of the Spirit was still saying within him, "You must yet go to America and preach the gospel." "So confident was I of my destiny" he remarks, "that I went on deck at midnight, and amidst the raging elements felt as calm as though I was sitting in a parlor at home. I believed I should reach America and perform my work."[4]

In studying the life of John Taylor we find there are three words that typify the characteristics of this great man. They are *converted, loyal,* and *articulate.* Let us look at experiences in his life that illustrate these three words.

CONVERSION

First, the word *conversion.* The story of the conversion of John Taylor and his wife, Leonora, begins with a missionary journey of Parley P. Pratt in April of 1836. Heber C. Kimball had prophesied that Brother Pratt should go to Upper Canada, even to the city of Toronto. There he would find people prepared for the fulness of the gospel. He would organize a branch of the Church among them that would spread into the regions round about, and many would be brought to a knowledge of the truth and be filled with joy.[5] Such a pronouncement by Elder Kimball impelled Elder Pratt to leave his sick wife, a partially completed home, and a mountain of debt in Kirtland to undertake the mission to Upper Canada.

At the outset he was uncertain how he should proceed. Penniless, he started off with Moses Nickerson, who bore his expenses as far as Niagara Falls, where their paths separated. Very shortly Elder Pratt met a stranger who gave him ten dollars and a letter of introduction to John Taylor, whom the man knew. When Elder Pratt arrived in

Toronto, he sought out the home of John Taylor. Here he found a handsome man, six foot tall, weighing about 180 pounds, who greeted Elder Pratt with a delightful accent that marked him as a native from northern England. The greeting was warm until Elder Pratt let him know that he was on a mission for the Mormon church. John Taylor then turned cool. During his service as a preacher in the Methodist Church he had heard derogatory reports about the new American sect and had closed his mind to it. John Taylor showed no interest in hearing the visitor's message, nor in helping him find lodging or a place in which to hold a meeting.

Disappointed at this rebuff, Elder Pratt checked into a public house and the next day canvassed the community trying to find accommodations for a public meeting. His efforts seemed fruitless. All doors were closed to him until a Mrs. Walton, a friend of the Taylors, allowed him to use her parlor for the meeting. Thus Elder Pratt began to proselytize among the group of Bible students in Toronto. John Taylor was one of the leaders of this group, most of whom had begun to question the tenets and practices of their church because these did not conform to biblical teachings.

Overcoming his initial reluctance to listen to Elder Pratt, John Taylor began attending the meetings held at Mrs. Walton's home as well as other homes where the visitor was invited to come and speak. Elder Pratt's skill and knowledge of the scriptures impressed John Taylor. To facilitate his study, he wrote down eight sermons that Elder Pratt had delivered and carefully compared them to the Bible. He also reviewed evidences of the authenticity of the Book of Mormon and the Doctrine and Covenants. Commenting later on these studies, the investigator said, "I made a regular business of it for three weeks . . . and followed Brother Parley from place to place."[6] Finally convinced of the truthfulness of what they had been hearing, both John and Leonora Taylor were baptized into The Church of Jesus Christ of Latter-day Saints on May 9, 1836. At the twilight of his life, John Taylor said of his conversion: "I have never doubted any principle of Mormonism since."[7] He became a leader of the newly formed branches in the Upper Canada regions.

The following spring John traveled to Church headquarters in Kirtland. The main purpose of the trip was for John to meet and receive counsel from the head of the Church, Joseph Smith. He was richly rewarded for his aim, as he not only met and received counsel from the young prophet but also was entertained in the Smith home. Such an intimate association with a man who conversed with Deity filled the new convert with a sense of awe that did not abate throughout his life.

In Kirtland, however, he found a spirit of darkness. The economic panic that swept through the country in 1837 caused hundreds of bank failures, including that of the Kirtland Safety Society, which had been organized by the Prophet and his associates. Many who lost money through this failure blamed the Prophet for it. Even Parley P. Pratt succumbed to the uproar in a measure and began to criticize and condemn Joseph Smith. When Elder Pratt expressed such feelings to John Taylor, he was sobered by the perceptive answer: "If the work was true six months ago, it is true today; if Joseph Smith was then a prophet, he is now a prophet."[8]

That strong witness permeated the life of John Taylor. His loyalty to the Church was challenged many times. He was required to make great sacrifices, suffering tribulation and persecution because of the faith he had embraced. In the fall of 1837 he received word from the Prophet that he should wind up his affairs in Canada and join the main body of Saints in Missouri. He gave up his comfortable home and his business affairs in Toronto and made the trip in the winter to Missouri.

He was called to be an Apostle, and on the evening of December 19, 1838, he was ordained to that calling under the hands of Brigham Young and Heber C. Kimball. Shortly afterwards, with his wife and family he was forced to flee eastward to the new gathering place of the Saints in Illinois. For a time he remained in Quincy. After the Prophet was released from prison in Missouri and assumed leadership in the city of Nauvoo, Elder Taylor and his family moved to that location. Not being able to find suitable living quarters, he crossed over the Mississippi River to the Iowa side and moved into one room of an old military barracks.

He was living in these humble circumstances when he was called to go to England on a mission, for which he departed in August 1839. He labored there as a missionary until April of 1841. "Prior to leaving England he published a report of his labors in the *Millennial Star*," a part of which reads:

I feel to rejoice before God that He has blessed my humble endeavors to promote His cause and Kingdom and for all the blessings I have received from this island; for although I have traveled 5,000 miles without purse or scrip, besides traveling so far in this country on railroads, coaches, steamboats, wagons, on horseback, and almost every way, and been amongst strangers in strange lands, I have never for once been at a loss for either money, clothes, friends or a home, from that day until now; neither have I ever asked a person for a far-thing. Thus I have proved the Lord, and I know that He is according to His word. And now as I am going away, I bear testimony that this work is of God—that He has spoken from the heavens—that Joseph Smith is a Prophet of the Lord—that the Book of Mormon is true; and I know that this work will roll on until "the kingdoms of this world become the Kingdoms of our God and his Christ."[9]

Upon arriving in Nauvoo, he found his family in rather depressing conditions. His wife was seriously ill, but through his faith and prayers and the prayers of others Leonora regained her strength. Soon he was able to build a better home for his family. A store, a printing office, and large barn were also erected; and he "had a farm on 106 acres, another 80 acres, forty of which were under cultivation, and forty in timber."[10]

But peace was not to come to this man and his family. After the death of the Prophet, persecution intensified and he was again forced to leave the comforts of his surroundings. On February 16, 1846, John Taylor and his family left Nauvoo, arriving at Winter Quarters on July 14. From there he and two other Apostles were sent on a special, short mission to England. Returning the following April, he remained for a time in Winter Quarters; then in June 1847 the family left for the Salt Lake Valley, with Elders Taylor and Parley P. Pratt presiding over the large group of 1,533 people. The party arrived in the Salt Lake Valley on October 5, 1847. Again Elder Taylor started the process of making a home for his family and attending to his responsibilities as a leader in the Church.

"At the October conference in 1849, John Taylor was called by the First Presidency to introduce the Gospel to the people of France." Arriving in Liverpool on May 27 of 1850, he remained in England for a few weeks and then went to France to open up the mission there. While he was there he made arrangements for publication of the Book of Mormon in the French language. In August, 1851, Elder Taylor went to Hamburg, Germany, where he was successful in getting the Book of Mormon translated into the German language.[11]

After nearly three years in Europe he returned again to Utah, making another weary trip across the plains. "Elder Taylor was now anxious to look after his personal affairs and improve his financial condition, after his long absence in Europe."[12] The First Presidency, however, having great confidence in his ability as a missionary, did not permit him to remain home very long. "In the summer of 1854 he was again sent east to 'preside over the Church in the eastern states,'"[13] from which he returned to Utah in August of 1857. For the next twenty years after arriving home from that mission he fulfilled various assignments, "both civil and religious, confined mostly to the valleys of the mountains."[14] He was willing to give up personal comforts time and time again under great stress and trials. He was true to his conversion to the Church of Jesus Christ and was loyal to it to the end of his days.

LOYALTY

The second word I think of when I hear the name of John Taylor is *loyalty*. It is interesting how the Lord prepares the leadership of the Church in every age that the gospel is on the earth. No two men were more loyal and strong in their defense of the Prophet Joseph Smith than were Brigham Young and John Taylor. A strong personal relationship developed between these two extraordinary men who were so much alike in some ways and yet so different. The similarities were on a spiritual level. The differences can be traced chiefly to their earthly backgrounds. Both Brigham Young and John Taylor were intelligent, strong-minded men who had joined the Church in their maturity, and whose conversion had been accompanied by a powerful spiritual manifestation. Both were staunchly loyal to the Prophet Joseph Smith and never deviated from his instructions and example, even after the Prophet's death. Both of them experienced an intellectual as well as a spiritual conversion and therefore were committed to the doctrines of the Church, including the doctrines of the gathering and the building up of the kingdom of God on earth.

But this pair came from widely differing backgrounds that affected their outlook and perceptions and gave balance to the early leadership of the Church. Elder Young spent his infancy, childhood, and young adulthood in the rural communities of Vermont and New York, which were comparatively unknown and undistinguished. These communities grew from untamed and uncultivated forest lands; therefore the first task of a farmer before he could apply his agricultural skills was to clear the land of trees, stumps, boulders, and underbrush. This tremendous work monopolized practically all the time of the farmer and his family. They were so preoccupied with the business of wresting a living from the soil that there was little time for cultural or intellectual pursuits, even if such opportunities had been available to them. Brigham Young grew up under such conditions and learned how to put his energies into physical demands that brought him not only a deep understanding of God's workings with the land but also the skill to tame the wild environment.

John Taylor, on the other hand, was born in England—a country that had been under cultivation for hundreds of years. Nearby were large commercial centers that over the centuries had acquired the jewels of civilization—libraries, museums, theaters, universities. This is the environment in which John Taylor had his early beginnings.

The two different environments in which Brigham Young and John Taylor were reared to maturity were calculated to prepare one to tame the wilderness and the other to combat the intellectual enemies of the Church with Latter-day Saint doctrine and philosophies in well-honed sentences and instruction. Each man was recognized and honored by the other for his special roles and abilities. Brigham Young, for instance, declared John Taylor to be the most powerful editor and writer in the Church, and at the general conference following Brigham Young's death Elder Taylor said of his departed leader, "Brigham Young needs no factitious aid to perpetuate his memory; his labors have been exhibited during the last forty-five years in his preaching, in his writing, in his counsels, in the wisdom and intelligence he has displayed, in . . . the building of cities throughout the length and breadth of this Territory."[15]

What a balance the Lord gave to His Church with these two early leaders in His kingdom!

John Taylor's strength, witness, conversion, and courage were illustrated by an event that occurred near Columbus, Ohio. A group of troublemakers, learning that he was scheduled to preach at a service there, decided to tar and feather him. Having heard about the plot, a few Church members went to John and urged him to cancel the meeting, for they lacked the strength to protect him. Expressing his thanks for their concern, Brother Taylor decided not to follow their counsel but to fulfill his assignment.

At the meeting, the English convert proceeded to lecture his audience about the blessings of freedom guaranteed in the American Constitution, about the valor of their forefathers in fighting for liberty, and about the yearnings of the downtrodden people around the world to live under the American flag. Having laid the groundwork, the artful speaker suddenly shifted his focus. "By the by," he said, "I have been informed that you purpose to tar and feather me, for my religious opinions. Is this the boon you have inherited from your fathers? Is this . . . your liberty?"

After letting the implications of these accusatory questions seep in, the speaker offered himself as a sacrifice for the liberty that they had enjoyed in the United States and for the faith he had in their religious freedom. He said: "Gentlemen, come on with your tar and feathers, your victim is ready; and ye shades of the venerable patriots, gaze upon the deeds of your degenerate sons! Come on, gentlemen! Come on, I say. I am ready."[16]

The would-be tormentors made no move. Instead they remained quiet and attentive while for three hours the speaker expounded on the doctrines of Mormonism.

His loyalty to the Prophet lasted right up until the final hours before Joseph Smith was murdered, he himself being wounded by the mob at that sad hour in the history of the Church and of America.

ARTICULATION

The third word I associate with John Taylor is *articulate*. The Prophet Joseph Smith found him to be intelligent, articulate, and a tough-minded leader in building the kingdom of our Father in Heaven. He was always given difficult assignments to articulate the gospel of our Lord and Savior, and he was able to subdue the false doctrines that were being published against the early Church. John Taylor received a difficult assignment from Brigham Young when he was given a special calling to go to New York City to organize and publish a newspaper whose purpose would be to present the doctrines and practices of the Church in a manner that would neutralize the groundswell of anti-Mormon feeling that had been mounting over the years. His confidence in the beliefs of the Church he had embraced caused him to establish his headquarters on the corner of Nassau and Ann Streets, between the offices of the city's media goliaths, the *New York Herald* and the *Tribune*. Titled *The Mormon*, this extraordinary little paper established its tone with the announcement of its policy in the first issue:

> We are Mormon, inside and outside, at home and abroad, in pub-
> lic and private, everywhere. We are so, however, from principle. We
> are such, not because we believe it to be more popular, lucrative, or
> honorable, (as the world has it); but because we believe it to be more
> true, more reasonable and scriptural, moral and philosophic; because
> we conscientiously believe that it is more calculated to promote the
> happiness and well being of humanity, in time, and throughout all
> eternity, than any other system which we have met with.[17]

His opening editorial brought abuse and criticism from almost every quarter. He went on to sketch for his readers the salient characteristics of a converted Mormon. He wrote: "He grasps at all truth, human and divine; he has no darling dogma to sustain or favorite creed to uphold; he has nothing to lose but error; nothing to gain but truth. He digs, labors, and searches for it as for hidden treasure; and while others are content with chaff and husks of straw, he seizes on the kernel, substance, the gist of all that is good, and clings to all that will ennoble and exalt the human family."[18]

His duties included not only the editing and publishing of the newspaper *The Mormon*, but also the heavy responsibility of presiding over the Eastern States Mission.

John Taylor had a dignified, impeccable style of speaking. His great gift and ability to communicate with the children of our Father in Heaven has given the Church much in gaining greater understanding of the mission of our Lord and Savior.

In addition to his great ability to communicate, he was skilled in the governing of the Saints according to the priesthood that had been restored. "He required bishops to hold weekly priesthood meetings in their wards, stake presidents to hold general priesthood meetings monthly in their respective stakes, and appointed quarterly conferences in all the stakes of Zion," and published "the dates of holding them for half a year in advance. . . . He personally attended as many of the quarterly conferences as he could" and sent the Twelve out where he could not go. "The results were a great spiritual awakening among the Saints" and more order established in the governing of the kingdom.[19]

With the great difficulties surrounding the Church during the early years of his administration, an order was issued for his arrest for the practice of polygamy. He was forced to go into seclusion and hence was found in public only a few times in his latter years. "He continued to direct the policies of the Church and from time to time issued Epistles addressed to the Saints. In a letter to his family, which had gathered in Salt Lake City to celebrate his seventy-eighth birthday on November 1, 1886, he did not complain of his exile." He wrote: "The protecting care of the Lord over me and my brethren has been very manifest since my absence from home, for which I feel to bless and praise His holy name. I always am very desirous to acknowledge His hand in all things, and I am very anxious that you should do the same. For to the Lord we are indebted for every blessing we enjoy, pertaining to this life, and the life which is to come."[20]

This was his last birthday message to his family. In the summer of 1887 his health began to fail, and he passed away peacefully at the home of Thomas F. Rouche in Kaysville, Utah, on July 25.

An article written for the *Deseret News* by his two counselors, George Q. Cannon and Joseph F. Smith, following his death, catches the spirit of this noble and great leader. They wrote:

> A faithful, devoted and fearless servant of God, the Church in his death has lost its most conspicuous and experienced leader. Steadfast to and immovable in truth, few men have ever lived who have manifest such integrity and such unflinching moral and physical courage as our beloved President who has just gone from us. He never knew the feeling of fear connected with the work of God. . . . The title of "Champion of Liberty," which he received at Nauvoo, was always felt to be most appropriate for him to bear.[21]

How blessed we are to have been taught by great prophets of God, each with his own unique abilities and experience. Each has delivered to us in his own way the fundamental doctrines and precepts we need to guide us through life and prepare us for the eternities to come. May we study their lives and apply in each of our own lives the principles they have taught.

NOTES

1. Preston Nibley, *The Presidents of the Church* (Salt Lake City: Deseret Book, 1941), p. 89.
2. Nibley, p. 90.
3. Nibley, p. 90.
4. B. H. Roberts, *The Life of John Taylor* (Salt Lake City: Bookcraft, 1963), pp. 28–29.
5. See Roberts, p. 35.
6. Roberts, p. 38.
7. Roberts, p. 38.
8. Roberts, p. 40.
9. Nibley, pp. 95–96.
10. Nibley, p. 100.
11. Nibley, p. 105.
12. Nibley, p. 106.
13. Nibley, p. 106.
14. Nibley, p. 109.
15. In *Journal of Discourses* 19:123.
16. Roberts, pp. 54–55.
17. *The Mormon*, February 17, 1855.
18. *The Mormon*, July 28, 1855.
19. Nibley, p. 116.
20. Nibley, pp. 117–18.
21. Nibley, pp. 119–20.

16

Elder Joseph B. Wirthlin

Newel K. Whitney
Faithful Steward,
Steadfast Saint

When Bishop Newel K. Whitney passed away in Salt Lake City on 23 September 1850 he was remembered in a *Deseret Weekly News* obituary as "one of the . . . most exemplary and useful members of the Church."[1] The tribute continues, describing Bishop Whitney as "a wise and able Counselor—. . . a thorough, straight-forward, business man," and concludes noting that "he has gone down to the grave, leaving a spotless name behind him, and thousands to mourn their loss of such a valuable man."[2]

In the small Kimball family cemetery, located in the center of the block immediately northeast of Temple Square in Salt Lake City, a sandstone obelisk atop a granite base marks the final resting place of Newel Kimball Whitney. The stone tablet honoring his name is found on the north side of the monument, opposite the tablet recounting the life of Heber C. Kimball.[3] In this peaceful place of quiet repose, one can ponder upon the good life of the man who served as the second ordained bishop of this dispensation and who was sustained as Presiding Bishop on 6 April 1847. I have always felt a certain closeness to Bishop Whitney. His life, as stated in his obituary, was truly "exemplary." All of us should strive to live as Newel K. Whitney did. We should live in such a way that when we pass from this mortal sphere we may leave a "spotless name behind [us]" and be remembered by those we have loved and served as wise, useful, and valuable.

Over the course of his fifty-five years Bishop Whitney passed through many days of triumph and trial. He was no stranger to both prosperity and adversity. As a skilled merchant he well understood the temporal principles of business and enterprise. He was an able provider for his family and a capable administrator in his many Church assignments. As a servant of the Lord, as one called to shepherd the flock and to "[search] after the poor to administer to their wants by humbling the rich and the proud" (D&C 84:112), he came to know, like the Savior he worshipped, "how to succor his people according to their infirmities" (Alma 7:12). As one who joined the Church in the first years of its history, he was subjected to all the persecution and forced relocations that tried and tempered those valiant pioneer Saints. To paraphrase the Apostle Paul, "Though he were a [bishop], yet learned he obedience by the things which he suffered" (Hebrews 5:8).

Newel K. Whitney was true to every stewardship entrusted to his care. He knew that the Lord requires "every steward to render an account of his stewardship, both in time and in eternity" (D&C 72:3), and he consistently and diligently magnified his office unto the Lord (see Jacob 1:19; D&C 84:33–36). During his twenty years as a member of the Church, his stewardships included serving as bishop's agent in Kirtland, bishop in Kirtland with responsibility for all the eastern states, bishop of the Nauvoo Middle Ward, trustee-in-trust for the Church following the death of Joseph Smith, Presiding Bishop of the Church, and bishop of the Salt Lake 18th Ward.

In Kirtland he was active in the School of the Prophets and played a key role in early attempts to establish the united order. He was given responsibility for the temple lot, he assisted in laying the cornerstones for the temple, and he worked tirelessly to see that the first house of the Lord to be constructed in this dispensation was completed. He was an elected alderman for the City of Nauvoo and was also elected to serve as a justice of the peace in Salt Lake City and treasurer of the newly formed territory of Deseret. Just prior to his death he assisted Brigham Young in locating and planning the city of Ogden, and his name was submitted to the federal government for approval to serve as an Associate Justice of the territorial supreme court.

Bishop Whitney was a constant and reliable man who could be

counted on by his family, his fellow Saints, his leaders, and his God. When I think of his "exemplary" life, the scripture that comes to my mind is 1 Nephi 2:10, wherein Father Lehi exhorts his rebellious son Lemuel to "be like unto this valley, firm and steadfast, and immovable in keeping the commandments of the Lord!" Newel K. Whitney was the kind of man Lehi wanted his son to be: firm, steadfast, and unwavering in his obedience to God's commands.

A HEARTFELT WITNESS

The foundation of Bishop Whitney's steadfast faithfulness was his powerful testimony. From the very beginning of his conversion to the Church, the power of the Holy Ghost bore witness to his heart that the work of the Restoration was true. Through both marvelous manifestations of the Spirit and close personal association, he knew with all his soul that Joseph Smith was a prophet of God. When difficult challenges arose and adversity overwhelmed the convictions of many, Newel Whitney stood firm.

Neither in word nor in deed would he deny the testimony that he knew had been given to him by a loving Father in Heaven as an answer to humble prayer and trusting faith. This knowledge, confirmed in his heart by the power of the Spirit, sustained him throughout the difficult trials of his life. He knew without a doubt that he was a Saint of the latter days, a faithful follower of the Lord Jesus Christ. Like Mormon of old he truly was "a disciple of Jesus Christ, the Son of God . . . called of him to declare his word among his people, that they might have everlasting life" (3 Nephi 5:13).

Several years after their marriage in 1822, Newel Whitney and his wife, Elizabeth Ann, joined the Campbellite congregation that met in Kirtland, Ohio, under the leadership of Sidney Rigdon. When Parley P. Pratt and other Mormon missionaries preached in Kirtland, Elizabeth was quick to accept their message. Reflecting on her conversion, Sister Whitney wrote: "I felt an earnest desire . . . to judge for myself; accordingly, I went immediately to hear, and as soon as I heard the Gospel as the Elders preached it, I knew it to be the voice of the Good Shepherd, and went home rejoicing to tell my husband the news."[4] Acting upon the joy she felt, Elizabeth was one of the first to be baptized in Kirtland.

Elizabeth's grandson, Orson F. Whitney, wrote of his grandmother that "hers was eminently a spiritual nature," while he characterized his grandfather as possessing "more of a business-like or temporal turn of mind."[5] With characteristic caution, then, Newel took some time to investigate this new religion when it was presented to him. Nevertheless he soon joined his wife in being baptized a member of the Church in November of 1830.

That the Whitneys had been prepared by the Spirit to receive the good news of the restored gospel there can be no doubt. Elizabeth recounted that some time prior to hearing the missionaries she and her husband had been praying fervently to be shown how they might obtain the gift of the Holy Ghost. In answer to their prayer, Newel and Elizabeth together received a vision wherein they heard a voice saying, "Prepare to receive the word of the Lord, for it is coming."[6] Shortly after this experience, Elder Parley P. Pratt and his missionary companions arrived in Kirtland.

FRIEND AND SERVANT TO THE PROPHET

Bishop Whitney's close association with Joseph Smith began unforgettably in February 1831. The Lord had commanded that "the church . . . should assemble together at the Ohio" (D&C 37:3), "and there I will give unto you my law; and there you shall be endowed with power from on high" (D&C 38:32). The Lord also promised that "inasmuch as my people shall assemble themselves at the Ohio, I have kept in store a blessing such as is not known among the children of men" (D&C 39:15). Obedient to the Lord's directive, the twenty-five-year-old prophet traveled with his wife, Emma, from Fayette, New York, to Kirtland. Upon his arrival Joseph entered the Gilbert & Whitney store, where Brother Whitney was the junior partner. To the surprise of Newel Whitney, who had never before met the Prophet, Joseph extended his hand and greeted him with the words, "Newel K. Whitney, thou art the man!"

Taken aback by this stranger who seemed to know him so well, Brother Whitney asked the visitor his name, to which Joseph replied: "I am Joseph the Prophet. You've prayed me here; now what do you want of me?"[7] Joseph later told Brother Whitney that he had seen him in a vision, praying for his coming to Kirtland. Joseph and Emma were immediately received into Newel and Elizabeth's home, where they resided for several weeks, enjoying all the comforts and hospitality that the Whitneys' prosperous business enabled them to provide.

Joseph himself described this first meeting in these words: "We arrived about the first of February, and were kindly received and welcomed into the house of Brother Newel K. Whitney. My wife and I lived in the family of Brother Whitney several weeks, and received every kindness and attention which could be expected, and especially from Sister Whitney."[8]

A close relationship was formed between the two families. Joseph Smith and Newel Whitney became fast friends. Newel Whitney "was one whom [Joseph Smith] trusted implicitly, not only in monetary matters, in which he often consulted him, but with many of his most secret thoughts, which he could confide but to few. But, though Joseph loved [Newel] as a bosom friend, he did not fail to correct him whenever occasion required, and the candor of his rebuke, and the outspoken nature of their friendship, served only to knit their souls more closely together."[9]

Throughout their close association Bishop Whitney sought not only to follow the Prophet's teachings but also to do all he could to lift the Prophet's burdens, to sustain him in bearing the weight of leading the Church.

During the time that Joseph Smith made Kirtland his home and established the headquarters of the Church there, Whitney family talents, means, resources, and assets were placed completely at the disposal of the Prophet to accomplish the work of the kingdom. In many ways Newel K. Whitney made it possible for the Prophet Joseph to accomplish what the Lord was directing him to do. While Joseph had the revealed vision and divine authority to direct the kingdom of God on earth, Bishop Whitney provided the administrative ability, practical knowledge, and financial skills so necessary to successfully manage the work of the Church.

Just as the First Presidency leans heavily upon the Presiding Bishopric today to administer the temporal affairs of a global Church, so Joseph relied heavily upon Bishop Whitney (and also upon Bishop Edward Partridge who presided in Missouri) to govern the day-to-day matters of getting the Lord's work done in the early Church. As I look at the role played by Bishop Whitney during those early years and review what we know about his accomplishments, I come to the conclusion that his able management and diligent labors powerfully sustained Joseph Smith in his role as "the Presiding High Priest over the High Priesthood of the Church" (D&C 107:66) and contributed significantly to the progress of the early Church.

While not always highly visible and not always a personal participant (as in the case of Zion's Camp), the steadying hand of Bishop Whitney was nonetheless apparent throughout such milestone accomplishments and endeavors as gathering the Saints to Kirtland, building Zion in Missouri, establishing the united order, organizing the march of Zion's Camp, constructing and dedicating the Kirtland Temple, publishing the first editions of the Doctrine and Covenants, international expansion of missionary work, and the eventual relocation of the Church to Nauvoo, Illinois. I will leave it to historians to recount all the details, but I would like to share some of the evidence that has led me to highly regard Bishop Whitney's contribution to this critical era, which established much of the foundation of the Lord's latter-day Church.

REVEALED CALLINGS

Brother Whitney's first calling came as a result of revelation received by the Prophet in late August 1831. In Doctrine and Covenants 63:42–45 the Lord directed that Brother Whitney "retain his store" and send as much money as he judged wise to Missouri for the work of establishing Zion. The Lord also directed that he "be ordained as an agent" to Bishop Partridge to serve the Saints who were to remain in Kirtland. Again, in Doctrine and Covenants 64:26 Brother Whitney was instructed, along with his partner, Sidney Gilbert, not to sell their store "until the residue of the church, which remaineth in this place [Kirtland], shall go up unto the land of Zion." Newel K. Whitney's call to serve as a bishop is recorded in Doctrine and Covenants 72:1–8. Despite his considerable qualifications, despite his preparatory service as an agent, and despite his powerful testimony, this call challenged Brother Whitney's faith.

COMFORTING REASSURANCE

As grand and glorious as were the revelations received by the Prophet Joseph to guide the Church and shape the coming forth of the latter-day work, all of which made a strong impression on Brother Whitney, perhaps of greatest personal significance to him was the revelation received on December 4, 1831, calling him to serve as bishop for the Church in Kirtland. As is often the case with many of us when we receive a call from the Lord to serve in His Church, Newel felt unworthy and unprepared for a position of such high trust and great responsibility. When he learned of the calling, he said to the Prophet, "I cannot see a Bishop in myself, Brother Joseph; but if you say it's the Lord's will, I'll try."[10] With kind words of reassurance and wise counsel Joseph gently reminded Brother Whitney that he need not rely on his words alone. Joseph directed him, "Go and ask Father for yourself."[11]

In answer to quiet, personal prayer, Newel Whitney, in "the solitude of his chamber . . . heard a voice from heaven: 'Thy strength is in me.' "[12] Once Brother Whitney's prayers for divine confirmation were answered, he laid his doubts aside and shouldered the weight of his calling with energy and commitment. If ever a calling from the Lord seems overwhelming—if we ever doubt our ability to serve—let us remember Joseph Smith's counsel to Bishop Whitney: "Go and ask Father for yourself." A loving Father in Heaven will not leave our sincere petition unanswered. He will send the Comforter to strengthen us and to give us the same conviction that characterized Bishop Whitney's service. He labored with zealous energy because he harbored no doubts as to the nature and source of his call to serve. By the witness of the Spirit, he knew that his call was from God.

Travels with the Prophet

In April and May of 1832 Bishop Whitney traveled with Joseph Smith to Missouri. On the return trip the horses bolted out of control, forcing both men to jump from the stagecoach. Joseph "cleared the wheels and landed in safety, but [Bishop Whitney] caught his foot in the wheel and was thrown to the ground with violence, breaking his leg and foot in several places."[13] They made their way to a public house near Greenville, Indiana, where a local doctor set Bishop Whitney's broken bones. "Joseph administered to his friend, and he recovered rapidly."[14]

Joseph stayed with Bishop Whitney during four weeks of recuperation. Over time, Joseph began to suspect that the keepers of the public house had murderous intentions for their guests. His suspicions were confirmed when he was fed poisoned food: "After dinner, one day, [Joseph] was seized with a violent attack of vomiting, accompanied by profuse hemorrhage. His jaw became dislocated through the violence of his contortions, but he replaced it with his own hands, and making his way to the bedside of Bishop Whitney, was administered to by him, and instantly healed. The effect of the poison . . . was so powerful as to loosen much of the hair of his head."[15]

With their lives in jeopardy, the two men had no choice but to leave right away. Bishop Whitney, though much improved, was not fully recovered and was "far from being in a fit condition to travel."[16] Joseph promised Newel that if he would agree to leave the next morning they would have a safe and pleasant journey home. Though he had not walked in nearly a month, Bishop Whitney, with faith in the promise of the Prophet of the Lord, agreed to leave. In fulfillment of that promise they arrived safely in Kirtland in July. During this journey Joseph would write to Emma describing Bishop Whitney as "chearful [sic] and patient and a true Brother to me."[17]

Bishop Whitney was commanded by revelation recorded in Doctrine and Covenants 84:112–16 to travel to New York City, Albany, and Boston to preach the gospel and to see to the needs of the poor by gathering funds from "the rich and the proud." In late September of 1832 he again set aside his personal business and traveled with the Prophet to fulfill the Lord's command and to move the work of the Church forward.

A PLACE OF REFUGE

In March of 1832 a mob dragged Joseph from the Johnson farmhouse in Hiram, Ohio, where he and Emma were staying with their eleven-month-old adopted twins. The Prophet was choked into unconsciousness, beaten, stripped of his clothing, scratched, and tarred and feathered. Several days after this incident one of the twins died. Threatened by further mob pursuit, Joseph fled from Hiram. When a beaten, grieving, fleeing Joseph was in need of a safe haven for his wife and surviving baby daughter, the Prophet turned to the family of his friend Newel K. Whitney.

Threatened by mobbers who pursued him from Hiram to Cincinnati
and seeing that the mob was not yet satiated, he now feared for the
immediate safety of Emma and his child, Julia. He instructed Emma
by letter that she quickly move back to Kirtland to stay with Newel
K. Whitney's family.[18]

Although the presence of a visiting relative made it impossible for
Sister Whitney to immediately accommodate Emma and Julia, shortly
after Newel and Joseph returned from Missouri the Smiths moved
into small quarters on the second story of the Whitney store.

For a period of about eighteen months starting in September of
1832, the rooms above the Whitney store served as the dwelling and
office space for Joseph and his family. A listing of significant Church
business transacted during this time is impressive:

The initial command to build the Kirtland Temple and much of the
subsequent planning occurred there. A survey of the high council
minutes reveals that at least eighteen meetings and conferences were
held in the store between December 3, 1832, and June 21, 1833. At
the Whitney store building, Joseph received seventeen revelations
that were compiled into the Doctrine and Covenants, continued his
translation of the Bible, conducted the School of the Prophets, and
organized the First Presidency. Great spiritual outpourings occurred
there, including visions of the Father and the Son. The store also
served as the first bishop's storehouse.[19]

For Joseph and Emma personally, this time living in the Whitney
store brought them the joy of their first surviving natural child. Their
son Joseph Smith III was born there on November 6, 1832,[20] just as
the Prophet and Bishop Whitney returned from their brief mission to
New York, Albany, and Boston.

"FOR WHOM THE LORD LOVETH
HE CHASTENETH"

In May of 1833 Joseph Smith received a revelation that is
recorded today in section 93 of the Doctrine and Covenants. In verse
50 the Lord lovingly but firmly directed his Kirtland bishop to give

more attention to his family: "My servant Newel K. Whitney also, a bishop of my church, hath need to be chastened, and set in order his family, and see that they are more diligent and concerned at home, and pray always, or they shall be removed out of their place."

All evidence we have indicates that Bishop Whitney took this counsel to heart and received it in the spirit of loving concern in which it was given. In keeping with the overall pattern of the "exemplary" life he led, he did not allow his pride to get in the way of his repentance. The Lord's revealed corrective counsel to Bishop Whitney serves now to remind all of us that our families cannot be ignored in the press of day-to-day demands on our time. Even the demands of Church service do not absolve us of the eternal responsibilities we have to tend to the material and spiritual nurturing of our families.

OTHER ASSIGNMENTS AND ACTIONS

Received in June 1833, Doctrine and Covenants 96:2 placed care of the French farm, which had been acquired by the Church, in the able hands of Bishop Whitney. The Lord clearly stated: "Therefore, let my servant Newel K. Whitney take charge of the place which is named among you, upon which I design to build mine holy house." This was the beginning of Bishop Whitney's tireless efforts, in which he worked closely with Hyrum Smith, to direct and coordinate nearly three years of labor requiring tremendous sacrifice from the faithful Saints that culminated in the glorious dedication of the Kirtland Temple on March 27, 1836.[21] In her later years Elizabeth Whitney described the work on the temple as a labor of love and faith, and reflected that to her it was a miracle that the temple was ever constructed.

Newel K. Whitney also served as one of several brethren who both witnessed and recorded revelations received by the Prophet Joseph Smith in Kirtland. After the first compilation of revelations was published, Newell K. Whitney "reviewed [the book] and testified that he had examined . . . [it], and the revelations contained in it he knew were true, for God had testified to him by his holy Spirit, for many of them were given under his roof and in his presence through President Joseph Smith, Junr. the Prophet of [the] Lord."[22]

In several of the revelations given to Joseph Smith, the Lord made it plain that a bishop in His church is to see to the needs of the poor, the sick, and the less fortunate (see D&C 42, 51, 84). A blessing given by Joseph Smith to Bishop Whitney indicated that he would "deal with a liberal hand to the poor and the needy, the sick and afflicted, the widow and the fatherless."[23] In January 1836 Bishop Whitney, working to fulfill the Lord's commands, organized a three-day feast for the poor. The Prophet attended the first day of the feast on Thursday, January 7, and gave this description of the event:

> Attended a sumptuous feast at Bishop Newel K. Whitney's. The feast was after the order of the Son of God—the lame, the halt, and the blind were invited, according to the instructions of the Savior. Our meeting was opened by singing, and prayer by Father Smith. . . . We then received a bountiful refreshment, furnished by the liberality of the Bishop.[24]

On Saturday Joseph was asked by his friend Bishop Whitney to return again to enjoy the last day of the feast. Bishop Whitney sent this invitation to the Prophet, which he accepted:

> Thus saith the voice of the Spirit to me—If thy brother Joseph Smith, Jun., will attend the feast at thy house, this day (at twelve o'clock), the poor and the lame will rejoice in his presence, and also think themselves honored.
> Yours in friendship and love, NEWEL K. WHITNEY[25]

Bishops must also serve as careful stewards to watch over the financial resources of the Church. During a period of great scarcity and financial hardship, Bishop Whitney, in September of 1837, issued an appeal to all members of the Church to come to the aid of the impoverished Saints in Kirtland. After much deliberation and extended counsel with the First Presidency, a letter was issued by the Bishop and his counselors to solicit funds from all members of the Church. A portion of that letter reveals not only the difficulties of the time but also the concern of a compassionate bishop who was striving with all his heart to move forward the work of his Lord and Master:

> The Saints in the city of Kirtland have been called to endure great affliction for the truth's sake, and to bear a heavy burden in order that the foundation of the kingdom of God might be laid on a sure

and certain basis. . . . The exertions of the enemy . . . have given to
the Saints great trouble, and caused them much expense. In addition
to this, they have had to publish the word of the Lord, which has
been attended with great expense. These things, together with building the House of the Lord, have [impoverished] them very much. . . .
And besides all this there have been a large number of poor who
have had to receive assistance from the donations of the Church. . . .
The Saints of God will rejoice in all that the Lord does, and in doing
all that the Lord requires. The sacrifice of righteousness which the
Lord requires will be offered with a willing heart and ready mind, and
with great joy. . . . Be admonished, then, O ye Saints! . . . Gather up
. . . all the means you have and send on to the Saints who are engaged in this great work of building the Zion of God.[26]

In section 64 of the Doctrine and Covenants, one of the revelations containing specific instructions for Newell K. Whitney, we find
counsel that obviously made a strong impression on Bishop Whitney.
The language and message of verse 34 are reflected in the above letter:
"Behold, the Lord requireth the heart and a willing mind; and the
willing and obedient shall eat the good of the land of Zion in these
last days."

Bishop Whitney's labors in the kingdom also reflected a profound
understanding of teachings found in verses 29 and 33 of section 64:
"Wherefore, as ye are agents, ye are on the Lord's errand; and whatever ye do according to the will of the Lord is the Lord's business. . . .
Wherefore, be not weary in well-doing, for ye are laying the foundation of a great work. And out of small things proceedeth that which is
great."

Bishop Whitney knew that he was "on the Lord's errand" and
went about doing "the Lord's business" with unwearying attention to
the important "small things" that did so much to lay "the foundation
of [the] great work" in which we are all engaged today.

During the tumult and apostasy of the later years of the Church's
Kirtland period Newel Whitney remained loyal to Joseph even in the
face of considerable personal persecution. Levi Hancock wrote that
Bishop Whitney "was cursed by some when he did his best to hold up
Joseph. He would suffer himself to be slandered to save the Prophet
from trouble."[27] It is no wonder, then, that Joseph on one occasion described the depth of his feelings for Bishop Whitney with these moving

words: "Thou art a faithful friend in whom the afflicted sons of men
can confide, with the most perfect safety. Let the blessings of the Eternal also be crowned upon his head. How warm that heart! how anxious that soul! for the welfare of one who has been cast out, and hated
of almost all men. Brother Whitney, thou knowest not how strong
those ties are that bind my soul and heart to thee."[28]

A SUSTAINING COMPANION

Almost always when a man distinguishes himself in faithful service to the Church, we find at his side a wife whose faith equals or
even transcends that of her husband. In Elizabeth Ann, Newel found
a companion who not only dearly loved him but who also deeply
loved the Lord and took great delight in striving always to do His will
(see Psalms 37:4; 40:8). In courting and marrying Elizabeth, young
Newel demonstrated the wisdom and good judgment that would serve
him well throughout his life. He avoided the pitfall of being "unequally yoked" (2 Corinthians 6:14) that often afflicts couples who do
not share the same beliefs, values, and commitments.

In honoring and sustaining her husband in his considerable and
often taxing responsibilities in the kingdom, Elizabeth took to heart
the counsel that the Lord gave to Emma Smith: "Let thy soul delight in
thy husband" (D&C 25:14). As she reflected back on her busy life with
an anxiously engaged Church-leader husband, she wrote: "My husband
traveled with Joseph the prophet, through many of the Eastern cities,
bearing their testimony and collecting means towards building a
Temple in Kirtland, and also to purchase lands in Missouri. . . . During
all these absences and separations from my husband, I never felt to
murmur or complain . . . I was more than satisfied to have him give all,
time, talents and ability into the service of the Kingdom of God."[29]

Elizabeth was a bastion of faith, a stalwart in her own right. She
endured well not only the absences of her husband but also the hardships of moving from Kirtland to Nauvoo to Salt Lake City. Throughout the toils of these wearisome journeys she remained not only faithful but also charitable. Upon her arriving in the Salt Lake Valley in
October of 1848, it was said of her that though "worn and weary with
fatigue and hardship, Sister Whitney still preserved the same sweet
spirit and equanimity of soul. She had always a word of consolation for

those who had not the same unbounded faith, and her charity for the weak and tired ones was most sublime."[30]

In addition to sustaining her husband and raising a large family of eleven children, Sister Whitney was always busy serving her brothers and sisters in the Church. She was always "anxiously engaged in a good cause, and [did] many things of [her] own free will, and [brought] to pass much righteousness" (D&C 58:27). This evident and energetic willingness to help others led to her being called to serve as a counselor to Emma Smith when the Relief Society was first organized in Nauvoo on May 17, 1842. Later in her life she was called again to the general presidency of the Relief Society, where she served as a counselor to Eliza R. Snow from 1880 to 1882.[31]

AN AFFECTIONATE HUSBAND, A KIND FATHER

As in all good partnerships, Bishop Whitney also did his part to reciprocate the strengthening, sustaining influence that his wife brought to their marriage. He was a caring husband and a nurturing father. Newel loved his good wife dearly and took seriously his role as husband and father. In their courtship and early marriage they saw themselves as "a happy couple, with bright prospects in store." As noted earlier, they were united in their faith, their "tastes and feelings were congenial."[32] Upon his death, he was fondly remembered by his family and friends as "an affectionate husband and a kind and generous father."[33]

Newel and Elizabeth could not have accomplished all that they did without the energizing, complementary strength that they found in each other. They are a great example of so many Latter-day Saint couples of both the past and the present who ably carry great burdens of heavy Church service, conscientiously provide for their family's needs, and diligently teach and successfully rear their children while still nurturing their eternal companionship. Such couples find true joy in each other, in their children, and in service to their brothers and sisters in the gospel. They exemplify the fulfillment that comes from righteous marriage. They demonstrate that man and woman are incomplete without each other (see 1 Corinthians 11:11; Matthew 19:5; Mark 10:8; D&C 49:16) and show us why the Lord has so clearly stated that "marriage is ordained of God unto man" (D&C 49:15).

FAITHFUL AND STEADFAST

Bishop Newel K. Whitney served with love and compassion. His understanding of the gospel was enlightened by his study, by his willingness to be instructed by those in authority over him, and by the Spirit, which he sought constantly and prayerfully to guide his life. He was faithful and loyal. He was diligent and persistent in seeking always to do the Lord's will. He was "firm and steadfast, and immovable in keeping the commandments of the Lord!" (1 Nephi 2:10.) Better than anything I might say, the following tribute speaks movingly of the "exemplary" life he led. After he departed this mortal life, Eliza R. Snow eloquently remembered Bishop Whitney with these words:

Lines on the Death of Bishop Newel K. Whitney

> A mighty man, a man of worth,
> A father and a friend,
> Has left the narrow sphere of earth,
> His upward course to wend.
>
> Firm as the hills—he was a stay,
> A bulwark, and a shield:
> Like a strong pillar, mov'd away
> To Zion's broader field.
>
> From understanding's deepest wells,
> Unmeasur'd draughts he drew;
> The light that with Jehovah dwells,
> Inspir'd his judgment too.
>
> With dignity he fill'd the sphere
> Allotted him below;
> His presence seem'd an impulse here
> To wisdom's genial flow.
>
> But now his noble form must lie
> And slumber in the dust,
> While he with honor joins the high
> Assemblies of the just.

With fondly cherish'd memory
His name will be belov'd
While virtue and integrity
Are by the Saints approv'd.

The stroke is with a heavy rod;
But while our hearts deplore
His loss, we'll own the hand of God,
That God whom we adore.[34]

—Eliza R. Snow
G.S.L. City, 1850

NOTES

1. *Deseret Weekly News,* 28 September 1850.
2. Ibid.
3. There was no immediate family relationship between Heber C. Kimball and Newel Kimball Whitney. They became fast friends over the years of their faithful service in the Church. This warm relationship led to two of their children forming a friendship that blossomed into romance: Heber's daughter, Helen Marr, married Newel's eldest son, Horace (Helen and Horace's son, Orson F. Whitney, served as an Apostle from 1906–1931). Also, Sarah Ann Whitney, Newel and Elizabeth's eldest daughter, was married to Heber. Hence, it was the close ties of friendship and interfamily marriage that led to Newel K. Whitney's burial in the Kimball family cemetery.
4. Elizabeth Ann Whitney, "A Leaf from an Autobiography," *The Woman's Exponent,* vol. 7 (Salt Lake City), 1878, p. 51.
5. Andrew Jenson, *Latter-day Saint Biographical Encyclopedia,* vol. 1 (Salt Lake City: Western Epics, 1971 reprint of 1901 original), p. 223.
6. Ibid.
7. Jenson, op. cit., p. 223.
8. Joseph Smith, *History of the Church* 1:145–46. Hereafter cited as *HC.*
9. Jenson, op. cit., p. 224.
10. Jenson, op. cit., p. 224.
11. Ibid.
12. Ibid.
13. Ibid.
14. Ibid.
15. Ibid., pp. 224–25.

16. Ibid., p. 225.

17. Larry N. Poulsen, "The Life and Contributions of Newel Kimball Whitney," MA Thesis, Brigham Young University, April 1966, as cited by Susan W. Easton, "Newel K. Whitney, Thou Art The Man," *Encyclia: The Journal of the Utah Academy of Sciences, Arts, and Letters*, vol. 62, 1985, p. 215.

18. Susan Easton Black, "Joseph's Experience in Hiram, Ohio: A Time of Contrasts," *Regional Studies in Latter-day Saint Church History—Ohio*, Department of Church History and Doctrine, Brigham Young University, 1990, p. 40.

19. Karl Ricks Anderson, *Joseph Smith's Kirtland: Eyewitness Accounts* (Salt Lake City: Deseret Book, 1989), p. 153.

20. Richard N. Holzapfel and T. Jeffery Cottle, *Old Mormon Kirtland and Missouri*, Fieldbrook Productions, 1991, p. 53.

21. See D&C 109 and HC 2:420–26.

22. Anderson, op. cit., p. 99.

23. HC 2:288.

24. HC 2:362.

25. HC 2:363.

26. HC 2:515–17.

27. "The Life of Levi Hancock," p. 51, as cited by Anderson, op. cit., p. 227.

28. HC 5:108.

29. Elizabeth Ann Whitney, "A Leaf from an Autobiography," *The Woman's Exponent*, vol. 7 (Salt Lake City, 1878), p. 71.

30. Emmeline B. Wells, "Elizabeth Ann Whitney," in *The Woman's Exponent*, vol. 10, March 15, 1882, p. 154.

31. See *Encyclopedia of Mormonism*, "Biographical Register of General Church Officers," vol. 4, Appendix 1, pp. 1649–50.

32. Jenson, op. cit., p. 223.

33. *Deseret Weekly News*, 28 September 1850.

34. Eliza R. Snow, *Poems: Religious, Historical and Political*, vol. 1 (Liverpool: F. D. Richards, 1856), pp. 207–8.

17

President Thomas S. Monson

Wilford Woodruff

On a beautiful summer day, July 17, 1993, I stood amidst a large crowd gathered at the Salt Lake City Cemetery to pay respects to Abraham Owen Woodruff and his wife, Helen May Winters Woodruff, as their remains were laid to rest eighty-nine years after their deaths from smallpox in 1904.

Owen Woodruff, a member of the Council of the Twelve Apostles and son of President Wilford Woodruff, along with his wife, Helen, were on assignment visiting the Mexican Mission when Helen contracted smallpox and died June 7, 1904, in Mexico City. Because of the fear of contagion, she was buried there in the American cemetery.

After his wife's death, the heartbroken Owen traveled to Ciudad Juarez, Mexico. There he, himself, began showing symptoms of smallpox. Taken to an El Paso, Texas, hospital, he died there just thirteen days after his beloved Helen. He was buried in El Paso.

Eighty-nine years later, after much effort on the part of descendants of Owen and Helen Woodruff, and following some miraculous events, the remains of Owen and Helen were returned to Salt Lake City and were buried alongside three of their deceased children and other members of the Woodruff family, including President Wilford Woodruff.

In my remarks to those assembled that day, I spoke the words penned by Elder John Taylor referring to the Prophet Joseph and his brother Hyrum, which seemed to apply so fittingly to Owen and

Helen: "In life they were not divided, and in death they were not separated." Two lines from Robert Louis Stevenson's "Requiem" also
seemed most appropriate:

> Home is the sailor, home from the sea,
> And the hunter home from the hill.

I concluded my remarks: "Welcome home, Owen. Welcome home,
Helen."

I felt privileged to be a part of the services held that July day in
1993 for President Wilford Woodruff's son and daughter-in-law, for I
have felt a closeness to President Woodruff that began when, as a
teenager, I was given a copy of one of his autobiographical works,
Leaves from My Journal.[1] I was fascinated as I read of his life, beginning with his boyhood in Connecticut, where even in his childhood
and teens he was much interested in religion and read his Bible stu-
diously. He had strong feelings that if the true church of Christ were
on the earth, it should have prophets, Apostles, and revelation. Such
astute observations undoubtedly helped young Wilford recognize the
true church when he came in contact with it. In December of 1833,
while he and his eldest brother, Azmon, were in Oswego County, New
York, they went to a meeting held by missionaries of The Church of
Jesus Christ of Latter-day Saints. Wilford said of that meeting, "The
Spirit of the Lord bore record to me that what I heard was true." He
and his brother were baptized just two days later, on December 31,
1833, when he was twenty-six years old.

Wilford Woodruff knew the Prophet Joseph Smith personally. In
1834 he went to Kirtland, Ohio, where he met the Prophet and other
early Church leaders and participated with them in the Zion's Camp
march to Missouri.

During that same year, 1834, Wilford felt a strong desire to serve a
mission. He did not express his desire to any of the authorities of the
Church, lest they think he was "seeking for an office."[2] Instead, he
went into the woods alone and prayed, asking that a way might be
opened for him to preach the gospel. He received a strong witness that
his prayer was heard and would be answered. As he left the woods and
returned to the well-traveled road, he met a high priest, Elias Higbee,
with whom he was well acquainted. Brother Higbee said to him, "The
Lord has revealed to me that it is your privilege to be ordained, and to

go and preach the gospel." A few days later, Wilford was called to serve a mission in Arkansas and Tennessee. Such was merely one example of the faith-promoting experiences that would fill the life of Wilford Woodruff.

At the close of his first year as a missionary, Wilford wrote: "The first year of my mission . . . I had traveled three thousand two hundred and forty-eight miles, held one hundred and seventy meetings, baptized forty-three persons—three of whom were Campbellite preachers—assisted [my companion] to baptize twenty more, confirmed thirty-five, organized three branches, ordained two Teachers and one deacon, procured thirty subscribers for the *Messenger and Advocate*, one hundred and seventy-three signers to the petition to the governor of Missouri for redress of wrongs done the Saints in Jackson County, had three mobs rise against me—but was not harmed, wrote eighteen letters, received ten."

This unflagging servant of the Lord returned from this first mission in the autumn of 1836. On April 13, 1837, he married Phoebe Whitmore Carter. Just a month later, he commenced a mission to the Fox Islands, situated east of the state of Maine. Once again this remarkable man—one of the most exceptional missionaries of our dispensation—had great success in bringing souls to Christ.

In the summer of 1838 Wilford Woodruff was informed that he was to fill a vacancy in the Council of the Twelve Apostles. He was ordained an Apostle by Brigham Young on April 26, 1839, at age thirty-two.

On August 8, 1839, afflicted with chills and fever, Elder Woodruff embarked upon his third mission. His wife, Phoebe, lay ill upon her bed. He administered to her and then left for England, in company with John Taylor. Both men felt weak and were feverish, but they made their way to New York, from which they sailed for Liverpool, England, on December 19, 1839, arriving there on January 11, 1840.

During this mission to England, Elder Woodruff was inspired to journey to Herefordshire to preach the gospel. There he went to the home of a wealthy farmer, John Benbow, and was received with "glad tidings" and informed that there was a group calling themselves the United Brethren—over six hundred in number—which had broken off from the Wesleyan Methodists. Among them were forty-five preachers. John Benbow told Elder Woodruff that the United Brethren had "gone as far as they could, and were calling upon the

Lord continually to open the way before them, and send them light
and knowledge that they might know the true way to be saved." Eventually all but one of the United Brethren were baptized by Elder
Woodruff. More than eighteen hundred were baptized in Herefordshire alone within the space of eight months.[3]

Elder Woodruff was to serve other missions for the Church. Following his death, President Heber J. Grant said of him, "I believe that
no other man who ever walked the face of the earth was a greater con-
verter of souls to the gospel of Jesus Christ."[4]

During my reading of *Leaves from My Journal*, two incidents in the
life of Wilford Woodruff particularly stood out. The first occurred in
1848. After journeying with the early pioneers to the Valley of the
Great Salt Lake—in fact being a member of the company that arrived
in the Valley on July 24, 1847—Elder Woodruff was assigned by the
First Presidency to take his family and go to Boston, there to "gather
up the remnant of the Latter-day Saints and lead them to the valleys
of the mountains." While on his way east to accomplish this task,
Elder Woodruff stopped at the home of one of the brethren in Indiana, where he put his carriage in the yard. He and his wife and one
child went to bed in the carriage, while the rest of the family slept in
the house. Shortly after he had retired for the night, the Spirit whispered a warning to him: "Get up, and move your carriage." He got up
as instructed and moved the carriage some distance from where it had
stood. As he was returning to bed, the Spirit spoke to him again,
telling him, "Go and move your mules away from that oak tree." This
he did. He then retired once again to his bed.

Not more than thirty minutes later a whirlwind caught the tree to
which his mules had been fastened, broke it off near the ground, and
carried it a hundred yards, sweeping away two fences in its course. The
enormous tree, with a trunk five feet in circumference, fell exactly
upon the spot where the carriage had originally stood. By listening to
the promptings of the Spirit, Elder Woodruff had saved his life and the
lives of his wife and child.

The second experience that so impressed me took place in 1850.
While returning to Utah with a large company of Saints from the
East, Elder Woodruff bought passage for himself and the company on a
steamer that was to sail down the Ohio River to St. Louis. As soon as
passage was secured, however, Elder Woodruff received a prompting
from the Spirit: "Go not on board of that steamer, neither you nor

your company." Elder Woodruff, obeying the inspiration which had come to him, decided to take the entire company on another steamer. The first steamer, after journeying down the Ohio River for five miles, caught fire. All on board died by either fire or drowning. Once again the life of Elder Woodruff and the lives of those in his care were spared as he obeyed the whisperings of the Spirit.

Throughout his life Wilford Woodruff was protected and guided and prepared for the time when he would preside over the Lord's church. His life was spared on countless occasions. When he was three years old he fell into a caldron of boiling water and was so badly scalded that it took nine months before he was considered to be out of danger. When he was five he fell from the beam of a barn, striking his face upon the floor and nearly breaking his neck. He experienced dozens of life-threatening accidents and illnesses throughout his life. In his later years he wrote: "I have broken both legs—one in two places—both arms, my breast bone and three ribs, and had both ankles dislocated. I have been drowned, frozen, scalded and bit by a mad dog—have been in two water wheels under full head of water—have passed through several severe fits of sickness, and encountered poison in its worst forms—have landed in a pile of railroad ruins—have barely been missed by the passing bullets, and have passed through a score of other hair-breadth escapes.

"It has appeared miraculous to me, that with all the injuries and broken bones which I have had, I have not a lame limb, but have been enabled to endure the hardest labor, exposures and journeys—have often walked forty, fifty, and on one occasion, sixty miles in a day. The protection and mercy of God has been over me, and my life thus far has been preserved; for which blessings I feel to render the gratitude of my heart to my Heavenly Father, praying that the remainder of my days may be spent in His service and in the building up of His kingdom."[5]

In January 1877, Wilford Woodruff offered the dedicatory prayer at the St. George Temple and was called to be the first president of that temple. He commenced endowment work for the dead, laid the foundations for our family genealogies, and systematized temple work. Inspiration from heaven guided him in his work.

Among his many remarkable accomplishments, Wilford Woodruff was one of the most prolific record keepers of the nineteenth century, eventually filling thirty-one handwritten volumes with his journal entries. He became clerk and historian of the Quorum of the Twelve in 1852 and served for thirty-four years as a historian in the Church Historian's Office. He wrote histories of eight of the first members of the Quorum of the Twelve. In 1890 he began weekday religious edu-cation classes, which led eventually to the seminary and institute pro-grams of the Church.

Elder Woodruff felt a keen sense of responsibility to provide vicar-ious ordinances for his ancestors. By the time he was seventy-eight years old 3,188 of his deceased relatives had been baptized vicariously and 2,518 had been endowed.

During his lifetime he organized 51 branches of the Church and ordained or assisted in ordaining 5,739 bearers of the priesthood.

The construction of the Salt Lake Temple, begun by President Brigham Young and continued during John Taylor's presidency, pro-ceeded in earnest after Wilford Woodruff was sustained as President of the Church on April 7, 1889. It became his task to deal with the fed-eral government, which had seized many Church properties and threatened to seize all of the Church's temples. He sought heavenly guidance in these matters. The risks decreased when he issued the Manifesto in September 1890 and it was sustained by the Saints in general conference. From that time forth efforts to complete the Salt Lake Temple were redoubled.

On April 6, 1893, when he was eighty-six years of age, President Woodruff presided at the first of forty-one dedicatory services in the Salt Lake Temple, culminating a forty-year epic of extreme sacrifice and monumental labor by the Saints in constructing the temple. Presi-dent Woodruff later wrote in his journal: "Near 50 years ago while in the City of Boston I had a vision of going with the Saints to the Rocky Mountains, building a temple, and I dedicated it."[6] Such was the inspiration of this great prophet, this giant of the Lord.

I have long been impressed by the prophetic comments made by President Woodruff in an 1894 meeting: "We cannot draw a veil over the events that await this generation. No man that is inspired by the Spirit and power of God can close his eyes and ears or his lips to these things. When I have the vision of night opened continually before my eyes, and can see the mighty judgments that are about to be poured out upon this world, when I know these things are true and are at the door, . . . can I withhold my voice from lifting up a warning to this people and to the nations of the earth? . . . Calamities and troubles are increasing in the earth, . . . Great changes are at our doors. . . . mighty changes among the nations of the earth. . . . I have felt oppressed with the weight of these matters, and I felt I must speak of them. . . . It's by the power of the gospel that we shall escape."[7]

On September 2, 1898, at the age of ninety-one, President Wilford Woodruff concluded his earthly sojourn, passing peacefully to the other side. Countless were the lives he had touched and inspired during his life. Countless, too, are the lives he has touched since—through his writings, his teachings, and his examples of total dedication to the Lord. I, for one, have been uplifted and inspired as I have studied his life.

Through the years I have felt a kinship with Wilford Woodruff. Not only have we each served in the Council of the Twelve Apostles, he being the fifteenth Apostle ordained in this dispensation and I the seventy-seventh, but we share other things in common as well, including a love for fly fishing. In August 1892 he wrote to *Forest and Stream* magazine about a fishing trip on the Weber River where he caught twenty trout in four hours—four of which weighed over four pounds! For a time he presided over the Saints in the eastern United States and eastern Canada. From 1959 to 1962 I served as president of what was then called the Canadian Mission, headquartered in Toronto, Ontario, Canada. There I walked where he had walked before me.

It was my privilege to sit in the Quorum of the Twelve for many years with Elder LeGrand Richards, who as a young boy heard President Wilford Woodruff speak on different occasions and who related to us precisely the words he had heard President Woodruff utter. He spoke to us of President Woodruff's last public address, which Elder Richards had heard when he was twelve years of age. More than eighty years later, Elder Richards still bore clear and strong testimony of that sacred occasion.

Among so many other qualities, I admire the ability President Woodruff had to dwell in harmony with those not of his faith. The evening before the first dedication service of the Salt Lake Temple, President Woodruff conducted nonmember guests on a tour through the building. This act was unprecedented at that time. It did much to rebuild harmony with nonmember neighbors after years of hostility. Even Charles S. Zane, the federally appointed Utah Territorial Supreme Court Justice and longtime critic of the Church, was impressed with the gesture, and he softened his stance toward the Church.

Another admirable characteristic of President Woodruff's was his desire to "do today" what needed to be done, without undue concern for what might occur in the future. On one occasion he was asked when the world was coming to an end. He replied, "Well, I don't know, but I am still planting cherry trees."[8]

It is an honor to pay tribute to one for whom I have such deep admiration—President Wilford Woodruff, fourth president of The Church of Jesus Christ of Latter-day Saints. Though he died twenty-nine years before I was born, his life has touched mine and has left me the better for it.

NOTES

1. *Leaves from My Journal* (Salt Lake City: Juvenile Instructor Office, 1881).

2. *Leaves from My Journal*, p. 8.

3. Matthias F. Cowley, *Wilford Woodruff,* . . . *History of His Life and Labors as Recorded in His Daily Journals* (Salt Lake City: *Deseret News*, 1909), pp. 117, 120.

4. Conference Report, June 1919, p. 8.

5. *Millennial Star* 27:392.

6. Wilford Woodruff Journal, box 5, fd. 2, p. 54, Church Historical Department.

7. *The Young Woman's Journal*, vol. V, no. 11, (Salt Lake City, August 1894), "The Temple Workers' Excursion," pp. 512, 513.

8. Harold B. Lee, *Stand Ye in Holy Places* (Salt Lake City: Deseret Book, 1974), p. 160.

18

Elder Neal A. Maxwell

Brigham Young

Many think of President Brigham Young as primarily a great colonizer and governor, and excellent he was in those roles. But President Young, much more than being a colonizer and a governor, was a seer and a profound teacher of gospel doctrines and principles. The more one encounters his key teachings, the larger he looms. This chapter is not a biography or history, however. Rather it contains a small, selected smorgasbord of his sermons, including some of the most informing and inspiring samples.

Of course it all began as Brigham began to be nourished by the Prophet Joseph Smith.

Brigham endured certain inconveniences in order to harvest from the Prophet Joseph so much of what Brigham taught in the decades to follow:

> In my experience I never did let an opportunity pass of getting with the Prophet Joseph and of hearing him speak in public or in private, so that I might draw understanding from the fountain from which he spoke, that I might have it and bring it forth when it was needed. . . . such moments were more precious to me than all the wealth of the world. No matter how great my poverty—if I had to borrow meal to feed my wife and children, I never let an opportunity pass of learning what the Prophet had to impart.[1]

Of this prophet-pupil relationship, Brigham, a future prophet himself, said: "An angel never watched [Joseph] closer than I did, and that is what has given me the knowledge I have today. I treasure it up, and ask the Father, in the name of Jesus, to help my memory when information is wanted."[2]

Apparently Joseph knew from the very beginning of their unique association that Brigham Young would one day preside over the Church.[3]

Seeing Brigham's frequently destitute condition, Joseph would "often ask me how I lived. I told him I did not know—that I did my best, and the Lord did the rest."[4]

Brigham Young observed, without particular complaint, that he had been driven from his "home five times," leaving "everything [he] had."[5] He knew poverty firsthand:

> I had spent hundreds of dollars, which I had accumulated on my mission, to help the brethren to emigrate to Nauvoo, and had but one sovereign left. I said I would buy a barrel of flour with that, and sit down and eat it with my wife and children, and I determined I would not ask anybody for work, until I had eaten it all up. Brother Joseph asked me how I intended to live. I said, "I will go to work and get a living." I tarried in Nauvoo from the year 1841 to 1846, the year we left. In that time I had accumulated much property, for the Lord multiplied everything in my hands, and blessed all my undertakings. But I never ceased to preach; and traveled every season, both in the winter, and in the summer. I was at home occasionally, and the Lord fed and clothed me. It has never entered into my heart, from the first day I was called to preach the Gospel to this day, when the Lord said, "Go and leave your family," to offer the least objection.[6]

Without the Restoration, however, Brigham Young probably would not have been much of a churchman for want of doctrinal satisfaction. "I was thought to be an infidel by the Christians, because I could not believe their nonsense. The secret feeling of my heart was that I would be willing to crawl around the earth on my hands and knees, to see such a man as was Peter, Jeremiah, Moses, or any man that could tell me anything about God and heaven. . . . until I saw Joseph Smith."[7]

Brigham Young, however, witnessed the Spirit's convincing power:

I saw a man without eloquence, or talents for public speaking, who could only say, "I know, by the power of the Holy Ghost, that the Book of Mormon is true, that Joseph Smith is a Prophet of the Lord," the Holy Ghost proceeding from that individual illuminated my understanding, and light, glory, and immortality were before me. I was encircled by them, filled with them, and I knew for myself that the testimony of the man was true. . . . My own judgment, natural endowments, and education bowed to this simple, but mighty testimony. There sits the man who baptized me, (brother Eleazer Miller.) It filled my system with light, and my soul with joy. The world, with all its wisdom and power, and with all the glory and gilded show of its kings or potentates, sinks into perfect insignificance, compared with the simple, unadorned testimony of the servant of God.[8]

Brigham Young also successfully endured a temptation to which others succumbed—to criticize the Prophet Joseph and to murmur: "I never called him in question, even in my feelings, for an act of his, except once. I did not like his policy in a matter, and a feeling came into my heart that would have led me to complain; but it was much shorter lived than Jonah's gourd, for it did not last half a minute. Much of Joseph's policy in temporal things was different from my ideas of the way to manage them. He did the best he could, and I do the best I can."[9]

President Young described that momentary "want of confidence in Brother Joseph Smith, . . . It was not concerning religious matters—. . . it was in relation to his financiering—to his managing the temporal affairs which he undertook. . . . [I] understood, by the spirit of revelation manifested to me, that if I was to harbor a thought in my heart that Joseph could be wrong in anything, I would begin to lose confidence in him, and that feeling would grow from step to step, and from one degree to another."[10]

The Restoration's surge of spiritual experience thus replaced Brigham's wonderment of earlier years. Before he joined the Church, being untouched by the restored gospel, Brigham was apparently somewhat discouraged about life. As a young man he disapproved of much of what he saw in the world but wondered what life held for him. Then his loving brother, Phineas, gave Brigham some prescient counsel in 1829: "Hang on, [Brigham], for I know the Lord is agoing to do something for us."[11] The rest is Moses-like history!

The small selection to follow will focus primarily on President Young's teachings about our moral agency and on God's plan of salvation with the inherent role of adversity. One senses how often he had thought deeply about the fundamental doctrines, and we are the beneficiaries of his summation.

The plan of salvation was often discussed in his sermons. President Young, for example, reassured us as follows: "When you understand the Gospel plan, you will comprehend that it is the most reasonable way of dealing with the human family."[12]

President Brigham Young observed concerning the practicality and simplicity of the gospel:

> If you could see things as they are, you would know that the whole plan of salvation, and all the revelations ever given to man on the earth are as plain as would be the remarks of an Elder, were he to stand here and talk about our every day business. . . . You may now be inclined to say, "O, this is too simple and child-like, we wish to hear the mysteries of the kingdoms of the Gods who have existed from eternity, and of all the kingdoms in which they will dwell; we desire to have these things portrayed to our understandings." Allow me to inform you that you are in the midst of it all now.[13]

President Young reminded us of the contrast: "The Lord Jesus Christ works upon a plan of eternal increase, of wisdom, intelligence, honor, excellence, power, glory, might, and dominion, and the attributes that fill eternity. What principle does the devil work upon? It is to destroy, dissolve, decompose, and tear in pieces."[14] Therefore, what a difference exists between the Lord's plan of happiness and the adversary's cunning plan of destruction! (See 2 Nephi 9:28.)

Through self-knowledge, and revealed knowledge of our fellowmen and of God, we have a more realistic sense of our true position, a clearer comprehension of "things as they really are" (Jacob 4:13).

> Then instead of concluding that the Lord has drawn us into difficulties, and compelled us to do that which is unpleasant to our feelings, and to suffer sacrifice upon sacrifice to no purpose, we shall understand that He has designed all this to prepare us to dwell in His presence. . . .

> He has so ordained it, that by the natural mind we cannot see and understand the things of God, therefore we must then seek unto the Lord, and get His Spirit and the light thereof, to understand His will. And when He is calling us to pass through that which we call afflictions, trials, temptations, and difficulties, did we possess the light of the Spirit, we would consider this the greatest blessing that could be bestowed upon us.[15]

At the heart of the plan of happiness is moral agency, which is essential to the plan itself. Brigham Young had a special sense of how deep God's commitment is to our moral agency, hence all the anxieties attendant to the exercise of that agency. "Yes; . . . it is [God's] earth, and he controlleth according to his pleasure, and it will yet be devoted to those who serve him. But, in consequence of the agency that is given to the intelligent children of our Father and God, it is contrary to his laws, government, and character for him to dictate us in our actions any further than we prefer."[16]

In Father's plan not only is "there . . . an opposition in all things," but all facts, said Brigham, are demonstrated by "their opposites," for "we find ourselves surrounded . . . by an almost endless combination of opposites, through which we must pass to gain experience and information to fit us for an eternal progression."[17] "When God organized intelligent beings, he organized them as independent beings to a certain extent, as he is himself. Whether we see an evil act or a good one performed by an intelligent being, that being has performed the act by his will, by his own independent organization, . . . But we have learned that in our organization we are as independent as the angels are in theirs."[18]

Concurring with Alma, Brigham stated that each principle of the gospel carries with it its own witness that it is true. "Every principle God has revealed carries its own convictions of its truth to the human mind."[19]

We should, of course, focus more on our possibilities than preen ourselves over our independencies, yet "man possesses the germ of all the attributes and power that are possessed by God. . . . that God possesses in perfection." Moreover, counseled sagely Brigham Young, "sin is . . . an inversion of the attributes God has placed in [man]."[20]

Out of the interplay of our agency and God's plan, true discipleship can be developed and bring true joy. "You all know that it takes intelligence to enjoy. . . . I say, if you want to enjoy exquisitely, become a Latter-day Saint, and then live the doctrine of Jesus Christ."[21]

Significantly, all the cardinal virtues can be developed or enhanced by the mortal experience. Moreover, all the described attributes flow from charity. "There is one virtue, attribute, or principle, which, if cherished and practiced by the Saints, would prove salvation to thousands upon thousands. I allude to charity, or love, from which proceed forgiveness, long-suffering, kindness, and patience."[22]

Brigham also wisely counseled regarding another vital attribute, submission, counseling us "to submit to the hand of the Lord, . . . and acknowledge his hand in all things, . . . then you will be exactly right; and until you come to that point, you cannot be entirely right. That is what we have to come to."[23]

Brigham Young, an exceptional disciple but one still in process, had faith strong enough to continue his struggle to improve to the end, including with regard to one of life's sternest challenges: "One of the hardest lessons for me to learn on earth is to love a man who hates me. . . . I do not think I have got this lesson by heart, and I do not know how long I shall have to live to learn it. I am trying."[24] We, too, must keep "trying"!

Since self-control brings emancipation, Brigham Young counseled us to control our tempers, even when we are provoked. "[N]ever suffer anger to find a seat in your breast, never get angry at all, treat all mildly, govern yourself, your passions, and it will give you power."[25] In the same way that aggressive, evil thoughts should not be offered a chair and invited to sit down, so anger should never be our tiring overnight guest!

> If you give way to your angry feelings, it sets on fire the whole course of nature, and is set on fire of hell; and you are then apt to set those on fire who are contending with you. When you feel as though you would burst, tell the old boiler to burst, and just laugh at the temptation to speak evil. If you will continue to do that, you will soon be so masters of yourselves as to be able, if not to tame, to control your tongues,— able to speak when you ought, and to be silent when you ought.[26]

Many of us do what Jesus never did: we talk too much. This, Brigham Young identified, saying, "You cannot hide the heart, when the mouth is open."[27]

Practical and spiritual Brigham wisely summarized of life, "we must endure all things that we cannot help."[28] How many times we fret and stew over that which we cannot change!

One day, however, full perspective will be ours:

> We talk about our trials and troubles here in this life: but suppose that you could see yourselves thousands and millions of years after you have proved faithful to your religion during the few short years in this time, and have obtained eternal salvation and a crown of glory in the presence of God; then look back upon your lives here, and see the losses, crosses, and disappointments, the sorrows . . . you would be constrained to exclaim, "But what of all that? Those things were but for a moment, and we are now here."[29]

Until then, however, said Brigham, in mortality we are "encumbered with this flesh,"[30] with its "weakness, blindness, and lethargy."[31] Among the influences of the flesh is its contribution to our "disposition to weep or mourn." Likewise, our "fear and trembling" arise from anxieties which drive us "to know how to save ourselves pertaining to the flesh." Even our fear of trials, continued President Young, "is on account of [our] tabernacles."[32]

Brigham Young said of life's tutoring experiences, "When chastisements come, let them be what they may, let us always be willing and ready to kiss the rod, and reverence the hand that administers it, acknowledging the hand of God in all things."[33] President Young did.

How marvelous when unjust criticism can be managed meekly! This was the case with Brigham Young. For one brief moment, the Prophet Joseph Smith unjustifiably reproved loyal Brigham. Of that brief episode, which involved the transgressions of William Smith, President Lorenzo Snow said, "Brigham Young was equal to the danger" and instantly and meekly yielded to the Prophet.[34]

President Brigham Young rightly observed that it is "not pleasant to our feelings" to receive a rebuke. We may realize our error, but "we do not like to have anyone tell us" about our mistakes.[35] In that same sermon, President Young continued by saying he wished the members of the Church, "when they are rebuked by a friend, to receive that rebuke kindly, and kiss the rod, and reverence the hand that administers it,—to learn that the rebuke of a friend is for our good."[36] Yet reproof is to be administered "in the spirit of meekness." There are "degrees of chastisement," and some are slow to respond to reproof, he wisely observed, whereas others have their hearts broken, because their feelings are "as an infant, and will melt like wax before the flames . . . [hence] you must chasten according to the spirit that is in the person. . . . There is a great variety. Treat people as they are."[37] Granted we have different bearing capacities and, therefore, different developmental needs, such as when "what becomes a trial to one person is not noticed by another."[38]

Thus some trials are customized:

> God never bestows upon His people, or upon an individual, superior blessings without a severe trial to prove them, . . . Then the greater the vision, the greater the display of the power of the enemy. . . . For this express purpose the Father withdrew His spirit from His Son, at the time he was to be crucified. Jesus had been with his Father, talked with Him, dwelt in His bosom, and knew all about heaven, about making the earth, about the transgression of man, and what would redeem the people, and that he was the character who was to redeem the sons of earth, and the earth itself from all sin that had come upon it. The light, knowledge, power, and glory with which he was clothed were far above, or exceeded that of all others who had been upon the earth after the fall, consequently at the very moment, at the hour when the crisis came for him to offer up his life, the Father withdrew Himself, withdrew His Spirit, and cast a veil over him. That is what made him sweat blood. If he had had the power of God upon him, he would not have sweat blood; but all was withdrawn from him, and a veil was cast over him, and he then plead with the Father not to forsake him.[39]

It follows, therefore, that while we will receive a fulness of God's blessings, likewise, "Every one will be rewarded and enjoy according to his capacity. Each vessel will be filled to overflowing, and hence all will be equal, in that they are full. Every man and woman will receive to a fulness, though the quantity will vary according to the extent of their capacity, and each will be crowned with glory and eternal life, if faithful."[40]

Again, one salutes President Young for his careful, thoughtful ponderings of the things that matter most.

One daily risk we run is being miffed with God over this or that part of the overall plan as it pertains to us. Brigham Young counseled us that when one is "a little distrustful with regard to the providences of God, in entertaining a misgiving in his heart and feeling with regard to the hand of the Lord towards him . . . his mind will begin to be darkened. . . . If there is a misgiving in the heart with regard to confidence in our God, do you not see that there is a chance for one to slide a hair's breadth from the truth? This gives power to the enemy, and if we are decoyed in the least from the path of duty, do you not perceive that it produces darkness?"[41]

Book of Mormon imagery apparently stuck with President Brigham Young such as when he later counseled us that "wherever the wisdom of God directs, let our affections and the labour of our lives be centered to that point, and not set our hearts on going east or west, north or south, on living here or there, on possessing this or that; but *let our will be swallowed up in the will of God*, allowing him to rule supremely within us until the spirit overcomes the flesh."[42]

On another occasion he said: "The same principle will embrace what is called sanctification. When the will, passions, and feelings of a person are perfectly submissive to God and His requirements, that person is sanctified. It is for my will to be swallowed up in the will of God, that will lead me into all good, and crown me ultimately with immortality and eternal lives."[43]

Our personal possessions and our material blessings are really not ours anyway: "How long have we got to live before we find out that we have nothing to consecrate to the Lord—that all belongs to the Father in heaven; that these mountains are His; the valleys, the timber, the water, the soil; in fine, the earth and its fulness?"[44]

Even so, if only inwardly, amid life's tests we may still sometimes wonder "Why me? Why this? Why now?" The remedy is for "the Spirit of revelation [to] be in each and every individual, to know the plan of salvation and keep in the path that leads them to the presence of God."[45]

Brigham had a special perspective about Latter-day Saints, as a people, and our need to endure:

> When the Latter-day Saints make up their minds to endure, for the kingdom of God's sake, whatsoever shall come, whether poverty or riches, whether sickness or to be driven by mobs, they will say it is all

right, and will honor the hand of the Lord in it, and in all things, and serve Him to the end of their lives, according to the best of their ability, God being their helper. If you have not made up your minds for this, the quicker you do so the better.[46]

We are involved in an unfolding which we can only see through a glass darkly, but which the Lord sees with the unique clarity of omniscience. For instance, President Brigham Young observed of certain political disorders and upheavals in the world with their attendant miseries and difficulties, that, even so, out of these there could come some benefit. We will see prophecies fulfilled, some of which cannot be fulfilled without accompanying dissonance. As to constraining political conditions in certain nations, "the Lord will yet revolutionize those nations until the door will be opened and the gospel will be preached to all."[47]

> It was revealed to me in the commencement of this Church, that the Church would spread, prosper, grow and extend, and that in proportion to the spread of the Gospel among the nations of the earth, so would the power of Satan rise.[48]

Brigham Young often counseled as to how our enduring is part of experiencing affliction personally, as in these words:

> It is like words in the wind to talk about the sweetness of the honeycomb to those who have not tasted the opposite. You may talk about the glory and comfort of the light to those who never knew darkness, and what do they know about it? Nothing. You might as well preach to those lamps. If we can realize that everything in all the eternities that ever were and ever will be is ordained of God for the benefit and glory of intelligent beings, we can understand why he said to Joseph, "Against none is my anger kindled, only those who do not acknowledge my hand in all things." Do I acknowledge his hand? Yes. I told you in your afflictions, drivings, persecutions, and all that has been grievous to be borne, that the hand of God was in that as much as it was in bringing forth his revelations and the Priesthood through Joseph. . . . So with "Mormonism:" every time they give it a kick, it rises in the scale of power and influence in the world.[49]

President Brigham Young observed: "Now, do not let your hearts faint; for all this will promote the kingdom of God, and it will increase upon the earth. Why? Because the world will decrease. We will be strengthened, while they will be weakened."[50]

Truly, President Brigham Young was remarkable, and I thank him for his deep influence upon me!

NOTES

1. In *Journal of Discourses* 12:269–70 (hereafter cited as *JD*).
2. Brigham Young Sermon, 8 October 1866, p. 6, Historian's Office Reports of Speeches, Church Historical Department.
3. See *Millennial Star* 25 (11 July 1863): 439.
4. In *JD* 7:230.
5. In *JD* 7:205.
6. In *JD* 2:19. See also *JD* 7:230.
7. Brigham Young, in *JD* 8:228.
8. In *JD* 1:90–91.
9. In *JD* 8:16.
10. In *JD* 4:297.
11. Phineas Young to Brigham Young, 11 August 1845, Brigham Young Papers, Church Historical Department.
12. In *JD* 8:115.
13. In *JD* 3:336.
14. In *JD* 1:116.
15. Brigham Young, in *JD* 2:303.
16. In *JD* 8:292.
17. In *JD* 11:42. See also 2 Nephi 2:11; D&C 122:7.
18. Brigham Young, in *JD* 6:146.
19. In *JD* 9:149. See also Alma 32:27–34.
20. In *JD* 10:251.
21. Brigham Young, in *JD* 18:246–47.
22. Brigham Young, in *JD* 7:133–34.
23. In *JD* 5:352.
24. In *JD* 14:97.
25. Wilford Woodruff Journal, 28 December 1843, Church Historical Department.
26. Brigham Young, in *JD* 6:75.
27. In *JD* 6:74.

28. In *JD* 19:97.
29. Brigham Young, in *JD* 7:275.
30. In *JD* 4:134.
31. In *JD* 4:131.
32. In *JD* 2:256–57.
33. In *JD* 2:280.
34. Abraham Cannon Journal, 9 April 1890, Harold B. Lee Library, Brigham Young University.
35. In *JD* 8:364–65.
36. In *JD* 8:364.
37. In *JD* 8:367.
38. In *JD* 9:292.
39. Brigham Young, in *JD* 3:205–6.
40. Brigham Young, in *JD* 7:7.
41. In *JD* 3:222.
42. In *JD* 9:106, emphasis added. See also Mosiah 15:7.
43. In *JD* 2:123.
44. Brigham Young, in *JD* 2:308.
45. Brigham Young, in *JD* 9:279.
46. In *JD* 1:338.
47. In *JD* 12:256.
48. In *JD* 13:280.
49. In *JD* 6:148.
50. In *JD* 4:369.

Index

— A —

Aaron (brother of Moses), 13
Aaronic Priesthood, 14, 15, 21, 163
Abinadi, on "will of the son," 29
Abraham, on "noble and great ones," 89
   on purpose of life, 35
Adam-ondi-Ahman, Mo., 140
Adversity, 222–23, 225–26
Agency, 223–24
Albany, N.Y., 102, 201
Alexandria, Egypt, 44
Allen, Charles, 75
Alma, 24
Anderson, Neils Christian, 49
Anger, 224
Anthon, Professor, 30
Apostasy. See Great Apostasy
Apostleship, of David W. Patten, 82
   of George A. Smith, 138
   of Heber C. Kimball, 58
   of Lorenzo Snow, 174
of Orson Hyde, 41
of Orson Pratt, 89
of Parley P. Pratt, 105
and priesthood keys, 46–47, 68
reorganized, 123–24
seniority in, 43–44
of Wilford Woodruff, 213
Arapahos Indians, 177
Arkansas, 213

— B —

Babcock, Phoebe Ann. See Patten, Phoebe Ann Babcock
Baptism, 101, 163–64
Baptists, 59, 102, 172
Barnaldwick, England, 66
Bavaria, 44
Bedford, England, 122
Benbow, John, 213
Bennett, John C., 94
Benson, Ezra T., 176
Benson, Ezra Taft, on dedication of Palestine, 46
   on welfare, 47

Bible, 4, 14, 72, 100, 101, 102,
    183, 185, 212
Bigler, Bathsheba. See Smith,
    Bathsheba Bigler
Billings, Titus, 73
Bill of Rights (United States), 10
Blackfoot Indians, 177
Boggs, Lilburn W., 4, 5, 67, 76
Book of Mormon, and David W.
    Patten, 82
  and Edward Partridge, 75
  in French, 187
  in German, 187
  and Hyrum Smith, 150, 154,
    157, 167
  in Italian, 175
  lost pages of, 27, 29
  and Orson Pratt, 91
  and Parley P. Pratt, 102–3, 185
  place of publication for, 25
  publication cost of, 30
  and Samuel Smith, 166
  taken to the Indians, 103
  translation of, 12–13, 17, 142,
    163
  and Willard Richards, 120, 132
  witnesses to, 14–15, 20, 21, 24,
    28, 29, 30–33, 164–65
Boston, Mass., 121, 201, 214
Botanic medicine, 119–20
Box Elder County, Utah, 176
Box Elder Stake, 177
Box Elder Tabernacle, 177
Brigham City, Utah, 176, 177
Brigham City Cooperatives, 177
Brigham City Mercantile and
    Manufacturing Association,
    176
British Mission, 49, 125, 174
Buffalo, N.Y., 102
Bullock, Thomas, 143
Burlington, N.Y., 100
Burnley, England, 125

— C —

Cahoon, Reynolds, 121, 138
Cairo, Egypt, 44
Caldwell County, Mo., 83
Calvin, John, 8
Campbellites, 37, 38, 101, 196, 213
Canaan, N.Y., 102
Canada, 41, 62–63, 106, 107,
    183–84
Canadian Mission, 217
Cannon, Fred E., 136–37
Cannon, George Q., 179
  on John Taylor, 192
  on Samuel Smith, 168
Carson Valley Nevada Mission, 49
Carter, Phoebe Whitmore. See
    Woodruff, Phoebe Whitmore
    Carter
Carthage, Ill., 2, 118, 127, 128–29,
    139, 143, 149, 156, 169–70
Charity, 224
Chatburn, England, 66
Chatham, N.Y., 119
Chile, 113
Church of Christ (William E.
    McLellin), 31
Ciudad Juarez, Mexico, 211
Clarkston, Utah, 32
Clay County, Mo., 74
Clayton, William, 143
Cleveland, Ohio, 101, 102
Clisbee, Lydia. See Partridge, Lydia
    Clisbee
Columbus, Ohio, 189
Congregational Church, 120, 132,
    136–37
Connecticut, 121, 212
Constantinople, 44
Constitution (United States), 10,
    47, 190
Corrill, John, 73
Council of Fifty, 139

Cowdery, Oliver, biographical
sketch of, 8–23
and Edward Partridge, 72
on Edward Partridge, 78
and George A. Smith, 140
and Hyrum Smith, 151
and Orson Hyde, 41, 49
and Parley P. Pratt, 103, 105
and Samuel Smith, 163
as scribe, 142
as a witness, 30
in Zion's Camp, 38
Crooked River, Mo., 4, 82, 87
Cry out of the Wilderness, A (pamphlet), 44

— D —

Dalby, Ezra, on Joseph Smith, 6
David (Bible king), 100
Dayton, Ohio, 40
Derby, Conn., 36
Deseret, State of, 112, 131
Deseret News, 131, 144, 192
Dille, David B., 31
Doctrine and Covenants, 28–29,
37, 185, 199
Downham, England, 65
Dundee, Mich., 81

— E —

Eastern States Mission, 191
Edmunds-Tucker Act, 178
Egbert G. Grandin Print Shop
(Palmyra, N.Y.), 150
Ein Ruf aus der Wüste (pamphlet),
44, 45
Elias, 14, 42
Elijah, 14, 42
El Paso, Tex., 211
Elyria, Ohio, 37
Emerald (ship), 109

Endurance, 87, 227–28
England, George A. Smith in, 138
Heber C. Kimball in, 61–66
John Taylor in, 186–87
Lorenzo Snow in, 174
Orson Hyde in, 41–42, 44
Parley P. Pratt in, 106, 108, 112
Willard Richards in, 118, 122, 126
Ensign Peak, Utah, 140
Erie Canal, N.Y., 25
Evil spirits, 64–65
Excommunication, 31

— F —

Fairbanks, Henry, 143
Faith, 83–84
Family, 203
Far West, Mo., 67, 68, 73, 87, 123,
138, 151
Fayette, N.Y., 30, 136
Fearlessness, 83
Fielding, James, 64, 122, 123
Fielding, Joseph, 41, 66, 121, 122,
124
Fielding family, 106
First Vision, 3, 11, 65, 162
Florence, Nebr., 111
Florence, Ohio, 37, 40
Fly fishing, 217
Forest and Stream (magazine), 217
Fox Islands, 213
France, 187
Frankfurt, Germany, 44
French farm (Ohio), 203
Frontier Guardian (newspaper), 49
Frost, Mary Ann. *See* Pratt, Mary
Ann Frost

— G —

Garrick (ship), 63
Germany, 44, 178

Gilbert, Sidney, 37, 199
Gilbert & Whitney store, 197
Goddard, Mary Adaline. *See* Snow,
    Mary Adaline Goddard
Goddess of Liberty (ship), 109
Gold plates, 11, 15, 164, 165
Goodson, John, 41, 122
Grandin building (Palmyra, N.Y.),
    25
Grant, Heber J., 180
    on Hyrum Smith, 150
    on Wilford Woodruff, 214
Great Apostasy, 8
Green County, Ind., 82
Greene, John P., 167
Greenville, Ind., 200
Groves, Elisha H., 82

— H —

Hale, England, 183
Halsal, Elder, 124
Halsey, Thankful. *See* Pratt,
    Thankful Halsey
Hamburg, Germany, 187
Hamilton, Mr., 170
Hancock, Levi, on Newel K. Whit-
    ney, 205
Hanover, N.H., 2
Harmony, Pa., 11, 163
Harris, Lucy, 27–28, 30
Harris, Martin, 11, 24–34, 41, 74
Harris, Martin, Jr., 32
Hartford, N.Y., 91
Haun's Mill, Mo., 4
Hawaii, 113, 176
Healings, 85, 155, 168, 175, 178
Hebrew School (Kirtland, Ohio),
    172
Henry (ship), 109
Herefordshire, England, 126, 213,
    214
Higbee, Elias, 212
Hill Cumorah, 25

Hiram, Ohio, 201
History, Church, 126–27, 135–36,
    141–46
"History of Joseph Smith," 127,
    141–46
*History of The Church of Jesus
    Christ of Latter-day Saints*, 124,
    127
"History of Willard Richards" (ar-
    ticle), 120
Hodgin, Alice, 124
Holy Ghost, 101, 173, 197
Holy Land, 177
Homer, William H., 31, 32
Hopkinton, Mass., 119
Horn, Joseph, 143
Humility, 156–59
Hyde, Emily Matilda, 44
Hyde, Laura Marinda, 42
Hyde, Marinda Nancy Johnson,
    40, 44, 49
Hyde, Myrtle Stevens, 45
Hyde, Nathan, 36
Hyde, Orson, 35–57, 64, 121, 122
    on Heber C. Kimball, 66
    on Samuel Smith, 168

— I —

Idaho, 180
Illinois, 111
Independence, Mo., 74, 107
Indiana, 82, 214
Indians, 177
Integrity, 152–55
Iowa, 48, 140, 156, 186
Israel, gathering of, 42, 44
Italy, 175, 176

— J —

Jackson County, Mo., 40, 73, 74, 76
James (Apostle), 3, 14, 15
Japan, 180

Jensen, Ella, 178
Jerusalem, 44–46
 dedicatory prayer in, 52–55
Jesus Christ, 8, 14, 15, 100, 179
Job (Biblical character), 90
John (Apostle), 3, 14, 15
Johnson, Luke, 40
Johnson, Lyman E., 40, 58
Johnson, Marinda Nancy. *See*
 Hyde, Marinda Nancy John-
 son
Johnson farm (Ohio), 201
John the Baptist, 3, 14, 15, 163
Jones, Dan, on Martyrdom, 158
Joseph (Bible prophet), 100

— K —

Kanesville, Iowa, 20, 49, 50
Kaysville, Utah, 192
Kentucky, 173
Kimball, Heber C., biographical
 sketch of, 58–70
 on David W. Patten, 84
 and John Taylor, 186
 keys bestowed on, 42
 and Lorenzo Snow, 174
 and Newel K. Whitney, 194
 and Oliver Cowdery, 20
 and Orson Hyde, 41
 and Parley P. Pratt, 106, 184
 and Samuel Smith, 167
 and Willard Richards, 121–22,
  123, 126, 131
 in Zion's Camp, 38
Kimball, Spencer W., 45
 on sacrifice, 92
Kimball, Vilate Murray, 59, 68–69
Kimball family cemetery, 194
Kirtland, Ohio, apostasy in, 31, 60,
 67, 87, 169, 186, 205
 Campbellites in, 196
 Edward Partridge in, 73, 74
 George A. Smith in, 137

Heber C. Kimball in, 59
John Taylor in, 185
Joseph Smith in, 2
Lorenzo Snow in, 172, 173, 174
Newel K. Whitney in, 194, 200,
 201
Orson Hyde in, 36, 37, 43, 50
Parley P. Pratt in, 104, 106, 197
persecution in, 4
Saints gathered to, 3
Wilford Woodruff in, 212
Willard Richards in, 121
Kirtland High Council, 151
Kirtland Safety Society, 60, 106–7,
 186
Kirtland Temple, 4, 14, 42, 62, 74,
 106, 139, 151, 155, 199, 202,
 203, 206
Knox, John, 8

— L —

Lake Erie, N.Y., 3, 152
Lane, Mrs., 85
Lang, William, 19
LaTour, Italy, 175
Leaves from My Journal (book),
 212, 214
Lebanon, N.H., 2
Lee, Ann, 31
Lee, Harold B., 39–40
Lehi, 196
Lemuel, 196
"Let Zion in Her Beauty Rise"
 (hymn), 74
Liberty, Mo., 2, 4–5, 6, 108
Liberty Jail (Mo.), 139, 153–54
Lima, Ill., 174
Liverpool, England, 63, 174, 183,
 187, 213
London, England, 175
Los Angeles, Calif., 113
Loyalty, 188–90
Luther, Martin, 8

Lyman, Angie Finlinson, 71
Lyman, Caroline Ely Partridge, 71
Lyon, T. Edgar, on Orson Pratt, 95

— M —

Mackinaw, Mich., 72
Maine, 213
Manchester, England, 174
Manchester, N.Y., 10, 11, 103
Manifesto (1890), 178, 216
"Man to Lead God's People, The"
    (talk), 39–40
Manti Temple, 49
Mantua, Ohio, 172, 173
Marks, William, 125, 130, 132
Marsh, Thomas B., 43, 138
Massachusetts, 71, 121, 126
Maxwell, Neal A., on Zion's
    Camp, 40
McKay, David O., "make good
    men better," 28
McLellin, William E., 31, 67
Medford (ship), 109
Medicine, 119–20
Melchizedek Priesthood, 14, 15,
    21, 85
Mendon, N.Y., 59
Mercer, James, 122
Messenger and Advocate (news-
    paper), 213
Methodists, 37, 41, 183, 185
Mexican Mission, 211
Mexico City, 211
Michigan, 21, 153
Millennial Star, 42, 108, 120, 126,
    142, 186
Miller, Eleazer, 221
Milnthorpe, England, 183
Missionary Training Center
    (Provo, Utah), 166
Missionary work, among Nez Perce
    Indians, 177
    of David W. Patten, 86

    of Edward Partridge, 73–74
    of George A. Smith, 137–38
    of Heber C. Kimball, 61–66
    of John Taylor, 187–88
    of Lorenzo Snow, 173, 174, 175
    of Orson Hyde, 38–39, 41–42,
        44–46
    of Parley P. Pratt, 103–4, 105–6,
        108, 112
    of Samuel Smith, 161–62,
        165–67
    of Wilford Woodruff, 212–14
Missouri, 4, 31, 40, 67, 73–74, 87,
    104, 105, 107, 199, 213
Mitchell, Professor, 30
Montrose, Iowa, 5
Morley, Isaac, 73, 74, 79
Moroni, 1, 3, 5, 25
Mormon, The (newspaper), 191
Moses, 14, 42
Mount of Olives, 44
Mount Pisgah, Iowa, 140, 174
Mulholland, James, 141–42
Murray, Mrs., 167
Murray, Vilate. *See* Kimball, Vilate
    Murray
Mutual Improvement Association,
    176

— N —

Nassau, N.Y., 119
Nauvoo, Ill., after the Martyrdom,
    130
    Edward Partridge dies in, 76
    George A. Smith in, 138,
        139–40, 143
    Heber C. Kimball in, 68
    John Taylor in, 186, 187
    Joseph Smith in, 5, 157
    Lorenzo Snow in, 174
    Newel K. Whitney in, 195
    Orson Hyde in, 48, 50
    Parley P. Pratt in, 108, 109

Willard Richards in, 118, 126
Nauvoo Legion, 174
Nauvoo Middle Ward, 195
Nauvoo Stake, 130
Nauvoo Temple, 5, 48–49, 68, 110, 118, 119, 139–40, 151, 155
Nephi, 24
"open your mouths," 166
New Hampshire, 2
Newman, John P., 95
New Orleans, La., 49
New York, 10, 40, 41, 100, 163, 188
New York City, 106, 121, 190, 201
New York Rochester Mission, 25
Nez Perce Indians, 177
Niagara Falls, N.Y., 184
Nickerson, Moses, 184

— O —

Oberlin Collegiate Institute (Ohio), 172
Ogden, Utah, 195
Ohio, 2, 3, 4, 27, 31, 50, 172, 197
"O How Happy Are They" (hymn), 104
Only Way to Be Saved, The (pamphlet), 174
Orson Hyde Memorial Garden (Jerusalem), 45
Oxford, Conn., 36

— P —

Page, Hiram, 17
Page, John E., 44, 123
Painesville, Ohio, 72
Palestine, 177
dedicatory prayer of, 52–55
mission to, 44–46
Palmyra, N.Y., 10, 25–26, 103, 150, 166
Palmyra Courier (newspaper), 28
Parker, Lucius, 120

Parley's Canyon, Utah, 112
Parowan, Utah, 140
Parrish, Warren, 31
Partridge, Caroline Ely. *See* Lyman, Caroline Ely Partridge
Partridge, Clisbee, 72
Partridge, Edward, 71–80, 198, 199
Partridge, Edward, Jr., 72
Partridge, Eliza Maria, 72
Partridge, Emily Dow, 72
Partridge, Harriet Pamelia, 72
Partridge, Lydia, 72
Partridge, Lydia Clisbee, 72
Patten, David W., 79, 81–88, 172
Patten, John, 82
Patten, Phoebe Ann Babcock, 81
Paul (Apostle), "Who shall separate us," 178
Pearl of Great Price, 142
Pennsylvania, 40
Penrith, England, 183
Perpetual Emigration Fund, 48, 68
Peter (Apostle), 3, 14, 15
Peterson, Ziba, 37, 72
Phelps, William W., 75, 127
"Praise to the Man," 5, 7
Pilkington, William, 27
Plural marriage. *See* Polygamy
Politics, and religion, 48
Polygamy, 59, 95, 111, 174, 177, 192
Polysophical Society, The, 176
Pond, Allie Young, 179
Potsdam, N.Y., 136
Practice of Medicine (book), 119
"Praise to the Man" (hymn), 5, 7
Pratt, Ann, on Parley P. Pratt, 111, 112
Pratt, Belinda Marden, 111
Pratt, Charity, 91, 100
Pratt, Jared, 91, 100
Pratt, Mary Ann Frost, 106
Pratt, Omner, 113–14
Pratt, Orson, 20, 38, 43, 44, 74, 89–98, 109

Pratt, Parley P., biographical
    sketch of, 99–117
  as editor, 126
  and Edward Partridge, 72, 73
  and John Taylor, 184–85, 186,
    187
  and Newel K. Whitney, 196, 197
  and Oliver Cowdery, 20
  and Orson Hyde, 41
  and Orson Pratt, 91
  and Willard Richards, 130
  in Zion's Camp, 38
Pratt, Parley P., Jr., 106
Pratt, Phoebe, 113
Pratt, Thankful Halsey, 101, 103,
    106
Pratt, William, 100, 101, 109
Premortality, 150
Preston, England, 42, 63–64, 65,
    122, 123, 124, 126
Price, Colonel, 107
Prichard, Sarah Ann. *See* Snow,
    Sarah Ann Prichard
Pride, 16–17
Priesthood, 85
  keys of the, 14, 42, 46–47, 68
  restoration of the, 3, 14, 15, 21,
    163
"Prophetic Warning to All the
    Churches . . ." (pamphlet), 41
Provo, Utah, 178

— Q —

Quillota, Chile, 113
Quincy, Ill., 4, 67, 76, 138, 186

— R —

Record keeping, 126–27, 135–36,
    141–46, 215–16
Reformation, 8–9
Relief Society, 207
Religion, and politics, 48

Remembering, 24
Restoration, 9–10
Reta, Professor, 175
Ribble Valley, England, 65
Richards, Franklin D., on George
    A. Smith, 137
Richards, Heber John, 125
Richards, Jennetta, 122–23, 124,
    125, 126, 127, 128
Richards, John, 123
Richards, Joseph, 119
Richards, LeGrand, 217
Richards, Levi, 119, 120, 121
Richards, Rhoda Howe, 119
Richards, Susan, 120
Richards, Willard, 20, 41, 42, 64,
    118–34, 141–43, 169, 170
Richmond, Mass., 120, 132
Richmond Jail (Mo.), 76, 107–8,
    151
Rigdon, Sidney, acted as scribe,
    142
  in Canada, 41
  and Edward Partridge, 73
  and George A. Smith, 139
  and Newel K. Whitney, 196
  and Orson Hyde, 37, 40
  and Parley P. Pratt, 101, 104
  seeks presidency, 119, 125, 130
  and Willard Richards, 121, 122
River Ribble, England, 42, 65
Rochester, N.Y., 102
Rocky Mountains, 5, 155
Role models, 96
Romney, Marion G., 42
Romney, Miles, 42
Rouche, Thomas F., 192
Russell, Isaac, 41, 64

— S —

Sacred Grove, 162
Sacrifice, 92
Salt Lake 18th Ward, 195

Salt Lake City, Utah, 31, 50, 140, 192, 194, 206, 214
Salt Lake City Cemetery, 211
Salt Lake Stake, 140
Salt Lake Tabernacle, 177
Salt Lake Temple, 49, 176, 178, 179, 180, 216, 217
Salt Lake Valley, Utah, 68, 112, 119, 131, 143, 174, 187
Samuel (Bible prophet), 100
Sandwich Islands. *See* Hawaii
San Francisco, Calif., 113
Sanpete-Sevier district (Utah), 49
Sanpete Stake, 49
School of the Prophets, 39, 89, 195, 202
Seneca Lake, 151
Service, 149–52
Shakers, 31
Shalersville, Ohio, 173
Sheldon, Vt., 59
Sherman, Lyman, 121
Sherwood, H. G., 173
Shoshone Indians, 177
Sidney (ship), 109
Smith, Bathsheba Bigler, 138, 139
Smith, Don Carlos, on Samuel Smith, 168
Smith, Emma, 11, 130, 150, 151, 197–98, 201, 202, 206
Smith, George A., 20, 43, 135–47, 177
   on Samuel Smith, 168
Smith, Hyrum, biographical sketch of, 148–60
   and David W. Patten, 82
   and Heber C. Kimball, 62
   humility of, 156–59
   integrity of, 152–55
   martyrdom of, 5, 47, 68, 109, 127, 128–29, 139, 143, 149, 156–59, 169, 174
   and Newel K. Whitney, 203
   and Parley P. Pratt, 103

service and love of, 149–52
   takes Oliver Cowdery's place, 18–19
   and Willard Richards, 122
Smith, Hyrum, Jr., 153
Smith, Jerusha, 153
Smith, John (father of George A.), 140
Smith, John (son of Hyrum), 148
Smith, Joseph, Jr., biographical sketch of, 1–7
   and Brigham Young, 219–21
   in Canada, 41
   and David W. Patten, 83
   description of, 103
   and Edward Partridge, 71, 73
   on Edward Partridge, 76, 78–79
   and George A. Smith, 135–37
   and Heber C. Kimball, 58, 61, 65, 67
   and Hyrum Smith, 150
   on Hyrum Smith, 149
   is poisoned, 200–201
   and John Taylor, 185–86, 188
   keys restored to, 42
   and Lorenzo Snow, 173
   lost gift to translate, 29
   and Martin Harris, 25–26, 31
   martyrdom of, 47, 60, 68, 127, 128–30, 143, 149, 156–59, 169, 174
   and Newel K. Whitney, 196, 197–98, 200–201, 202, 203–4, 205
   and Oliver Cowdery, 8–20
   and Orson Hyde, 37, 38, 44, 45
   and Orson Pratt, 94
   and Parley P. Pratt, 107–8, 109, 110
   and record keeping, 126–27, 135–36, 141–42
   reorganized Twelve, 123
   and Samuel Smith, 162–63
   and Wilford Woodruff, 212

and Willard Richards, 121, 126,
    128–29, 141–42
Smith, Joseph, Sr., 1, 79, 136, 148,
    150, 173
Smith, Joseph III, 202
Smith, Joseph F., 97, 179
    on John Taylor, 192
Smith, Joseph Fielding, on Consti-
    tution, 47
    on Hyrum Smith, 151–52, 156
    on Martyrdom, 159
Smith, Julia, 202
Smith, Lucy Mack, 11, 32, 148,
    149, 153
    on Edward Partridge, 72–73
    on Joseph Smith, Jr., 162
    on Lucy Harris, 27
    on Martyrdom, 158–59
    on Samuel Smith, 168, 170
Smith, Mary (daughter of Hyrum),
    153
Smith, Nathan, 2
Smith, Samuel Harrison, 11, 37,
    38, 161–71
Smith, William, 20, 31, 225
Smithfield, Utah, 32
Snow, Charlotte Squires, 174,
    175–76
Snow, Eliza R., 143, 172, 207
    on Charlotte Snow, 175–76
    on Newel K. Whitney, 208–9
Snow, Harriet Amelia Squires, 174
Snow, Leonora, 172
Snow, LeRoi, 178, 180
Snow, Lorenzo, 172–82
    on Brigham Young, 225
    on David W. Patten, 86
    Jesus Christ appeared to, 179
Snow, Mary Adaline Goddard, 174
Snow, Oliver G., 177
Snow, Sarah Ann Prichard, 174
Snyder, John, 41
Society Islands, 113
South Royalton, Vt., 9

Spring City, Utah, 50
Squires, Charlotte. *See* Snow,
    Charlotte Squires
Squires, Harriet Amelia. *See* Snow,
    Harriet Amelia Squires
St. George, Utah, 140, 177,
    179–80
St. George Tabernacle, 180
St. George Temple, 215
St. Louis, Mo., 49
Stenhouse, Elder, 175
Stevenson, Edward, 31
Stevenson, Robert Louis, "Home is
    the sailor," 212
Strang, James J., 31
Susquehanna River, 163

— T —

Tahiti, 113
Tarring and feathering, 74–75,
    189–90, 201
Taylor, Agnes, 183
Taylor, Edward, 183
Taylor, James, 183
Taylor, John, articulation of,
    190–93
    biographical sketch of, 183–93
    called as Apostle, 123
    in Carthage Jail, 128–29,
        157–58, 169
    conversion of, 184–88
    on Hyrum Smith, 149
    on Joseph and Hyrum, 212
    loyalty of, 188–90
    and Oliver Cowdery, 20
    on Orson Hyde, 43–44
    on Orson Pratt, 93
    and Parley P. Pratt, 41, 106, 107,
        112
    on Parley P. Pratt, 99, 116
    and Wilford Woodruff, 213
    and Willard Richards, 118, 130
Taylor, Leonora, 184, 185, 187

Temple work, 155, 215–16
Tennessee, 213
Testimony, 221
Theresa, N.Y., 81
Thompson, Robert B., on Heber
   C. Kimball, 62–63
Thomson, Samuel, 119, 120
Thomsonian Infirmary (Boston,
   Mass.), 120
Thornley, England, 122
Thorpe, Sally, 36
Times and Seasons, The (newspa-
   per), 126
Tithing, 180
Tolstoy, Leo, on truth, 97
Toronto, Canada, 41, 184–85, 217
Toronto, Joseph, 175
"Two Minutes in Jail" (article), 128
Tyler, Daniel, 152

— U —

Umatilla Indians, 177
United Brethren, 213–14
United Order, 177, 195, 199
University of Deseret, 176
Utah War, 141

— V —

Valparaiso, Chile, 113
Van Buren, Ark., 116
Vermont, 2, 9, 188
Voice of Joseph, The (pamphlet),
   175
Voice of Warning (pamphlet), 106

— W —

Walton, Mrs., 185
Ward, Thomas, 174
Washington, D.C., 141
Weber River, 217
Welfare program, 47

Wells, Vt., 9
Wesleyan Methodists, 213
"We Thank thee, O God, for a
   Prophet" (hymn), 6
Wheeler, Nathan, 36
Whitaker, William H., 165
Whitehead, James, 124
Whitmer, David, 15, 22, 30, 41
Whitmer, John, 142
Whitmer, Peter, Jr., 37, 72
Whitmer farm (Fayette, N.Y.), 6,
   30–31, 164
Whitney, Elizabeth Ann, 196, 197,
   198, 203
   on Newel K. Whitney, 206
Whitney, Newel K., 37, 39, 130,
   194–209
Whitney, Orson F., on Edward
   Partridge, 76
   "the good ship Zion," 60
   on Heber C. Kimball, 69
   on his grandparents, 197
   on Orson Pratt, 93
Widtsoe, John A., on Orson Hyde,
   43
Wight, Lyman, 73, 79
Williams, Frederick G., 37
Winter Quarters, 68, 112, 119,
   131, 140, 187
Winters, Helen May. *See*
   Woodruff, Helen May Winters
Witnesses, 13–15, 20, 21, 24, 28,
   29, 30–33, 164
Woodruff, Abraham Owen,
   211–12
Woodruff, Azmon, 212
Woodruff, Helen May Winters,
   211–12
Woodruff, Phoebe Whitmore
   Carter, 213
Woodruff, Wilford, biographical
   sketch of, 211–18
   called to the Twelve, 123
   as Church President, 178

on David W. Patten, 84
death of, 179
on destiny of the Church, 38
on Edward Partridge, 78
on the "History of Joseph
    Smith," 145
kept journals, 144
and the Nauvoo Temple, 48
and Oliver Cowdery, 20
on Oliver Cowdery, 15
on Orson Pratt, 95
recorded history, 143
and Willard Richards, 126
Woodward, Jabez, 175
Wooster, Nathan, 36
Word of Wisdom, 154–55
Wycliffe, John, 8

— Y —

Young, Brigham, on adversity,
    222–23
on anger, 224
in Canada, 41
on charity, 224
on endurance, 227–28
and George A. Smith, 139, 140,
    141
and Heber C. Kimball, 61, 68
on Heber C. Kimball, 58–59,
    66–67
on his poverty, 220
on his testimony, 221
on Hyrum Smith, 149
and John Taylor, 186, 188, 189,
    190

and Joseph Smith, 219–21
and Lorenzo Snow, 173, 174,
    177
and Martin Harris, 32
and Newel K. Whitney, 195
and Oliver Cowdery, 20
on Oliver Cowdery, 22
and Orson Hyde, 43, 49
and Orson Pratt, 94
on Orson Pratt, 96
and Parley P. Pratt, 112
on religion and politics, 48
and Samuel Smith, 167
on simplicity of the gospel, 222
on submission, 224
on trials, 225–26
and Wilford Woodruff, 213
and Willard Richards, 118–19,
    120–21, 123, 126, 130, 131
on Willard Richards, 131–32
in Zion's Camp, 38
Young, Brigham, Jr., 22
Young, Joseph, 41
Young, Lorenzo, 155
Young, Lucy P., on Oliver Cow-
    dery, 22
Young, Mary Ann, 68
Young, Phineas, 19, 167, 221–22

— Z —

Zane, Charles S., 217
Zion, 4, 45, 74, 199
Zion's Camp, 31, 38, 40, 60, 82,
    89, 105, 138, 139, 150, 199,
    212